P9-BYG-826

BREAK THE
CALORIE CODE—
TAKE THE MYSTERY
OUT OF DIETING

Accurate, detailed, this book leaves absolutely nothing to guesswork. Every food you're ever likely to eat, in all its various forms, is listed here to help you plan your way to a healthier, trimmer tomorrow.

The double compilation, providing standard household measure and the metric system, makes this the one calorie book you can carry confidently into the future.

Here, at last, is the book that will answer your every question about counting calories and making calories count.

THE COMPLETE CALORIE COUNTER

Elaine Chaback

A DELL BOOK

Published by
Dell Publishing Co., Inc.
1 Dag Hammarskjold Plaza
New York, New York 10017

Dell ® TM 681510, Dell Publishing Co., Inc.

ISBN: 0-440-11134-X
Printed in the United States of America

March 1979
20 19 18 17 16 15

WFH

TABLE OF CONTENTS

Foreword:
COUNTING CALORIES

Dieting is never exactly a breeze, but this calorie counter should make it practically painless. As the title notes, it is a *complete* calorie counter, which means that between these covers you will find complete calorie data on all the foods you are ever likely to eat, and then some. The very detailed way that foods are listed leaves absolutely nothing to chance or to the imagination. Moreover the double compilation—in standard and metric measures—makes this calorie counter one you can carry into the future.

Calories are the cornerstone of dieting, as every battler of the bulge knows. Other methods of weight reduction do get results, of course, but, for one reason or another, are simply not as reliable over the long haul. Fad diets—for instance, any of the high-protein or low-carbohydrate plans —quickly bore many dieters into quitting. Gimmicky crashes, which may be ideal for an instant five-pound drop, are medically unsound over lengthy periods of time. And it is nearly impossible for anyone feeding a family to adhere to the graceful diet menus described by writers in women's magazines. Realistically, then, if you are serious about slimming and want an effective, no-nonsense way to diet, counting calories is absolutely your best bet!

In essence, all low-calorie diets operate on the same basic principle. By cutting down on the dieter's caloric intake, they force the body to burn its own stored fat for energy. Calling on the body's reserves to supply energy *not* coming from food calories results in weight loss.

Pounds start to fall away. The dieter becomes slimmer.

On low-calorie diets what you eat actually doesn't matter! Choose raw carrot sticks, or indulge yourself with a slice of sweet carrot cake. Just as long as you keep within your daily caloric limit, you are succeeding. No doubt you have heard of 1,500-calorie or 1,000-calorie or 800-calorie diets. These are typical daily regimes. Obviously the more narrowly you restrict your caloric intake, the faster fat will disappear. An 800-calorie diet is considered rather extreme, whereas 1,500 calories a day makes for fairly comfortable dieting with a great number of options at mealtime.

Many people are puzzled by the idea of calories when it is really such a simple notion. Calories are a scientific measure denoting the differing energy values of foods. You have probably heard of caloric stoves; "calorie" means heat. It is the quantity of heat released by a food when it burns that reveals how much energy that food contains. The more heat, the more energy—the higher the number of calories.

By the same token, to function the human body uses energy, a quantity also measurable in calories. Even if you were to sit completely motionless, calories would be burned up in keeping your heart beating, your breathing continuous, and your temperature normal. (That calorie figure, by the way, is known as your basal metabolism rate.) Of course, no one operates at that basic minimum level. The simple motions of raising your arm and moving your fingers call for additional calories, or energy.

You get calories from food and you spend them in the business of living. In a perfect world the calories you eat equal exactly the calories you use. In other words, the energy flow is balanced. When you are overweight, that energy equation is out of kilter. Having taken in more than it needs, your body is forced to do something with that surplus energy; so it stores it up for a rainy day. The unfortunate form it takes is fat.

Dieting means ridding the body of those reserves of fat. Scientists have determined that one pound of body fat is equal to 3,500 calories. Thus, if you are ten pounds overweight, you have overeaten by 35,000 calories. Twenty pounds over the mark signifies that a 70,000-calorie bonus has settled on your frame. Every pound you plan to lose means a loss of 3,500 calories. The way you lose is by shifting the balance of the energy equation. Now instead of consuming *more* calories than your body needs, you consume *fewer*. Caught up short, the body is literally forced to draw that fat into action.

Clearly, before you can cut down on calories, it is crucial to know how many calories your body actually needs daily. The number is different for everyone and is based on age, sex, body type, and level of daily activity. You can be medically tested to determine your daily maintenance requirement, but you can be reasonably accurate if you consult the calorie maintenance chart on page 269.

The hitch is the term *desirable weight*. If you are unaware of what you should weigh, you can refer to a second chart on page 268 which lists desirable weights by height, build, and sex. Doctors generally advise that your correct weight is what you weighed in your early twenties (provided, of course, you were not overweight then).

Now you have a few sets of numbers and can readily determine your diet plan. As an example, take the case of 34-year-old Betty who weighs 141 pounds—about 20 pounds too much for her. Since her ideal weight is 120 pounds, she finds that her daily requirement is 2,000 calories. Weekly her body needs 14,000 calories to maintain her ideal weight. However, to lose 2 pounds a week, Betty must cut down to 1,000 calories per day, or a total weekly cutback of 7,000 calories—the equivalent of 2 pounds.

Consult your physician for the best low-calorie plan to serve your own particular needs. Based on your sex, age, weight, and general physical health, your doctor will prescribe a daily calorie quota for you to follow. He may also specify foods that you should include in your diet or avoid. It is inadvisable for anyone to diet without medical supervision.

Armed with your magic number—1,200, 1,000, 800, or whatever—you are ready to start the calorie count. And that is where this book will come in handy.

Introduction:
MAKING
CALORIES
COUNT

This calorie counter lists just about every edible food. Ever tasted an alewife? Or bit into a cherimoyer? Their specific calorie counts appear here, as do 96 separate calorie listings for choice-grade beef alone! And spelling it out in detail eliminates areas of potential confusion for the dieter. Slimmers are interested in speed—in hurrying those pounds off—so accuracy is important.

Beyond its comprehensiveness, this calorie counter is unique because it presents each food in both standard household measures and metric measures. (Note that the book is divided accordingly at page 134.)

Following a worldwide trend, the United States has been steadily "going metric," that is, changing the official system of measurement to the simpler decimal system which is in prominent use throughout the rest of the world. The conversion from feet, pounds, and quarts to meters, grams, and liters has been gradual, but sure. At this point we are not even midway in the changeover process. Still, the telltales are everywhere, from the highway signs now indicating kilometers as well as miles to the American canned goods listing both ounces and grams.

As of this writing, dieters most likely will not feel

pressed to use metric measures when monitoring their food calories. However, the metric measures are truly invaluable if you want the most exact calorie readings possible.

Let us say, for example, that your diet is rich in fresh fruits and vegetables and calls for eating a raw apple every day of the week. Consulting the section on "Standard Household Measures," you would find four listings for one apple with skin. Four sizes are noted by their diameters. Well, frankly, it is tricky to measure fruit with a ruler or a tape measure; so your calorie count is bound to be only approximate. But, consulting the section on "Metric Household Measures," under "apples, commercial varieties, with skin" you discover that gram weights are specified for the same four apples. You, having invested in an inexpensive gram scale, are in business! Weighing your own apple, you find that it is 135 grams—which is about 60 percent larger than the 115-gram apple. So, you adjust the caloric value by 60 percent and figure you are about to consume 72 calories. With all that certainty, no diet could possibly fail!

For those content with the more approximate way of losing weight, the metric calorie counter may provide a key to all the popular imported foods currently stacked on supermarket shelves. And lucky travelers abroad will be able to tally up the calories in spaghetti and meatballs —and diet while enjoying the sights.

Eventually, thinking in terms of metric measures will become second nature to all of us, just as a second language somehow sinks in. At first a conscious effort will be necessary to translate our familiar measures into metric equivalent, but soon you will be thinking in metrics without hesitation.

The basic metric units are grams, meters, and liters— terms that most people recognize. The *gram* (abbreviated *g.*) measures weight; the *meter* (abbreviated *m.*) measures length; and the *liter* (abbreviated *l.*) measures volume. Often these measures are prefixed to designate a smaller or larger unit of the basic measure. For the purposes of using this counter, you need to know only that *centi* means a hundred times smaller. Thus, one *centimeter* (which is abbreviated *cm.*) is 1/100 of a meter and one *milliliter* (*ml.*) is 1/1000 of a liter.

Get accustomed to translating our basic standard measuring units into metric measures, and vice versa. The following table lists equivalents for the standard and metric measures used in this book:

STANDARD TO METRIC

1 ounce = 28.35 grams
1 pound = 453.60 grams
1 fluid ounce = 29.57 milliliters
1 cup (8 fluid ounces) = 236.56 milliliters
1 quart (32 fluid ounces) = .95 liter
1 inch = 2.54 centimeters

METRIC TO STANDARD

1 gram = .03 ounce
100 grams = 3.53 ounces
1 kilogram = 2.20 pounds
1 milliliter = .03 fluid ounce
1 liter = 1.06 quarts
1 centimeter = .39 inch

With the information above, you will know when looking at the metric section of this book that a 250-milliliter cup is larger, and will contain more, than our standard 8-fluid-ounce cup, which is equivalent to only 236.56 milliliters. More information on standard-to-metric equivalents, and vice versa, prefaces each of the two main sections of this book.

Now back to your diet and those omnipresent calories. Knowing how to utilize this calorie counter properly will insure the success of your weight-loss program.

All the foods are listed in ordinary household measures —standard or metric. For dieting purposes, the important ground rule is this: When comparing two foods, you must compare *like* measures. Take this example: Suppose you want to include a starch of some kind on your dinner menu, but cannot make up your mind whether to have rice or noodles. You decide to check the calorie counts of each food and serve whichever is less fattening. One cup of cooked long-grain white rice has 179 calories, you find. Checking under noodles, you see that a 4-ounce portion of dry egg noodles has 440 calories.

What is the problem here? You cannot compare these two figures. Why not? Because a cup is a measure of *capacity* (that is, how much space something occupies) and an ounce is a measure of *weight* (how heavy something is). The very confusing point is that because one cup equals eight ounces, many people believe you can compare. But it is not at all the same eight ounces. One cup is eight *fluid* ounces—a measure of capacity and not weight. This visual picture may help. Think of an ordinary one-cup kitchen measuring cup. Imagine filling it with dry noodles. You would have eight (fluid) ounces worth. Now, think of a scale. Imagine putting on it enough noodles to weigh eight ounces. You would end up with the equivalent of one whole box of noodles, or about three times the amount in the measuring cup.

So, the point is made. *Don't compare foods listed in dissimilar measures,* though you *can* convert a unit of measure to a smaller or larger amount in order to simplify the comparison of like measures. (For instance, to compare four ounces of porterhouse steak with a pound of sirloin steak, convert the pound to sixteen ounces and divide the calorie count of the sirloin by four.)

As you track calories (by the way, a small pocket notebook is a great organizer), refer closely to this calorie counter to check that your food description is accurate. Don't just take the first listing you see. Are those snacking peanuts shelled or unshelled? Raw or roasted? Candy or chocolate coated? Because there are so many entries, you will have to read carefully. A serious diet should be an accurate one. All measures listed within these pages are level measures—that is, one level teaspoon, one level cup, and so on. Even when you are tempted to cheat, to put that little extra bit of sugar in your coffee, don't! For itself, self-discipline is dull, but it will help you to slim faster.

Making the actual decision to diet is the first step in any diet—and the hardest. Full-fledged commitment is the real key to the success of your diet (and other kinds of success, too). That you have bought this book proves you are well on your way to a brand-new figure. This calorie counter can make the road pleasant, even fun.

Low-calorie diets permit you to reduce on the foods you like. Take full advantage of this! Plan tempting menus that will satisfy not only your hunger, but your palate, too. And if you are struck with the urge—splurge! Last night's devilish devil's food cake with ice cream can be atoned for with a skinny salad lunch today. Leaf through the listings to acquaint yourself with the full range and variety of foods from which you can select. Diet time can be a time to adventure.

One of the valuable bonuses of low-calorie dieting is that you come away with a real feeling for food values. Soon you will know instinctively the calorie counts for hundreds of different foods. That kind of knowledge can do much, much more than help you to slim down to a gorgeous new shape—it can help you to keep it forever.

Foods are generically listed. The United States Department of Agriculture is the source of nearly all the calorie data. Although individual brand-name products are not included in this counter, where an item is almost always commercially packaged (such as frozen vegetables, candy bars, or matzos), the data represent an average of the major brand-name products. If you come upon a listing that reads "home recipe," be aware that it is meant as a guide since home recipes vary—often greatly—from kitchen to kitchen. All the home recipes in this book were provided by the USDA and may be obtained by writing to the Assistant Public Printer (Superintendent of Documents), U.S. Government Printing Office, Washington, D.C. 20402 (a fee may be required).

STANDARD HOUSEHOLD MEASURES

There are probably very few, if any, foods you can think of that have not been thought of and included in this calorie counter. Do you want to diet in the North Woods or on a South Sea island? It's easy when you can find calorie listings for mealtime helpings of beaver meat and breadfruit!

This section lists foods alphabetically in standard (U.S.) household measures—ounces, cups, teaspoons, etc. These are the measures Americans have grown up with. They are as familiar to us as the alphabet, so you should have few difficulties in computing calories for foods listed here.

As noted earlier, you can compare foods listed in a similar measure, and you can convert a unit of measure to a smaller or a larger amount. You may find the following chart useful in making such conversions:

EQUIVALENTS BY CAPACITY
(all measurements level)

1 quart = 4 cups
1 cup = 8 fluid ounces
= ½ pint
= 16 tablespoons
2 tablespoons = 1 fluid ounce
1 tablespoon = 3 teaspoons

EQUIVALENTS BY WEIGHT

1 pound = 16 ounces
3.53 ounces = 100 grams
1 ounce = 28.35 grams

Remember: All measures in this section are level. If the calorie counter specifies one teaspoon, it means not one giant heaping teaspoon but a level or moderate teaspoon. Dieting is a battle of the will, a war on your nerves, and a real fight to the finish. Determination is the thing you will need in heaping quantities if you are serious about wanting to change the shape of your shape. Do stick with your diet. If it is any comfort, thousands have traveled this rocky road before you and have come out successful —and thin. Once those beautiful results start to show, you will see that the discomfort was worthwhile.

ABBREVIATIONS AND SYMBOLS USED IN THIS SECTION

diam.	diameter	oz.	ounce
fl.	fluid	pkg.	package
"	inch	qt.	quart
lb.	pound	tbsp.	tablespoon
	tsp.	teaspoon	

CALORIE COUNTER: STANDARD HOUSEHOLD MEASURES

A

food and measure	calories

Abalone, raw:
in shell, 1 lb. 187
meat only, 4 oz. 111
Abalone, canned:
4 oz. 91
Acerola juice, fresh:
1 cup 56
juice from 1 lb. cherries 71
Acerolas (West Indian cherries), fresh:
whole, with pits, 1 lb. 104
pitted, 4 oz. 32
10 cherries (1″ in diam.; about 3½ oz.) 23
Alcoholic beverages:
beer, 4.5% alcohol, 12-fl.-oz. can or bottle 151
beer, 4.5% alcohol, 1 cup 101
pure distilled liquor (gin, rum, whiskey, vodka, etc.):
    80 proof, 1½-fl.-oz. jigger 97
    86 proof, 1½-fl.-oz. jigger 105
    90 proof, 1½-fl.-oz. jigger 110

94 proof, 1½-fl.-oz. jigger	116
100 proof, 1½-fl.-oz. jigger	124
wine, dessert, 18.8% alcohol, 3½-fl.-oz. glass	141
wine, table or dry, 12.2% alcohol, 3½-fl.-oz. glass	87

Alewife, raw:

whole, 1 lb.	282
meat only, 4 oz.	144

Alewife, canned:

with liquid, 8 oz.	320

Almond meal:

partially defatted, 1 oz.	116

Almonds, dried:

in shell, 1 lb.	1,383
in shell, 1 cup	187
in shell, 10 nuts	60
shelled, 4 oz.	678
shelled, 1 oz.	170
shelled, whole, 1 cup	849
shelled, chopped, 1 cup	777
shelled, chopped, 1 tbsp.	48
shelled, slivered, 1 cup loosely packed	688

Almonds, roasted and salted:

roasted in oil, 4 oz.	711
roasted in oil, 1 oz.	178
roasted in oil, 1 cup	984

Almonds, sugar- or chocolate-coated, see Candy

Amaranth, fresh:

whole, with stems, 1 lb.	103
leaves, 1 lb.	163

Anchovies, canned:

flat or rolled, 2-oz. can drained	79
flat, 5 average anchovies	35

Anchovy paste:

1 tbsp.	42

Apple brown Betty, home recipe:

8 oz.	343
1 cup	325

Apple butter, commercial:

12-oz. jar	632
1 oz.	53

1 cup	525
1 tbsp.	33

Apple drink, canned:

1 cup	116

Apple juice, canned or bottled:

5½-fl.-oz. can	80
1 cup	117

Apple pie, see Pies

Apples, commercial varieties:

freshly harvested and stored:

with skin, 1 lb.	242
with skin, 1 apple (3¼″ in diam.; about 2 per lb.)	123
with skin, 1 apple (3″ in diam.; about 2½ per lb.)	96
with skin, 1 apple (2¾″ in diam.; about 3 per lb.)	80
with skin, 1 apple (2½″ in diam.; about 4 per lb.)	61
with skin, quarters or finely chopped pieces, 1 cup	73
with skin, sliced (¼″ thick) or diced, 1 cup	64
pared, 1 apple (3¼″ in diam.; about 2 per lb.)	107
pared, 1 apple (3″ in diam.; about 2½ per lb.)	84
pared, 1 apple (2¾″ in diam.; about 3 per lb.)	70
pared, 1 apple (2½″ in diam.; about 4 per lb.)	53
pared, quarters or finely chopped pieces, 1 cup	68
pared, sliced (¼″ thick) or diced, 1 cup	59

Apples, canned, see Applesauce

Apples, dehydrated:

uncooked, 8 oz.	801
uncooked, 1 cup	353
cooked, sweetened, 8 oz.	173
cooked, sweetened, 1 cup	194

Apples, dried:

uncooked, 8 oz.	625
uncooked, 1 cup	234
cooked, unsweetened, 8 oz.	177
cooked, unsweetened, 1 cup	199
cooked, sweetened, 8 oz.	254
cooked, sweetened, 1 cup	314

Apples, frozen:

sliced, sweetened, 8 oz.	210

Applesauce, canned:

unsweetened, 8 oz.	93
unsweetened, 1 cup	100

Applesauce, continued

sweetened, 8 oz. 207
sweetened, 1 cup 232

Apricot nectar, canned or bottled:

5½-fl.-oz. can 99
1 cup 143

Apricot-orange juice drink, see **Orange-apricot juice drink**

Apricots, fresh:

whole, 1 lb. 217
whole, 3 apricots (about 12 per lb.) 55
pitted, halves, 1 lb. 231
pitted, halves, 1 cup 79

Apricots, candied:

1 oz. 96

Apricots, canned:

in water, with liquid, 8 oz. 86
in water, with liquid, halves, 1 cup 93
in water, 3 halves and 1¾ tbsp. liquid 32
in juice, with liquid, 8 oz. 123
in heavy syrup, whole, with liquid, 8 oz. 184
in heavy syrup, halves, with liquid, 8 oz. 195
in heavy syrup, whole or halves, with liquid, 1 cup 222
in heavy syrup, 2 whole apricots and 2 tbsp. liquid 78
in heavy syrup, 3 halves and 1¾ tbsp. liquid 73

Apricots, dehydrated (nugget type):

uncooked, 8 oz. 753
uncooked, 1 cup 332
cooked, sweetened, 8 oz. 270
cooked, sweetened, 1 cup 337

Apricots, dried (halves):

uncooked, 8 oz. 590
uncooked, 1 cup (about 37 medium halves) 338
uncooked, 10 large halves (1½″ in diam.) 125
uncooked, 10 medium halves (1⅓″ in diam.) 91
cooked, unsweetened, with liquid, 8 oz. 193
cooked, unsweetened, with liquid, 1 cup 213
cooked, sweetened, 8 oz. 277
cooked, sweetened, 1 cup 329

Apricots, frozen:

sweetened, 8 oz. 223
sweetened, 1 cup 256

Artichoke hearts, frozen:
3 average 22

Artichokes, globe or French, fresh:
raw, whole, 1 lb. 85
stored, boiled, drained, 1 whole bud (about 13½ oz.) 67

Artichokes, Jerusalem, see Jerusalem artichokes

Asparagus spears, fresh:
raw, whole spears, 1 lb. 66
raw, cut spears (1½"–2" pieces), 1 cup 35
boiled, drained, 4 large spears (¾"-diam. base) 20
boiled, drained, 4 medium spears (½"-diam. base) 12
boiled, drained, 4 small spears (⅜"-diam. base) 8
boiled, drained, cut spears (1½"–2" pieces), 1 cup 29

Asparagus spears, canned (green or white):
with liquid, 8 oz. 41
with liquid, 1 cup 44
cut spears, with liquid, 8 oz. 41
cut spears, with liquid, 1 cup 43
drained, 8 oz. 48
drained, 1 cup 51
cut spears, drained, 1 cup 49
dietary (low-sodium) pack, with liquid, 8 oz. 37
dietary (low-sodium) pack, cut spears, with liquid, 1 cup 38
dietary (low-sodium) pack, drained, 8 oz. 46
dietary (low-sodium) pack, drained, cut spears, 1 cup 47

Asparagus spears, frozen:
unthawed, 10-oz. pkg. 68
boiled, drained, 8 oz. 52
boiled, drained, 1 cup 44
boiled, drained, 4 large spears (¾"-diam. base) 18
boiled, drained, 4 medium spears (½"-diam. base) 14
boiled, drained, 4 small spears (⅜"-diam. base) 9
cuts and tips, unthawed, 10-oz. pkg. 65
cuts and tips, boiled, drained, 8 oz. 50
cuts and tips, boiled, drained, 1 cup 40

Avocados, California, fresh:
whole, with peel and pit, 1 lb. 589
peeled and pitted, average half (3⅛" in diam.) 185
cubed (½" pieces), 1 cup 257
mashed, 1 cup 393

Avocados, Florida, fresh:
whole, with peel and pit, 1 lb. 389
peeled and pitted, average half (3⅝" in diam.) 196
cubed (½" pieces), 1 cup 192
mashed, 1 cup 294

B

food and measure	calories

Bacon, Canadian-style:
unheated, 1 lb. 980
fried, drained, about 12 oz. (yield from 1 lb. raw) 921
fried, drained, 4 oz. 311
fried, drained, 1 slice (3⅜" in diam.) 58
Bacon, cured, sliced:
raw, 1 lb. 3,016
fried, drained, about 5.1 oz. (yield from 1 lb. raw) 860
fried, drained, 2 thick slices (about 12 slices per lb. raw) 143
fried, drained, 2 medium slices (about 20 slices per lb. raw) .. 86
fried, drained, 2 thin slices (about 28 slices per lb. raw) 61
canned, 1 lb. can (17–18 slices) 3,107
Bagels, egg or water:
1 medium (3" in diam.) 165
Baking powder:
SAS, 1 tbsp. 14
SAS, 1 tsp. 4
phosphate, 1 tbsp. 15
phosphate, 1 tsp. 5
tartrate, 1 tbsp. 7
tartrate, 1 tsp. 2
low-sodium, commercial, 1 tbsp. 23
low-sodium, commercial, 1 tsp. 7
Bamboo shoots, raw:
8 oz. 61
cuts (1" pieces), 1 cup 41
Banana custard pie, see Pies
Bananas, baking-type, see Plantains

Bananas, common varieties, fresh:
whole, with skin, 1 lb. 262
whole, 1 large (9¾" long) 116
whole, 1 medium (8¾" long) 101
whole, 1 small (7¾" long) 81
sliced, 1 cup 136
mashed, 1 cup 191

Bananas, dehydrated:
flakes, 4 oz. 388
flakes, 1 oz. 96
flakes, 1 cup 340
flakes, 1 tbsp. 21

Bananas, red, fresh:
whole, with skin, 1 lb. 278
whole, 1 average (7¼" long) 118
sliced, 1 cup 135

Barbados cherries, see Acerolas

Barbecue sauce:
8 oz. 207
1 cup 228

Barley, pearled:
light, uncooked, 8 oz. 792
light, uncooked, 1 cup 698
pot or Scotch, uncooked, 8 oz. 790
pot or Scotch, uncooked, 1 cup 696

Barracuda, Pacific, raw:
meat only, 4 oz. 129

Basella, see Vine spinach

Bass, black sea:
raw, whole, 1 lb. 165
raw, meat only, 4 oz. 106
baked fillets, stuffed with bacon, butter, celery, and bread cubes:
4 oz. 204
1 piece (3½" x 4½" x 1½") 531

Bass, smallmouth and largemouth, raw:
whole, 1 lb. 146
meat only, 4 oz. 118

Bass, striped:
raw, whole, 1 lb. 205
raw, meat only, 4 oz. 120
oven-fried fillets, prepared with milk, bread crumbs, and butter:

9

    4 oz. 223
    1 piece (8¾" x 4½" x ⅝") 392

Bean curd, see Soybean curd
Bean flour (lima):
    8 oz. 779
    sifted and spooned, 1 cup 432

Bean soup, see Soups
Bean sprouts, mung:
    uncooked, 8 oz. 80
    uncooked, 1 cup 37
    boiled, drained, 8 oz. 64
    boiled, drained, 1 cup 35

Bean sprouts, soy:
    uncooked, 8 oz. 105
    uncooked, 1 cup 48
    boiled, drained, 8 oz. 86
    boiled, drained, 1 cup 48

Beans, baked, canned, solids and liquid:
    in tomato sauce, meatless, 8 oz. 272
    in tomato sauce, meatless, 1 cup 306
    with pork, in molasses sauce, 8 oz. 340
    with pork, in molasses sauce, 1 cup 383
    with pork, in tomato sauce, 8 oz. 277
    with pork, in tomato sauce, 1 cup 311
    with sliced frankfurters, 8 oz. 327
    with sliced frankfurters, 1 cup 367

Beans, black, dry:
    uncooked, 8 oz. 768

Beans, broad, see Broad beans
Beans, great northern, dry:
    uncooked, 8 oz. 771
    uncooked, 1 cup 612
    cooked, 8 oz. 268
    cooked, 1 cup 212

Beans, green or snap, fresh:
    raw, whole, 1 lb. 128
    raw, trimmed, 1 lb. 145
    raw, cuts (1"–2" lengths), 1 cup 34
    boiled, drained, cuts or French-style, 1 cup 31

Beans, green or snap, canned:

with liquid, 8 oz.	41
with liquid, 1 cup	43
drained, 8 oz.	55
drained, cuts (pieces under 1½"), 1 cup	32
drained, French-style, 1 cup	31
dietary (low sodium) pack, with liquid, 8 oz.	37
dietary (low-sodium) pack, with liquid, 1 cup	38
dietary (low-sodium) pack, drained, 8 oz.	50
dietary (low-sodium) pack, drained, 1 cup	30

Beans, green or snap, frozen:

cuts, unthawed, 10-oz. pkg.	74
cuts, boiled, drained, 9.2 oz. (yield from 10-oz. pkg.)	65
cuts, boiled, drained, 1 cup	34
French-style, unthawed, 10-oz. pkg.	77
French-style, boiled, drained, 8.8 oz. (yield from 10-oz. pkg.)	65
French-style, boiled, drained, 1 cup	34

Beans, lima, immature seeds, fresh:

in pods, raw, 1 lb.	223
shelled, raw, 8 oz.	279
shelled, raw, 1 cup	191
boiled, drained, 8 oz.	252
boiled, drained, 1 cup	189

Beans, lima, immature seeds, canned:

with liquid, 8 oz.	161
with liquid, 1 cup	176
drained, 8 oz.	214
drained, 1 cup	163
dietary (low-sodium) pack, with liquid, 8 oz.	159
dietary (low-sodium) pack, with liquid, 1 cup	174
dietary (low-sodium) pack, drained, 8 oz.	216
dietary (low-sodium) pack, drained, 1 cup	162

Beans, lima, immature seeds, frozen:

Fordhook, unthawed, 10-oz. pkg.	290
Fordhook, boiled, drained, 10.4 oz. (yield from 10-oz. pkg.)	283
Fordhook, boiled, drained, 1 cup	168
baby, unthawed, 10-oz. pkg.	346
baby, boiled, drained, 11.1 oz. (yield from 10-oz. pkg.)	339
baby, boiled, drained, 1 cup	212

Beans, lima, mature seeds, dry:

uncooked, 8 oz.	783

Beans, lima, mature seeds, continued

uncooked, Fordhook (large-seeded), 1 cup 621
uncooked, baby (small-seeded), 1 cup 656
cooked, 8 oz. 313
cooked, 1 cup 262

Beans, mung, dry:
uncooked, 8 oz. 771
uncooked, 1 cup 714

Beans, pea or navy, dry:
uncooked, 8 oz. 771
uncooked, 1 cup 697
cooked, 1 cup 224

Beans, pinto or red Mexican, dry:
uncooked, 8 oz. 792
uncooked, 1 cup 663

Beans, red kidney:
dry, uncooked, 8 oz. 778
dry, uncooked, 1 cup 635
dry, cooked, 1 cup 218
canned, with liquid, 8 oz. 204
canned, with liquid, 1 cup 230

Beans, wax or yellow, fresh:
raw, 1 lb. 122
raw, cuts (1″–2″ pieces), 1 cup 30
boiled, drained, whole or cuts, 8 oz. 50
boiled, drained, cuts (1″–2″ pieces), 1 cup 28

Beans, wax or yellow, canned:
with liquid, 8 oz. 43
with liquid, 1 cup 45
drained, 8 oz. 55
drained, cuts, 1 cup 32
drained, French-style, 1 cup 31
dietary (low-sodium) pack, with liquid, 8 oz. 34
dietary (low-sodium) pack, with liquid, 1 cup 36
dietary (low-sodium) pack, drained, 8 oz. 48
dietary (low-sodium) pack, drained, 1 cup 28

Beans, wax or yellow, frozen:
cuts, unthawed, 9-oz. pkg. 71
cuts, boiled, drained, about 8.2 oz. (yield from 9-oz. pkg.) 63
cuts, boiled, drained, 1 cup 36

Beans, white, dry:
uncooked, 8 oz. 771
cooked, 1 cup 224
Beaver:
roasted, 8 oz. 563
Beechnuts:
in shell, 4 oz. 393
shelled, 4 oz. 644
Beef, choice-grade, retail trim:
chuck, arm, roast or steak, boneless, lean with fat:
    raw, 1 lb. 1,012
    braised, drained, 10.7 oz. (yield from 1 lb. raw) 879
    braised, drained, 4 oz. 328
    braised, drained, chopped or diced, 1 cup 405
    braised, drained, ground, 1 cup 318
chuck, arm, roast or steak, boneless, lean only (fat trimmed):
    braised, drained, 9.1 oz. (yield from 1 lb. raw with fat) 498
    braised, drained, 4 oz. 219
    braised, drained, chopped or diced, 1 cup 270
    braised, drained, ground, 1 cup 212
chuck, rib, roast or steak, boneless, lean with fat:
    raw, 1 lb. 1,597
    braised, drained, 10.7 oz. (yield from 1 lb. raw) 1,298
    braised, drained, 4 oz. 484
    braised, drained, chopped or diced, 1 cup 598
    braised, drained, ground, 1 cup 470
chuck, rib, roast or steak, boneless, lean only (fat trimmed):
    braised, drained, 7.4 oz. (yield from 1 lb. raw with fat) 523
    braised, drained, 4 oz. 282
    braised, drained, chopped or diced, 1 cup 349
    braised, drained, ground, 1 cup 274
chuck, stewing, boneless, lean with fat:
    raw, 1 lb. 1,166
    stewed, drained, 10.7 oz. (yield from 1 lb. raw) 994
    stewed, drained, 4 oz. 371
    stewed, drained, chopped or diced, 1 cup 458
chuck, stewing, boneless, lean only (fat trimmed):
    raw, 1 lb. 717
    stewed, drained, 10.7 oz. (yield from 1 lb. raw) 651
    stewed, drained, 4 oz. 243
    stewed, drained, chopped or diced, 1 cup 300

club steak, with 16% bone, lean with fat:
- raw, 1 lb. 1,443
- broiled, 9.8 oz. (yield from 1 lb. raw) 1,262
- broiled, 4 oz. without bone 515

club steak, with 16% bone, lean only (fat trimmed):
- broiled, 5.7 oz. (yield from 1 lb. raw with fat) 393
- broiled, 4 oz. without bone 277

flank steak, boneless, all lean:
- raw, 1 lb. 653
- braised, drained, 10.7 oz. (yield from 1 lb. raw) 596
- braised, drained, 4 oz. 222
- braised, drained, 1 piece (2½" x 2½" x ¾") 167

ground, lean with 10% fat:
- raw, 1 lb. 812
- broiled well-done, 12 oz. (yield from 1 lb. raw) 745
- raw, 4-oz. patty 202
- broiled well-done, 3-oz. patty (yield from 4 oz. raw) 186

ground, lean with 21% fat:
- raw, 1 lb. 1,216
- broiled rare to medium, 11.5 oz. (yield from 1 lb. raw) 932
- raw, 4-oz. patty 303
- broiled rare to medium, 2.9-oz. patty (yield from 4 oz. raw) .. 235

plate, boneless, lean with fat:
- raw, 1 lb. 1,615
- simmered, drained, 10.7 oz. (yield from 1 lb. raw) 1,313
- simmered, drained, 4 oz. 490

plate, boneless, lean only (fat trimmed):
- simmered, drained, 6.5 oz. (yield from 1 lb. raw with fat) .. 368
- simmered, drained, 4 oz. 226

porterhouse steak, with 9% bone, lean with fat:
- raw, 1 lb. 1,603
- broiled, 10.6 oz. (yield from 1 lb. raw) 1,400
- broiled, 4 oz. without bone 527

porterhouse steak, with 9% bone, lean only (fat trimmed):
- broiled, 6.1 oz. (yield from 1 lb. raw with fat) 385
- broiled, 4 oz. without bone 254

rib roast, boneless, lean with fat:
- raw, 1 lb. 1,819
- roasted, 11.7 oz. (yield from 1 lb. raw) 1,456
- roasted, 4 oz. 499

roasted, chopped or diced, 1 cup 616
roasted, ground, 1 cup 484
rib roast, boneless, lean only (fat trimmed):
   roasted, 7.5 oz. (yield from 1 lb. raw with fat) 511
   roasted, 4 oz. 273
   roasted, chopped or diced, 1 cup 337
   roasted, ground, 1 cup 265
round steak, boneless, lean with fat:
   raw, 1 lb. 894
   braised or broiled, 11.1 oz. (yield from 1 lb. raw) 820
   braised or broiled, 4 oz. 296
round steak, boneless, lean only (fat trimmed):
   braised or broiled, 9.5 oz. (yield from 1 lb. raw with fat) 507
   braised or broiled, 4 oz. 214
rump roast, boneless, lean with fat:
   raw, 1 lb. 1,374
   roasted, 11.7 oz. (yield from 1 lb. raw) 1,149
   roasted, 4 oz. 394
   roasted, chopped or diced, 1 cup 486
   roasted, ground, 1 cup 382
rump roast, boneless, lean only (fat trimmed):
   roasted, 8.8 oz. (yield from 1 lb. raw with fat) 516
   roasted, 4 oz. 236
   roasted, chopped or diced, 1 cup 291
   roasted, ground, 1 cup 229
sirloin steak, double-bone, 18% bone, lean with fat:
   raw, 1 lb. 1,240
   broiled, 9.6 oz. (yield from 1 lb. raw) 1,110
   broiled, 4 oz. without bone 463
sirloin steak, double-bone, 18% bone, lean only (fat trimmed):
   broiled, 6.3 oz. (yield from 1 lb. raw with fat) 387
   broiled, 4 oz. without bone 245
sirloin steak, hip-bone, 15% bone, lean with fat:
   raw, 1 lb. 1,585
   broiled, 9.9 oz. (yield from 1 lb. raw) 1,368
   broiled, 4 oz. without bone 552
sirloin steak, hip-bone, 15% bone, lean only (fat trimmed):
   broiled, 5.5 oz. (yield from 1 lb. raw with fat) 372
   broiled, 4 oz. without bone 272
sirloin steak, round-bone, 7% bone, lean with fat:
   raw, 1 lb. 1,316

Beef, continued

    broiled, 10.9 oz. (yield from 1 lb. raw) 1,192

    broiled, 4 oz. without bone 439

  sirloin steak, round-bone, 7% bone, lean only (fat trimmed):

    broiled, 7.2 oz. (yield from 1 lb. raw with fat) 420

    broiled, 4 oz. without bone 235

  T-bone steak, 11% bone, lean with fat:

    raw, 1 lb. 1,596

    broiled, 10.4 oz. (yield from 1 lb. raw) 1,395

    broiled, 4 oz. without bone 537

  T-bone steak, 11% bone, lean only (fat trimmed):

    broiled, 5.8 oz. (yield from 1 lb. raw with fat) 368

    broiled, 4 oz. without bone 253

Beef, corned, medium-fat:

  raw, 1 lb. 1,329

  cooked, 10.7 oz. (yield from 1 lb. raw) 1,131

  cooked, 4 oz. 422

  canned, 12-oz. can 734

  canned, 4 oz. 245

  canned, 1 slice (3″ x 2″ x ⅜″) 86

Beef, corned, hash (with potatoes), canned:

  15½-oz. can 795

  8 oz. 410

  1 cup 398

Beef, dried (chipped), commercial:

  uncooked, 2½-oz. jar 144

  uncooked, 5-oz. jar 288

Beef, dried, cooked (creamed), home recipe:

  8 oz. 350

  1 cup 377

Beef, potted, canned:

  5½-oz. can 387

  1 oz. 70

  1 cup 558

  1 tbsp. 32

Beef, roast, canned (see also **Beef, rib roast** or **rump roast**):

  8 oz. 508

Beef heart, see **Hearts**

Beef kidney, see **Kidneys**

Beef liver, see **Liver**

Beef pot pie, home recipe:
    baked, 1 whole pie (9″ in diam.) 1,550
    baked, ⅓ of 9″ pie 517
    baked, 8 oz. 558

Beef pot pie, frozen:
    8-oz. pie 436

Beef soup, see Soups

Beef tongue, see Tongue

Beef-vegetable stew, home recipe:
    cooked with lean chuck, 8 oz. 202
    cooked with lean chuck, 1 cup 218

Beef-vegetable stew, canned:
    15-oz. can 336
    8 oz. 179
    1 cup 194

Beer, see Alcoholic beverages

Beet greens, fresh:
    raw, trimmed, 1 lb. 61
    boiled, drained, 8 oz. 41
    boiled, drained, 1 cup 26

Beets, fresh:
    raw, trimmed, 1 lb. 137
    raw, whole, 1 medium beet (2″ in diam.) 21
    raw, diced, 1 cup 58
    boiled, drained, whole, 2 medium beets (2″ in diam.) 32
    boiled, drained, diced, 1 cup 58
    boiled, drained, sliced, 1 cup 66

Beets, canned:
    with liquid, 8 oz. 77
    with liquid, 1 cup 84
    drained, 8 oz. 84
    drained, whole, small, 1 cup 59
    drained, diced, 1 cup 60
    drained, sliced, 1 cup 65
    dietary (low-sodium) pack, with liquid, 8 oz. 73
    dietary (low-sodium) pack, with liquid, 1 cup 79
    dietary (low-sodium) pack, drained, 8 oz. 84
    dietary (low-sodium) pack, whole, small, 1 cup 59
    dietary (low-sodium) pack, diced or sliced, 1 cup 63
    Harvard, with liquid, 1 cup 110
    pickled, with liquid, 1 cup 150

Beverages, see individual listings

Biscuit dough, canned:
chilled, 4 oz. 318
frozen, 4 oz. 263

Biscuit mix, baked:
made with milk, 1-oz. biscuit (2" in diam., 1¼" high) 91

Biscuits, baking-powder, home recipe:
baked, 1-oz. biscuit (2" in diam, 1¼" high) 103

Blackberries, fresh:
1 lb. 250
1 cup 84

Blackberries, canned:
in water, with liquid, 8 oz. 91
in water, with liquid, 1 cup 98
in heavy syrup, with liquid, 8 oz. 207
in heavy syrup, with liquid, 1 cup 233

Blackberries, frozen, see Boysenberries, frozen

Blackberry juice, canned:
unsweetened, 1 cup 91

Blackberry pie, see Pies

Black-eyed peas, see Cowpeas

Blackfish, see Tautog

Blueberries, fresh:
1 lb. 259
1 cup 90

Blueberries, canned:
in water, with liquid, 8 oz. 89
in heavy syrup, with liquid, 8 oz. 230
in heavy syrup, with liquid, 1 cup 253

Blueberries, frozen:
unsweetened, 10-oz. pkg. 156
unsweetened, 1 cup 91
sweetened, 10-oz. pkg. 298
sweetened, 1 cup 242

Blueberry pie, see Pies

Bluefish, fillets:
raw, meat only, 1 lb. 531
broiled with butter, 12⅞ oz. (yield from 1 lb. raw) 580
broiled with butter, 4 oz. 180

fried, with egg, milk, bread crumbs, 13⅗ oz.
(yield from 1 lb. raw) 789
fried, with egg, milk, bread crumbs, 4 oz. 232

Blood sausage (pudding), see Sausages

Bockwurst:
1 lb. (about 7 links) 1,198
1 link (about 2.3 oz.) 172

Bologna:
without binders, chub, 1 slice (3″ in diam., ⅛″ thick) 36
without binders, ring, 12-oz. ring (15″ long, 1⅜″ in diam.) 942
without binders, sliced, 8-oz. pkg. 629
without binders, sliced, 6-oz. pkg. 471
without binders, sliced, 1-oz. slice (4½″ in diam., ⅛″ thick) .. 79
without binders, sliced, ¾-oz. slice (4″ in diam., ⅛″ thick) .. 61
with cereal, chub, 1 slice (3″ in diam., ⅛″ thick) 34
with cereal, ring, 12-oz. ring (15″ long, 1⅜″ in diam.) 891
with cereal, sliced, 8-oz. pkg. 595
with cereal, sliced, 6-oz. pkg. 445
with cereal, sliced, 1-oz. slice (4½″ in diam., ⅛″ thick) 74
with cereal, sliced, ¾-oz. slice (4″ in diam., ⅛″ thick) 58

Bonito, raw:
meat only, 4 oz. 192

Borscht, see Soups

Boston cream pie, see Pies

Bouillon, dry form:
cubes, ½″ cube 5
powder (instant), 1 oz. 34
powder (instant), 1 packet 8
powder (instant), 1 tsp. 2

Boysenberries, fresh, see Blackberries, fresh

Boysenberries, canned:
in water, with liquid, 8 oz. 82
in water, with liquid, 1 cup 88

Boysenberries, frozen:
unsweetened, 10-oz. pkg. 136
unsweetened, 1 cup 60
sweetened, 10-oz. pkg. 272
sweetened, 1 cup 137

Brains, fresh (all types):
raw, 8 oz. 284

Bran, wheat, see Wheat bran

19

Bran flakes, see Cereals, ready-to-eat
Braunschweiger (smoked liverwurst):
rolls, 8-oz. roll (5½" long, 2" in diam.) 724
rolls, 1 slice (2" in diam., ¼" thick) 32
slices, 6-oz. pkg. (6 slices) 542
slices, 1 slice (3⅛" in diam., ¼" thick) 90
Brazil nuts:
in shell, 1 lb. 1,424
in shell, 1 cup 383
in shell, 3 large or 3½ medium nuts (1 oz.) 89
shelled, 4 oz. 741
shelled, 1 cup 916
shelled, 6 large or 8 medium nuts (1 oz.) 185
Bread crumbs:
dry, grated, 1 cup 392
dry, grated, 1 oz. 111
soft, 1 cup 122
Bread cubes, white bread:
firm-crumb type, 1 cup 83
soft-crumb type, 1 cup 81
Breadfruit, fresh:
raw, untrimmed, 1 lb. 360
raw, trimmed, peeled, 4 oz. 117
Breads, commercial
Boston brown, 1 slice (3" x ¾") 101
corn, see Cornbread
cracked-wheat, 1-lb. loaf 1,193
cracked-wheat, 1 slice (18 slices per loaf) 66
cracked-wheat, 1 slice (20 slices per loaf) 60
French, 1-lb. loaf 1,316
French, 1 slice (2½" x 2" x ½") 44
French, 1 slice (5" x 2½" x 1") 102
Italian, 1-lb. loaf 1,252
Italian, 1 slice (4½" x 3¼" x ¾") 83
Italian, 1 slice (3¼" x 2½" x ½") 28
pumpernickel, 1-lb. loaf 1,117
pumpernickel, 1 slice (5" x 4" x ⅜") 79
pumpernickel, snack size, 8-oz. loaf 558
pumpernickel, snack size, 1 slice (2½" x 2" x ¼") 17
raisin, 1-lb. loaf 1,188
raisin, 1 slice (18 slices per loaf) 66

raisin, 1 slice (20 slices per loaf) 60
rye, light, 1-lb. loaf 1,102
rye, light, 1 slice (4¾" x 3¾" x 7/16") 61
rye, light, 1 slice (20 slices per loaf) 56
rye, light, snack size, 8-oz. loaf 552
rye, light, snack size, 1 slice (2½" x 2" x ¼") 17
Vienna, 1-lb. loaf 1,316
Vienna, 1 slice (4¾" x 4" x ½") 73
white, firm-crumb type, 1-lb. loaf 1,247
white, firm-crumb type, 1 slice (20 slices per loaf) 63
white, firm-crumb type, 1 slice (30 slices per loaf) 41
white, soft-crumb type, 1-lb. loaf 1,225
white, soft-crumb type, 1 slice (18 slices per loaf) 68
white, soft-crumb type, 1 slice (22 slices per loaf) 54
whole-wheat, firm-crumb type, 1-lb. loaf 1,102
whole-wheat, firm-crumb type, 1 slice (18 slices per loaf) 61
whole-wheat, firm-crumb type, 1 slice (20 slices per loaf) 56
whole-wheat, soft-crumb type, 1-lb. loaf 1,093
whole-wheat, soft-crumb type, 1 slice (16 slices per loaf) 67

Bread sticks:
regular, 1 oz. 109
regular, 1 stick (4½" long, ½" in diam.) 38
Vienna, 1 oz. 86
Vienna, 1 stick (6½" long, 1¼" in diam.) 106

Bread stuffing, mix:
dry form, 8-oz. pkg. 842
dry form, coarse crumbs, 1 cup 260
dry form, cubes, 1 cup 111
prepared with butter and water, 8 oz. 812
prepared with butter and water, 1 cup 501
moist, prepared with egg, butter, and water, 8 oz. 472
moist, prepared with egg, butter, and water, 1 cup 416

Broad beans, raw:
immature seeds, 8 oz. 238
mature seeds, 8 oz. 767

Broccoli, fresh:
raw, 1 lb. (2 large, 3 medium, or 4 small stalks or spears) 89
raw, trimmed, 1 lb. 145
boiled, drained, 8 oz. 59
boiled, drained, 1 large spear (about 10 oz.) 73
boiled, drained, 1 medium spear (about 6.5 oz.) 47

Broccoli, fresh, continued

    boiled, drained, 1 small spear (about 5 oz.) 36

    boiled, drained, cuts (½″ pieces), 1 cup 40

Broccoli, frozen:

    spears, unthawed, 10-oz. pkg. 80

    spears, boiled, drained, about 8.8 oz. (yield from 10-oz. pkg.) .. 65

    spears, boiled, drained, 1 average (4½″–5″ long) 8

    chopped, unthawed, 10-oz. pkg. 82

    chopped, boiled, drained, about 9 oz. (yield from 10-oz. pkg.) .. 65

    chopped, boiled, drained, 1 cup 48

Brown-and-serve sausages, see Sausages

Brownies, see Cookies

Brussels sprouts, fresh:

    raw, whole, 1 lb. (about 24 medium sprouts, 1¼–1½″ in diam.) 204

    raw, trimmed, 1 lb. 188

    boiled, drained, 8 oz. (about 10½ medium sprouts) 82

    boiled, drained, 1 cup (about 7–8 medium sprouts) 56

    boiled, drained, 4 medium sprouts 30

Brussels sprouts, frozen:

    unthawed, 10-oz. pkg. 102

    boiled, drained, 10 oz. (yield from 10-oz. pkg.) 94

    boiled, drained, 1 cup 51

Buckwheat flour, see Flour

Bulgur (parboiled wheat):

    club wheat, dry, 8 oz. 814

    club wheat, dry, 1 cup 628

    hard red winter wheat, dry, 8 oz. 802

    hard red winter wheat, dry, 1 cup 603

    white wheat, dry, 8 oz. 810

    white wheat, dry, 1 cup 553

    canned, hard red winter wheat, unseasoned, 8 oz. 382

    canned, hard red winter wheat, unseasoned, 1 cup 227

    canned, hard red winter wheat, seasoned, 8 oz. 412

    canned, hard red winter wheat, seasoned, 1 cup 246

Buns, see Rolls and buns

Butter, regular:

    1 cup or 8 oz. 1,625

    1 stick or 4 oz. 812

    1 tbsp. 102

    1 tsp. 34

    1 pat (1″ x ⅓″; 90 pats per lb.) 36

Butter, whipped:

8-oz. container	1,625
1 cup	1,081
1 stick or ½ cup	541
1 tbsp.	67
1 tsp.	23
1 pat (1¼" x ⅓"; 120 pats per lb.)	27

Butterfish, raw:

gulf, meat only, 4 oz.	108
northern, meat only, 4 oz.	192

Buttermilk, see Milk

Butternuts:

in shell, 4 oz.	100
shelled, 4 oz.	713
4–5 nuts	94

Butter oil:

1 tbsp.	123

Butterscotch, see Candy

Butterscotch pie, see Pies

C

food and measure	calories

Cabbage, Chinese (celery cabbage), fresh:

raw, 1 lb.	62
raw, trimmed, 1 lb.	64
raw, cuts (1" pieces), 1 cup	11
raw, strips, 1 cup	8

Cabbage, common varieties, fresh:

raw, whole, 1 lb.	98
raw, trimmed, 1 lb.	109
raw, chopped or finely shredded, 1 cup	22
raw, sliced or coarsely shredded, 1 cup	17
raw, ground, 1 cup	36
shredded, boiled in small amount water, drained, 1 cup	29
wedges, boiled in large amount water, drained, 1 cup	31

Cabbage, common varieties, dehydrated:

1 oz.	87

Cabbage, red:

fresh, raw, 1 lb. 127

fresh, raw, trimmed, 1 lb. 141

raw, chopped or finely shredded, 1 cup 28

raw, sliced or coarsely shredded, 1 cup 22

canned, sweet-and-sour, 1 cup 150

Cabbage, savoy, fresh:

raw, 1 lb. 98

raw, trimmed, 1 lb. 109

raw, sliced or coarsely shredded, 1 cup 17

Cabbage, spoon (pakchoy), **fresh:**

raw, 1 lb. 73

raw, trimmed, 1 lb. 69

raw, cuts (1″ pieces), 1 cup 11

boiled, drained, cuts (1″ pieces), 1 cup 24

Cabbage salad, see Coleslaw

Cake icings, see Icings

Cake mixes, commercial, prepared (baked), 3½ oz.-serving:

angel food, made with water, flavorings 259

chocolate malt, made with eggs, water, uncooked white icing .. 346

coffeecake, made with eggs, milk 322

devil's-food, made with eggs, water, chocolate icing 339

gingerbread, made with water 276

honey spice, made with eggs, water, caramel icing 352

marble, made with eggs, water, boiled white icing 331

white, made with egg whites, water, chocolate icing 351

yellow, made with eggs, water, chocolate icing 337

Cakes, baked from home recipe, 3½-oz. serving:

angel food 269

Boston cream pie, see **Pies**

caramel, without icing 385

caramel, with caramel icing 379

chocolate (devil's-food), without icing 366

chocolate (devil's-food) with chocolate icing 369

chocolate (devil's-food), with uncooked vanilla icing 369

cottage pudding, without sauce 344

cottage pudding, with chocolate sauce 318

cottage pudding, with fruit (strawberry) sauce 292

fruitcake, dark 379

fruitcake, light 389

gingerbread 317

    fondant, mint, chocolate-coated, 1 oz. 116
    fondant, mint, chocolate-coated, 1 large (2½" in diam.) 144
    fondant, mint, chocolate-coated, 1 small (1⅜" in diam.) 45
    fondant, mint, chocolate-coated, 1 miniature (¾" in diam.) ... 10
    fudge, chocolate, 1 oz. 113
    fudge, chocolate, 1 piece (1" cube) 89
    fudge, chocolate, with nuts, 1 oz. 121
    fudge, chocolate, with nuts, 1 piece (1" cube) 89
    fudge, vanilla, 1 oz. 113
    fudge, vanilla, 1 piece (1" cube) 84
    fudge, vanilla, with nuts, 1 oz. 120
    fudge, vanilla, with nuts, 1 piece (1" cube) 89
    fudge, with caramel and nuts, chocolate-coated, 1 oz. 123
    fudge, with nuts and caramel, chocolate-coated, 1 oz. 130
    gumdrops, 1 oz. 98
    hard candy, 1 oz. 109
    honey with peanut butter, chocolate-coated, 1 oz. 131
    jellybeans, 1 oz. 104
    jellybeans, ½ cup 404
    marshmallow, 1 oz. 90
    marshmallow, regular, 1 average (1⅛" x ¾") 23
    marshmallow, soft, 1 average (1⅛" x ¾") 19
    marshmallow, miniature, 1 cup loosely packed 147
    mints, uncoated, 1 oz. 103
    mints, chocolate-coated, see **Candy, fondant**
    nougat and caramel, chocolate-coated, 1 oz. 118
    peanut bar, 1 oz. 146
    peanut brittle, 1 oz. 119
    peanuts, chocolate-coated, 1 oz. 159
    peanuts, whole, chocolate-coated, ½ cup 477
    raisins, chocolate-coated, 1 oz. 120
    raisins, whole, chocolate-coated, ½ cup 404
    vanilla creams, chocolate-coated, 1 oz. 123

Cantaloupe, fresh:
    ½ melon (5" in diam.) 58
    cubed or diced, 1 cup 48

Cape gooseberries, see Ground cherries

Capers, in jars:
    1 tbsp. 6

Capicola:
4½-oz. pkg. (about 6 slices) 639
1 slice (4¼" x 4¼" x 1/16") 105
1 oz. 141

Carambolas, fresh:
raw, whole, 1 lb. 149
raw, peeled and seeded, 4 oz. 40

Carissas (natal plums), fresh:
raw, whole, 1 lb. 273
raw, peeled and seeded, 4 oz. 79
raw, sliced (⅛" thick), 1 cup 105

Carob flour, see Flour

Carrots, fresh:
raw, whole, with tops, 1 lb. 112
raw, packaged, whole, without tops, 1 lb. 156
raw, whole, trimmed and scraped, 8 oz. 95
raw, whole, 1 medium (5½" x 1") 21
raw, chunks, 1 cup 58
raw, diced, 1 cup 60
raw, grated or shredded, 1 cup 46
raw, slices, 1 cup 53
raw, strips, 1 cup 49
raw, strips, 6 strips (about ¼" x 3") 12
boiled, drained, chunks, 1 cup 51
boiled, drained, diced, 1 cup 43
boiled, drained, slices, 1 cup 47

Carrots, canned:
with liquid, 8 oz. 64
with liquid, 1 cup 69
drained, 8 oz. 68
drained, diced, 1 cup 44
drained, slices, 1 cup 47
dietary (low-sodium) pack, with liquid, 8 oz. 50
dietary (low-sodium) pack, with liquid, 1 cup 54
dietary (low-sodium) pack, drained, 8 oz. 57
dietary (low-sodium) pack, slices, drained, 1 cup ... 39

Carrots, dehydrated:
1 oz. 97

Casaba melon, fresh:
whole, with rind, 1 lb. 61

wedge (7¾" x 2")	22
cubed or diced, 1 cup	46
Cashew nuts, shelled, roasted in oil:	
4 oz.	639
1 cup	785
1 oz. (about 14 large, 18 medium, or 26 small nuts)	159
dry-roasted, 1 oz.	173
Catfish, freshwater:	
raw, fillets, 4 oz.	117
Catsup, tomato, canned or bottled:	
8 oz.	241
1 cup	289
1 tbsp.	16
1 packet (½ oz.)	15
Cauliflower, fresh:	
raw, whole, 1 lb.	48
raw, flowerets, 1 lb.	122
raw, flowerets, whole, 1 cup	27
raw, flowerets, chopped, 1 cup	31
raw, flowerets, sliced, 1 cup	23
boiled, drained, flowerets, 1 cup	28
Cauliflower, frozen:	
unthawed, 10-oz. pkg.	62
boiled, drained, 9.5 oz. (yield from 10-oz. pkg.)	49
boiled, drained, 1 cup (about 7 flowerets)	32
Caviar, sturgeon:	
granular, 1 oz.	74
granular, 1 tbsp.	42
pressed, 1 oz.	90
pressed, 1 tbsp.	54
Celeriac root, fresh:	
whole, with skin, 1 lb.	156
pared, 4 oz.	45
pared, 4–6 roots	40
Celery, fresh:	
raw, untrimmed, with leaves, 1 lb.	58
raw, packaged, trimmed, 1 lb. (about 7 stalks)	61
raw, 1 large outer stalk (8" long)	7
raw, 3 small inner stalks (5" long)	9
raw, chopped or diced, 1 cup	20

corn, puffed, presweetened, unflavored, 1 cup 114
corn, puffed, presweetened, cocoa-flavored, 1 oz. 110
corn, puffed, presweetened, cocoa-flavored, 1 cup 117
corn, puffed, presweetened, fruit-flavored, 1 oz. 112
corn, puffed, presweetened, fruit-flavored, 1 cup 119
corn flakes, 1 oz. 109
corn flakes, 1 cup 97
corn flakes, crumbs, 1 cup 328
corn flakes, sugar-coated, 1 oz. 109
corn flakes, sugar-coated, 1 cup 154
corn flakes, with protein concentrates, 1 oz. 107
corn, rice, and wheat flakes, 1 oz. 110
corn, shredded, 1 oz. 110
corn, shredded, 1 cup 97
oat flakes, with soy flour and rice, 1 oz. 113
oats and corn, puffed, sugar-coated, 1 oz. 112
oats and corn, puffed, sugar-coated, 1 cup 139
oats, puffed, 1 oz. 113
oats, puffed, 1 cup 99
oats, shredded, 1 oz. 107
oats, shredded, 1 cup 171
rice flakes, 1 oz. 110
rice, oven-popped, 1 oz. 113
rice, oven-popped, 1 cup 117
rice, oven-popped, presweetened, 1 oz. 110
rice, oven-popped, presweetened, 1 cup 175
rice, puffed, 1 oz. 113
rice, puffed, 1 cup 60
rice, puffed, presweetened, with honey or cocoa, 1 oz. 110
rice, puffed, presweetened, with honey or cocoa, 1 cup 140
rice, shredded, 1 oz. 111
rice, shredded, 1 cup 98
rice, shredded, with protein concentrates, casein, 1 oz. 108
rice, shredded, with protein concentrates, casein, 1 cup 325
rice, shredded, with protein concentrates, wheat gluten, 1 oz. . 109
rice, shredded, with protein concentrates, wheat gluten, 1 cup 77
wheat flakes, 1 oz. 100
wheat flakes, 1 cup 106
wheat germ, toasted, 1 oz. 111
wheat germ, toasted, 1 tbsp. 23

wheat, puffed, 1 oz. 103
wheat, puffed, 1 cup 54
wheat, puffed, with sugar and/or honey, 1 oz. 107
wheat, puffed, with sugar and/or honey, 1 cup 132
wheat, shredded, 1 oz. 100
wheat, shredded, 1 oblong biscuit (3¾" x 2¼" x 1" or
   2½" x 2" x 1¼") 89
wheat, shredded, 1 round biscuit (3" in diam., 1" thick) 71
wheat, shredded, spoon size, 1 cup (about 50 biscuits) 177
wheat, shredded, crumbled, 1 cup 124
wheat, shredded, finely crushed, 1 cup 266
wheat, shredded, with malt and sugar, 1 oz. 104
wheat, shredded, with malt and sugar, bite-size squares, 1 cup 201
wheat, shredded, with malt and sugar, shreds, 1 cup 146
wheat and malted barley, flakes, 1 oz. 111
wheat and malted barley, flakes, 1 cup 157
wheat and malted barley, granules, 1 oz. 111
wheat and malted barley, granules, 1 cup 430

Cervelat, dry:
  5⅓-oz. roll (about 6" long, 1½" in diam.) 677
  4 slices (1½" in diam., ⅛" thick) 54
  1 oz. 128

Cervelat, soft, see Thuringer cervelat

Chard, Swiss:
  raw, whole, 1 lb. 113
  raw, trimmed, 1 lb. (weighed whole) 104
  boiled, drained, leaves and stalks, 1 cup 26
  boiled, drained, leaves only, 1 cup 32

Cheese food, processed:
  American, 1 oz. 92
  American, 1" cube 57
  American, 1 tbsp. 45

Cheeses, natural:
  bleu or blue, 1 oz. 104
  bleu or blue, 1" cube 64
  bleu or blue, crumbled, 1 cup loosely packed 497
  bleu or blue, crumbled, 1 cup packed 916
  brick, 1 oz. 105
  brick, 1" cube 64
  brick, packaged, 1 slice (10 slices per lb.) 167
  Camembert, domestic, 1 oz. 85

Camembert, domestic, 1" cube 51
Camembert, domestic, packaged, 1 piece (12 pieces per lb.) .. 114
Cheddar, domestic, 1 oz. 113
Cheddar, domestic, 1" cube 68
Cheddar, domestic, packaged, 1 slice (10 slices per lb.) 179
Cheddar, domestic, diced, 1 cup 521
Cheddar, domestic, shredded, 1 cup 450
Cheddar, domestic, grated, 1 tbsp. 28
cottage, creamed, large- or small-curd, 1 oz. 30
cottage, creamed, 12-oz. container 360
cottage, creamed, large-curd, 1 cup loosely packed 239
cottage, creamed, small-curd, 1 cup loosely packed 223
cottage, uncreamed, 1 oz. 24
cottage, uncreamed, 12-oz. container 292
cottage, uncreamed, 1 cup loosely packed 125
cottage, uncreamed, 1 cup packed 172
cream, 1 oz. 106
cream, 1" cube 60
cream, 1 cup 868
cream, 1 tbsp. 52
cream, whipped, 1 oz. 106
cream, whipped, 1 cup 580
cream, whipped, 1 tbsp. 37
Edam, 1 oz. 105
Fontina, 1 oz. 114
Gorgonzola, 1 oz. 112
Gouda, 1 oz. 108
Gruyère, 1 oz. 110
Limburger, 1 oz. 98
Limburger, 1" cube 62
Monterey Jack, 1 oz. 103
Mozzarella, low-moisture, part skim, 1 oz. 85
Muenster, 1 oz. 100
Parmesan, 1 oz. 111
Parmesan, grated, 1 oz. 132
Parmesan, grated, 1 cup loosely packed 467
Parmesan, grated, 1 cup packed 654
Parmesan, grated, 1 tbsp. 23
Parmesan, shredded, 1 oz. 120
Parmesan, shredded, 1 cup loosely packed 338

Parmesan, shredded, 1 cup packed 464
Parmesan, shredded, 1 tbsp. 21
Port du Salut, 1 oz. 100
Provolone, 1 oz. 99
ricotta, moist, 1 oz. 45
Roquefort, 1 oz. 104
Roquefort, 1" cube 64
Roquefort, crumbled, 1 cup loosely packed 497
Roquefort, crumbled, 1 cup packed 916
Swiss, domestic, 1 oz. 105
Swiss, domestic, 1" cube 56
Swiss, domestic, 1 slice (14 slices per lb.) 130

Cheeses, processed:
American, 1 oz. 105
American, 1" cube 65
American, diced, 1 cup loosely packed 518
American, shredded, 1 cup loosely packed 418
American, diced or shredded, 1 cup packed 944
American, grated, 1 tbsp. 28
Muenster, 1 oz. 102
pimento, American, 1 oz. 105
pimento, American, 1" cube 65
Swiss, 1 oz. 101
Swiss, 1" cube 64

Cheese spread, processed:
American, 1 oz. 82
American, 1" cube 50
American, diced, 1 cup loosely packed 403
American, shredded, 1 cup loosely packed 325
American, 1 cup packed 734
American, 1 tbsp. 40
American, canned, pressurized, 4 oz. can 389

Cheese straws:
10 pieces (5" long) 272
1 oz. 128

Cherimoyers, raw:
whole, with skin and seeds, 1 lb. 247
peeled and seeded, 4 oz. 107

Cherries, fresh:
sour, red, whole, with pits and stems, 1 lb. 213
sour, red, whole, 1 cup 60

    sour, red, pitted, 1 cup 90
    sweet, whole, with pits and stems, 1 lb. 286
    sweet, whole, 1 cup 82
    sweet, pitted, 1 cup 102
    sweet, 10 cherries 47

Cherries, canned, with liquid:
    sour, red, in water, pitted, 8 oz. 98
    sour, red, in water, pitted, 1 cup 105
    sweet, in water, with pits, 8 oz. 92
    sweet, in water, with pits, 1 cup 109
    sweet, in heavy syrup, with pits, 8 oz. 155
    sweet, in heavy syrup, with pits, 1 cup 191
    sweet, in heavy syrup, pitted, 8 oz. 189
    sweet, in heavy syrup, pitted, 1 cup 208

Cherries, frozen:
    sour, red, unsweetened, unthawed, 8 oz. 125
    sour, red, sweetened, unthawed, 8 oz. 254

Cherries, candied:
    1 oz. 96
    10 cherries 119

Cherries, maraschino, bottled:
    with liquid, 1 oz. 33
    1 average cherry 8

Cherry pie, see Pies

Chervil:
    raw, 1 oz. 16

Chestnut flour:
    4 oz. 410

Chestnuts, fresh:
    in shell, 1 lb. 713
    in shell, 1 cup 189
    in shell, 10 nuts 141
    shelled, 4 oz. 220
    shelled, 1 cup 310

Chestnuts, dried:
    shelled, 4 oz. 428

Chewing gum, sweetened:
    1 oz. 90
    1 stick 9
    candy-coated, 1 piece (¾" x ½" x ¼") 5

Chicken, fresh:

Chicken, potted, canned:
5½-oz. can	387
1 cup	558
1 tbsp.	32
1 oz.	70

Chicken à la king, home recipe:
8 oz.	433
1 cup	468

Chicken chow mein, see Chow mein, chicken

Chicken fricassee, home recipe:
8 oz.	365
1 cup	386

Chicken gizzards, see Gizzards

Chicken hearts, see Hearts

Chicken liver, see Liver

Chicken pot pie, home recipe:
Baked, 1 whole pie (9″ in diam.)	1,640
baked, ⅓ of 9″ pie	545
baked, 8 oz.	533

Chicken pot pie, frozen:
8-oz. pie	497

Chicken soup, see Soups

Chick-peas (garbanzos), dry:
raw, 8 oz.	817
raw, 1 cup	720

Chicory, witloof, see Endive, French or Belgian

Chicory greens, fresh:
untrimmed, 1 lb.	74
cuts, 1 cup	11
10 inner leaves	5

Chili con carne, canned:
with beans, 8 oz.	302
with beans, 1 cup	339
without beans, 8 oz.	454
without beans, 1 cup	510

Chili powder:
seasoned, 1 oz.	96
seasoned, 1 tbsp.	52

Chili sauce, tomato, canned or bottled:
8 oz.	236

Clam fritters, home recipe:
    1 fritter (2″ in diam., 1¾″ thick) 124
Clam juice or liquor, canned or bottled:
    1 cup 46
    1 fl. oz. 6
Clams, fresh, raw:
    hard or round, meat only, 1 pt. 363
    hard or round, meat only, 8 oz. 182
    hard or round, meat only, 4 cherrystones or 5 littlenecks 56
    soft, meat only, 1 pt. 372
    soft, meat only, 8 oz. 186
Clams, canned:
    with liquid, 8 oz. 118
    drained, 8 oz. 223
    drained, chopped or minced, 1 cup 157
Club soda, see **Soft drinks**
Cocoa and chocolate-flavored mixes, dry:
    high-fat or breakfast, processed, 1 oz. 84
    high-fat or breakfast, processed, 1 tbsp. 18
    medium-fat, processed, 1 oz. 74
    medium-fat, processed, 1 tbsp. 16
    low-medium-fat, processed, 1 oz. 61
    low-medium-fat, processed, 1 tbsp. 13
    low-fat, 1 oz. 53
    low-fat, 1 tbsp. 11
    mix, with nonfat dry milk, 1 oz. 102
    mix, with nonfat dry milk, 1 tbsp. 32
    mix, without milk, 1 oz. 98
    mix, without milk, 1 tbsp. 31
    mix, for hot chocolate, 1 oz. 111
    mix, for hot chocolate, 1 tbsp. 35
Coconut, fresh:
    in shell, 1 coconut (4⅝″ in diam.; about 27 oz.) 1,373
    shelled, meat only, 4 oz. 392
    shelled, meat only, 1 piece (2″ x 2″ x ½″) 156
    shredded or grated, 1 cup loosely packed 277
    shredded or grated, 1 cup packed 450
Coconut, dried, shredded:
    unsweetened, 4 oz. 751
    unsweetened, 1 cup 622

sweetened, 4 oz.	621
sweetened, 1 cup	515

Coconut, chocolate-covered, see Candy

Coconut cream (liquid from grated coconut meat):

1 cup	802
1 tbsp.	50

Coconut milk (liquid from grated coconut meat and coconut water):

1 cup	605

Coconut water (liquid from coconuts):

1 cup	53

Coconut custard pie, see Pies

Cod, fresh:

raw, fillets, 8 oz.	176
broiled, with butter, 1 steak (5½" x 4" x 1¼")	352
broiled, with butter, fillets, 4 oz.	192
broiled, with butter, 1 fillet (5" x 2½" x ⅞")	111

Cod, canned:

drained, 8.5 oz. (yield from 11-oz. can)	204
drained, 4 oz.	97
drained, flaked, 1 cup	119

Cod, frozen:

cakes, breaded, reheated, 4 oz.	308
fillets, 4 oz. or 2 average fillets	84
sticks, breaded, 4 oz. or 5 average sticks	276

Cod, dehydrated and dried:

dehydrated, lightly salted, 4 oz.	424
dehydrated, lightly salted, shredded, 1 cup	158
dried, salted, 4 oz.	148
dried, salted, 1 piece (5½" x 1½" x ½")	104

Codfish cakes, see Cod, frozen and Fish cakes

Coffee, instant:

regular, dry, 1 tbsp.	3
regular, dry, 1 tsp.	1
freeze-dried, dry, 1 tbsp.	5
freeze-dried, dry, 1 tsp.	1

Cola, see Soft drinks

Coleslaw:

homemade, with French dressing, 4 oz.	147
homemade, with French dressing, 1 cup	155
commercial, with French dressing, 4 oz.	108
commercial, with French dressing, 1 cup	114

commercial, with mayonnaise, 4 oz. 164
commercial, with mayonnaise, 1 cup 173
commercial, with mayonnaise-type salad dressing, 4 oz. 113
commercial, with mayonnaise-type salad dressing, 1 cup 119

Collards, fresh:

raw, with stems, 1 lb. 181
raw, leaves only, 1 lb. 204
leaves only, boiled in small amount water, drained, 1 cup 63
leaves only, boiled in large amount water, drained, 1 cup 59
with stems, boiled in small amount water, drained, 1 cup 42

Collards, frozen:

chopped, unthawed, 10-oz. pkg. 91
chopped, boiled, drained, 8.8 oz. (yield from 10-oz. pkg.) 75
chopped, boiled, drained, 1 cup 51

Consommé, see Soups

Cookie crumbs:

gingersnap, 1 cup 483
graham cracker, 1 cup loosely packed 326
graham cracker, 1 cup packed 403
vanilla wafer, 1 cup 370

Cookies:

animal crackers, 1 oz. 128
animal crackers, 10 average 112
assorted, 11-oz. pkg. (about 36 cookies) 1,498
assorted, 1 oz. 136
brownies with nuts, home recipe, 1 oz. 137
brownies with nuts, home recipe, 1 brownie (3" x 1" x ⅞") .. 97
brownies with nuts, iced, frozen, 1 oz. 119
brownies with nuts, iced, frozen, 1 brownie (1½" x 1¾" x ⅞") 103
butter, thin, rich, 1 oz. 130
butter, thin, rich, 10 cookies (2"–2½" in diam., ¼" thick) .. 229
chocolate, 1 oz. 126
chocolate chip, home recipe, 1 oz. 146
chocolate chip, home recipe, 4 cookies (2⅓" in diam.) 206
chocolate chip, commercial, 1 oz. 134
chocolate chip, commercial, 10 cookies (2¼" in diam.) 495
chocolate chip, commercial, 10 cookies (1¾" in diam.,
   ½" thick) 344
chocolate chip, commercial, 10 cookies (1¾" in diam.,
   ⅜" thick) 250

Cookies, continued

   self-rising, whole-ground, dry, 8 oz. 788
   self-rising, whole-ground, dry, 1 cup 465
   self-rising, degermed, dry, 8 oz. 790
   self-rising, degermed, dry, 1 cup 491

Corn muffins, see Muffins

Corn salad:
   raw, whole, 1 lb. 91
   raw, trimmed, 1 lb. 96

Cornstarch:
   4 oz. 413
   stirred, 1 cup 463
   stirred, 1 tbsp. 29

Corn syrup, see Syrups

Cowpeas (black-eyed peas):
   immature seeds, in pods, raw, 1 lb. 317
   immature seeds, shelled, raw, 8 oz. 288
   immature seeds, shelled, raw, 1 cup 184
   immature seeds, boiled, drained, 1 cup 178
   young pods, with seeds, raw, 1 lb. 182
   young pods, with seeds, boiled, drained, 1 cup 154
   mature seeds, dry, uncooked, 8 oz. 779
   mature seeds, dry, uncooked, 1 cup 583
   mature seeds, dry, cooked, 1 cup 190

Cowpeas (black-eyed peas), canned:
   with liquid, 8 oz. 159
   with liquid, 1 cup 179

Cowpeas (black-eyed peas), frozen:
   unthawed, 10-oz. pkg. 372
   boiled, drained, 9.2 oz. (yield from 10-oz. pkg.) 338
   boiled, drained, 1 cup 221

Crab, fresh:
   steamed, in shell, 1 lb. 202
   steamed, meat only, 8 oz. 211
   steamed, meat only, pieces, 1 cup loosely packed 144
   steamed, meat only, flaked, 1 cup loosely packed 116
   steamed, meat only, pieces or flaked, 1 cup packed 195

Crab, canned:
   drained, 8 oz. 229
   claw, drained, 1 cup loosely packed 116

saltines, 4 crackers (1⅞″ square) 48
soda, 1 oz. 124
soda, 10 biscuits (2⅜″ x 2⅛″ x ¼″) 221
soda, 10 crackers (1⅞″ square) 125
whole-wheat, 1 oz. 114
zwiebacks, 1 oz. 121
zwiebacks, 1 piece (3½″ x 1½″ x ½″) 30

Cranberries:
fresh, whole, with stems, 1 lb. 200
fresh, without stems, 1 cup 52
fresh, chopped, 1 cup 51
dehydrated, 1 oz. 104

Cranberry juice cocktail, canned or bottled:
6 fl. oz. 124
1 cup 164

Cranberry-orange relish:
uncooked, 4 oz. 202
uncooked, 1 cup 498

Cranberry sauce:
canned, strained, 1 oz. 41
canned, strained, 1 cup 404
homemade, unstrained, 1 cup 493

Crayfish:
raw, in shell, 1 lb. 39
raw, meat only, 4 oz. 82

Cream:
half and half, 1 cup 324
half and half, 1 tbsp. 20
light, table or coffee, 1 cup 506
light, table or coffee, 1 tbsp. 32
whipping, light, 1 cup unwhipped 717
whipping, light, 1 tbsp. unwhipped 45
whipping, light, 1 cup whipped 357
whipping, light, 1 tbsp. whipped 23
whipping, heavy, 1 cup unwhipped 837
whipping, heavy, 1 tbsp. unwhipped 53
whipping, heavy, 1 cup whipped 419
whipping, heavy, 1 tbsp. whipped 27

Cream, imitation:
creamer, powdered, 1 tbsp. 30

creamer, frozen, liquid, 1 tbsp.	20
sour-cream dressing, 1 tbsp.	20
Cream, sour:	
1 cup	485
1 tbsp.	26
Cress, garden:	
raw, untrimmed, 1 lb.	103
raw, trimmed, 4 oz.	36
boiled in small amount water, drained, 1 cup	31
boiled in large amount water, drained, 1 cup	30
Cress, water, see Watercress	
Croaker, Atlantic:	
raw, whole, 1 lb.	148
raw, meat only, 4 oz.	109
baked, 4 oz.	152
Croaker, white:	
raw, meat only, 4 oz.	95
Croaker, yellow:	
raw, meat only, 4 oz.	101
Cucumber, fresh:	
with skin, 1 lb.	65
with skin, 1 large (8¼" long; about 1½ per lb.)	45
with skin, 1 small (6⅜" long; about 2⅔ per lb.)	25
with skin, sliced, 6 large or 8 small slices (about 1 oz.)	4
with skin, sliced, 1 cup	16
pared, 1 lb.	64
pared, 1 large (8¼" long)	39
pared, 1 small (6⅜" long)	22
pared, sliced, 6½ large or 9 small slices (about 1 oz.)	4
pared, sliced or diced, 1 cup	20
Cucumber, pickled, see Pickles	
Cupcakes, baked from home recipe:	
chocolate, without icing, 1 cupcake (2¾" in diam.)	121
chocolate, without icing, 1 cupcake (2½" in diam.)	92
chocolate, with chocolate icing, 1 cupcake (2¾" in diam.) ...	162
chocolate, with chocolate icing, 1 cupcake (2½" in diam.) ...	125
chocolate, with uncooked white icing, 1 cupcake (2¾" in diam.)	162
chocolate, with uncooked white icing, 1 cupcake (2½" in diam.)	122
plain, without icing, 1 cupcake (2¾" in diam.)	120
plain, without icing, 1 cupcake (2½" in diam.)	91
plain, with chocolate icing, 1 cupcake (2¾" in diam.)	173

plain, with chocolate icing, 1 cupcake (2½" in diam.)	132
plain, with boiled white icing, 1 cupcake (2¾" in diam.)	155
plain, with boiled white icing, 1 cupcake (2½" in diam.)	116
plain, with uncooked white icing, 1 cupcake (2¾" in diam.)	172
plain, with uncooked white icing, 1 cupcake (2½" in diam.)	128

Cupcakes, baked from mix:

with egg, milk, without icing, 1 cupcake (2¾" in diam.)	116
with egg, milk, without icing, 1 cupcake (2½" in diam.)	88
with egg, milk, chocolate icing, 1 cupcake (2¾" in diam.)	172
with egg, milk, chocolate icing, 1 cupcake (2½" in diam.)	129
yellow, with eggs, chocolate icing, 1 cupcake (2¾" in diam.)	155
yellow, with eggs, chocolate icing, 1 cupcake (2½" in diam.)	118

Currants, fresh:

black, with stems, 1 lb.	240
black, trimmed, 1 cup	60
red or white, with stems, 1 lb.	220
red or white, trimmed, 1 cup	55

Cusk:

raw, meat only, 4 oz.	85
steamed, meat only, 4 oz.	120

Custard, see Pies and Puddings

D

food and measure	calories

Dandelion greens, fresh:

raw, fully trimmed, 1 lb.	204
boiled, drained, 1 cup loosely packed	35
boiled, drained, 1 cup packed	70

Danish pastry, plain, commercial:

ring, 12-oz. pkg. (8" in diam.; 2"-diam. hole)	1,435
ring, ⅛ of 12-oz. ring (3⅛" arc)	179
ring, 5-oz. pkg. (7" in diam.; 4"-diam. hole)	599
ring, ¼ of 5-oz. ring (5½" arc)	150
rectangular, 1 piece (6½" x 2¾" x ¾")	317
round, 1 piece (4¼" in diam., 1" thick)	274
4-oz. piece	480

Dates, Chinese, see Jujubes

Dates, domestic:
with pits, 1 lb. 1,081
pitted, 1 lb. 1,243
chopped, 1 cup 488
10 average dates 219

Deviled ham, see Ham, deviled

Dewberries, see Blackberries

Dinners, frozen, see Plate dinners

Distilled liquor, see Alcoholic beverages

Dock or sorrel:
raw, with stems, 1 lb. 89
boiled, drained, 1 cup 38

Doughnuts, cake-type, plain:
1 doughnut (3⅝" in diam., 1¼" thick; about 2 oz.) 227
1 doughnut (3½" in diam., 1" thick; about 1½ oz.) 164
1 doughnut (3¼" in diam., 1" thick; about ⅞ oz.) 98
1 doughnut (1½" in diam., ¾" thick; about ½ oz.) 55

Doughnuts, yeast, plain:
1 doughnut (3¾" in diam., 1¼" thick; about 1½ oz.) 176

Drum:
freshwater, raw, whole, 1 lb. 143
freshwater, raw, meat only, 4 oz. 138
red, raw, whole, 1 lb. 149
red, raw, meat only, 4 oz. 91

Duck:
domesticated, raw, meat only, 4 oz. 188
domesticated, roasted, meat only, 4 oz. 352
wild, raw, meat only, 4 oz. 157

E

food and measure	calories

Eclairs, custard-filled:
with chocolate icing, 1 éclair (5" x 2" x 1¾") 239
with chocolate icing, 4 oz. 272

Eel:

domestic, raw, meat only, 4 oz. 264

smoked, 4 oz. 376

Eggnog, commercial, dairy-packed:

6% butterfat, 1 cup 300

8% butterfat, 1 cup 342

Eggplant, fresh:

raw, whole, 1 lb. 92

raw, diced, 1 cup 50

boiled, drained, 4 oz. 22

boiled, drained, diced, 1 cup 38

Eggs, chicken, fresh:

raw, whole, 1 lb. (8 extra large, 9 large, or 10 medium eggs) .. 739

raw, whole, 1 extra large egg 94

raw, whole, 1 large egg 82

raw, whole, 1 medium egg 72

raw, white of 1 extra large egg 19

raw, white of 1 large egg 17

raw, white of 1 medium egg 15

raw, yolk of 1 extra large egg 66

raw, yolk of 1 large egg 59

raw, yolk of 1 medium egg 52

boiled or poached, 1 extra large egg 94

boiled or poached, 1 large egg 82

boiled or poached, 1 medium egg 72

fried, 1 extra large egg 112

fried, 1 large egg 99

fried, 1 medium egg 86

scrambled or omelet, 1 extra large egg 126

scrambled or omelet, 1 large egg 111

scrambled or omelet, 1 medium egg 97

Eggs, chicken, dried:

whole, ½ cup 320

whole, 1 oz. 168

whole, 1 tbsp. 41

white, flakes, 1 oz. 99

white, powdered, 1 oz. 105

white, powdered, 1 tbsp. 26

yolk, 1 oz. 188

yolk, 1 tbsp. 47

Eggs, duck, fresh:
  raw, whole, 1 lb. (about 6½ eggs) 866
  raw, whole, 1 egg 134
Eggs, goose, fresh:
  raw, whole, 1 lb. (about 3⅛ eggs) 839
  raw, whole, 1 egg 266
Eggs, turkey, fresh:
  raw, whole, 1 lb. (about 5-7/10 eggs) 771
  raw, whole, 1 egg 135
Elderberries, fresh:
  with stems, 1 lb. 307
  without stems, 4 oz. 82
Endive, curly, see **Escarole**
Endive, French or Belgian, bleached, fresh:
  trimmed, 1 lb. 68
  1 head (5″–7″ long) 8
  10 small leaves 5
  chopped (½″ pieces), 1 cup 14
Escarole, fresh:
  untrimmed, 1 lb. 80
  4 large outer leaves 20
  7 small leaves 4
  cuts or small pieces, 1 cup 10
Eulachon (smelt), raw:
  meat only, 4 oz. 135

F

food and measure   calories

Farina, see **Cereals, cooking-type**
Fats, cooking (see also **Lard, Oils,** etc.):
  vegetable shortening, 8 oz. 2,005
  vegetable shortening, 1 cup 1,768
  vegetable shortening, 1 tbsp. 111
Fennel leaves, raw:
  1 lb. (weighed untrimmed) 118
  trimmed, 4 oz. 32

Figs, raw:
whole, 1 lb. 363
1 large (2½" in diam.; about 7 per lb.) 52
1 medium (2¼" in diam.; about 9 per lb.) 40
1 small (1½" in diam.; about 11 per lb.) 32

Figs, candied:
1 oz. 85

Figs, canned:
in water, with liquid, 8 oz. 109
in water, with liquid, 1 cup 119
in water, 3 figs and 1¾ tbsp. liquid 38
in heavy syrup, with liquid, 8 oz. 191
in heavy syrup, with liquid, 1 cup 218
in heavy syrup, 3 figs and 1¾ tbsp. liquid 71

Figs, dried:
4 oz. 311
1 fig (2" x 1") 57

Filberts (hazelnuts):
in shell, 4 oz. 331
in shell, 10 nuts 87
shelled, 4 oz. 719
shelled, whole, 1 cup 856
shelled, whole, 1 oz. (about 20 nuts) 180
shelled, chopped, 1 cup 729
shelled, chopped, 1 tbsp. 44
shelled, ground, 1 cup 476

Finnan haddie:
meat only, 4 oz. 117

Fish, see individual listings

Fish cakes, fried, home recipe:
made with canned fish, potato, egg, 4 oz. 195
made with canned fish, potato, egg, 1 cake (3" in diam.,
5⁄8" thick) 103
made with canned fish, potato, egg, 1 bite-size cake
(1¼" in diam.) 21

Fish cakes, fried, frozen:
reheated, 4 oz. 306
reheated, 1 cake (3" in diam., 5⁄8" thick; or
2½" in diam., 7⁄8" thick) 162
reheated, 1 bite-size cake (1¼" in diam., 5⁄8" thick) 33

Fish flakes, canned:
7-oz. can 220
1 cup 183

Fish flour:
from whole fish, 1 oz. 95
from fish fillets, 1 oz. 113
from fish-fillet waste, 1 oz. 86

Fish loaf, home recipe, cooked:
whole loaf (8¾″ x 4⅛″ x 2½″) 1,507
1 slice (4⅛″ x 2½″ x 1″; ⅛ of whole loaf) 186

Fish sticks, breaded, fried, frozen:
reheated, 8-oz. pkg. 400
reheated, 1 stick (4″ x 1″ x ½″) 50

Flat fish, see Flounder, Sand dab, and Sole

Flounder, fillets:
raw, 4 oz. 89
baked with butter, 4 oz. 229
baked with butter, 1 fillet (8¼″ x 2¾″ x ¼″) 202
baked with butter, 1 fillet (6″ x 2½″ x ¼″) 115

Flour (see also individual listings):
buckwheat:
    whole-grain, 4 oz. 382
    whole-grain, sifted, 1 cup 335
    dark, 4 oz. 380
    dark, sifted, spooned into cup, 1 cup 326
    light, 4 oz. 395
    light, sifted, spooned into cup, 1 cup 340
carob (St.-John's-bread), 4 oz. 205
carob (St.-John's-bread), 1 cup 252
carob (St.-John's-bread), 1 tbsp. 14
corn, 4 oz. 419
corn, 1 cup 431
rye:
    dark, 4 oz. 373
    dark, spooned into cup, 1 cup 419
    light, 4 oz. 407
    light, unsifted, spooned into cup, 1 cup 364
    light, sifted, spooned into cup, 1 cup 314
    medium, 4 oz. 399
    medium, sifted, spooned into cup, 1 cup 308

Flour, continued
  soybean:
    full-fat, 4 oz. 478
    full-fat, not stirred, 1 cup 358
    full-fat, stirred, 1 cup 295
    low-fat, 4 oz. 401
    low-fat, stirred, 1 cup 313
    defatted, 4 oz. 370
    defatted, stirred, 1 cup 326
  sunflower seed, partially defatted, 4 oz. 386
  wheat, patent (white):
    all-purpose, 4 oz. 415
    all-purpose, unsifted, dipped with cup, 1 cup 499
    all-purpose, unsifted, spooned into cup, 1 cup 455
    all-purpose, sifted, spooned into cup, 1 cup 419
    all-purpose, instant-blending, unsifted, 1 cup 470
    bread, 4 oz. 416
    bread, unsifted, dipped with cup, 1 cup 500
    bread, sifted, spooned into cup, 1 cup 420
    cake or pastry, 4 oz. 415
    cake or pastry, unsifted, dipped with cup, 1 cup 430
    cake or pastry, unsifted, spooned into cup, 1 cup 397
    cake or pastry, sifted, spooned into cup, 1 cup 349
    gluten (45%), 4 oz. 431
    gluten (45%), unsifted, dipped with cup, 1 cup 529
    gluten (45%), unsifted, spooned into cup, 1 cup 510
    self-rising, 4 oz. 401
    self-rising, unsifted, spooned into cup, 1 cup 440
    self-rising, sifted, spooned into cup, 1 cup 405
  wheat, whole (hard wheat), 4 oz. 380
  wheat, whole (hard wheat), stirred, spooned into cup, 1 cup .. 400
Frankfurters, canned:
  12-oz. can (7 frankfurters) 751
  1 frankfurter (4⅞″ long, ⅞″ in diam.) 106
Frankfurters, chilled or refrigerated:
  without binders (all meat):
    not smoked, 1-lb. pkg. (8 or 10 frankfurters) 1,343
    not smoked, 5½-oz. pkg. (about 16 frankfurters) 462
    not smoked, 1 frankfurter (5″ long, ⅞″ in diam.; 8 per lb.) . 169
    not smoked, 1 frankfurter (5″ long, ¾″ in diam.; 10 per lb.) 133
    not smoked, 1 frankfurter (1¾″ long., ½″ in diam.; ⅓ oz.) . 30

half smoked, 11-oz. pkg. (about 5 frankfurters) 924
half smoked, 1 frankfurter (5" long, 1" in diam.) 184
smoked, 12-oz. pkg. (8 or 10 frankfurters) 1,006
smoked, 5-oz. pkg. (about 16 frankfurters) 420
smoked, 1 frankfurter (4¾" long, ¾" in diam.; 8 per lb.) .. 124
smoked, 1 frankfurter (4½" long, ¾" in diam.; 10 per lb.) . 101
smoked, 1 frankfurter (1¾" long, ⅝" in diam ; ⅓ oz.) 27

with nonfat dry milk:

  1 lb. pkg. (8 or 10 frankfurters) 1,361
  1 frankfurter (5" long, ⅞" in diam.; 8 per lb.) 171
  1 frankfurter (5" long, ¾" in diam.; 10 per lb.) 135

with cereal:

  1 lb. pkg. (8 or 10 frankfurters) 1,125
  1 frankfurter (5" long, ⅞" in diam.; 8 per lb.) 141
  1 frankfurter (5" long, ¾" in diam.; 10 per lb.) 112

Frogs' legs, raw:

  whole, with bone, 1 lb. 215
  meat only, 4 oz. 83

Frostings, see Icings

Frozen dinners, see Plate dinners

Fruit, see individual listings

Fruit, mixed, frozen:

  sweetened, 8-oz. pkg. 250

Fruitcake, see Cakes

Fruit cocktail, canned:

  in water, with liquid, 8 oz. 84
  in water, with liquid, 1 cup 91
  in heavy syrup, with liquid, 8 oz. 173
  in heavy syrup, with liquid, 1 cup 194

Fruit salad, canned:

  in water, with liquid, 8 oz. 80
  in water, with liquid, 1 cup 80
  in heavy syrup, with liquid, 8 oz. 170
  in heavy syrup, with liquid, 1 cup 191

Fruit salad, dairy-packed:

  8 oz. 136

Fudge syrup, see Chocolate syrup

food and measure   calories

Garbanzos, see Chick-peas
Garlic, raw:
  whole, 2 oz. (weighed with skin) 68
  peeled, 1 oz. 39
  peeled, 5 cloves 14
Gelatin:
  unflavored, dry, 1 oz. 95
  unflavored, dry, 1 tbsp. 33
Gelatin dessert, flavored, commercial:
  dry, 3-oz. pkg. 315
  prepared with water, 2¼ cups (yield from 3-oz. pkg.) 315
  prepared with water, 1 cup 142
  prepared, fruit (bananas and grapes) added, 1 cup 161
Ginger, crystallized (candied):
  1 oz. 96
Ginger root, fresh:
  unpeeled, 1 lb. 207
  peeled, 1 oz. 14
Gizzards:
  chicken, raw, 1 lb. 513
  chicken, simmered, 11⅞ oz. (yield from 1 lb. raw) 497
  chicken, simmered, 4 oz. 168
  chicken, simmered, chopped or diced, 1 cup 215
  goose, raw, 1 lb. 631
  turkey, raw, 1 lb. 712
  turkey, simmered, 11⅞ oz. (yield from 1 lb. raw) 659
  turkey, simmered, 4 oz. 222
  turkey, simmered, chopped or diced, 1 cup 284
Gluten flour, see Flour, wheat
Goat's milk, see Milk, goat's
Goose, domesticated:
  raw, whole, ready-to-cook, 1 lb. 1,172
  roasted, whole, 8½ oz. (yield from 1 lb. raw) 1,022
  roasted, meat only, 4 oz. 266
  roasted, meat and skin, 4 oz. 503

Gooseberries, fresh:
1 lb. 177
1 cup 59

Gooseberries, canned:
in water, with liquid, 8 oz. 59
in heavy syrup, with liquid, 8 oz. 204

Gourd, see **Towel gourd**

Granadillas, purple (passion fruit), raw:
whole, in shell, 1 lb. 212
whole, 1 average fruit 16
shelled, 4 oz. 102

Grape drink, canned:
1 cup 135

Grapefruit, fresh:
pink or red, seeded:
whole, with skin, 1 lb. 87
½ large (4⅜" in diam.) 68
½ medium (4 3/16" in diam.) 58
½ small (3 15/16" in diam.) 51
sections, 1 cup 80
sections, with 2 tbsp. juice, 1 cup 92
pink or red, seedless:
whole, with skin, 1 lb. 93
½ large (3 15/16" in diam.) 55
½ medium, 3¾" in diam.) 49
½ small (3 9/16" in diam.) 41
sections, 1 cup 80
sections, with 2 tbsp. juice, 1 cup 92
white, seeded:
whole, with skin, 1 lb. 84
½ large (4⅜" in diam.) 66
½ medium (4 3/16" in diam.) 56
½ small (3 15/16" in diam.) 49
sections, 1 cup 82
sections, with 2 tbsp. juice, 1 cup 94
white, seedless:
whole, with skin, 1 lb. 87
½ large (3 15/16" in diam.) 51
½ medium (3¾" in diam.) 46
½ small (3 9/16" in diam.) 38

Grapefruit-orange juice, see Orange-grapefruit juice

Grapefruit-pineapple juice drink, see Pineapple-grapefruit juice drink

Grapefruit peel, candied:
1 oz. 90

Grape juice, canned or bottled:
1 cup 167

Grape juice concentrate, frozen:
sweetened, undiluted, 6-fl.-oz. can 395
sweetened, diluted with 3 parts water, 1 cup 133

Grapes, fresh:
all varieties, seeds removed, halves, 1 cup 117
American-type (slipskin), Concord, Delaware, Niagara, etc.:
seeded, whole, 1 lb. 197
seeded, 1 cup 70
seeded, 10 grapes (¾" in diam.) 18
European-type (adherent skin), Malaga, muscat, Thompson
seedless, etc.:
whole, 1 lb. 270
seeded, 1 cup 102
seedless, 1 cup 107
seedless, 10 grapes (⅝" in diam.) 34

Grapes, canned (Thompson seedless):
in water, with liquid, 8 oz. 116
in water, with liquid, 1 cup 125
in heavy syrup, with liquid, 8 oz. 175
in heavy syrup, with liquid, 1 cup 197

Griddlecakes, see Pancakes

Grits, see Corn grits

Ground cherries (cape gooseberries or pohas):
raw, with husks, 1 lb. 221
raw, without husks, 1 lb. 240
raw, without husks, 1 cup 74

Grouper, raw:
whole, 1 lb. 170
meat only, 4 oz. 99

Guavas, common, fresh:
whole, with stems, 1 lb. 273
trimmed, 4 oz. 70
1 small (about 2¾ oz.) 48

Guavas, strawberry, fresh:
  whole, with stems, 1 lb. 289
  trimmed, 4 oz. 74
Guinea hen, raw:
  whole, ready-to-cook, 1 lb. 594
  meat and skin, 4 oz. 179
Gum, see Chewing gum

H

Haddock, fresh:
  raw, whole, 1 lb. 172
  raw, fillets, 1 lb. 360
  fillets, breaded, fried, 12⅘ oz. (yield from 1 lb. raw) 597
  fillets, breaded, fried, 4 oz. 187
Haddock, frozen:
  fillets, 4 oz. 88
Haddock, smoked, see Finnan haddie

Half and half, see Cream

Halibut, Atlantic or Pacific, fresh:
  raw, whole, 1 lb. 268
  raw, fillets, 1 lb. 452
  fillets, broiled with butter, 12⅞ oz. (yield from 1 lb. raw) 624
  fillets, broiled with butter, 4 oz. 194
Halibut, frozen:
  steak, 4 oz. 144
Halibut, smoked:
  4 oz. 254
Ham, retail cuts (see also Pork):
  fresh, lean with fat:
    raw, with bone and skin, 1 lb. 1,188
    baked, with bone and skin, 9.2 oz. (yield from 1 lb. raw) .. 980
    raw, without bone and skin, 1 lb. 1,397
    baked, without bone and skin, 10.9 oz. (yield from 1 lb. raw) .1,152
    baked, without bone and skin, 4 oz. 424

baked, chopped or diced, 1 cup 524
baked, ground, 1 cup 411
fresh, lean only (trimmed of fat):
baked, with bone and skin, 6.8 oz.
(yield from 1 lb. raw with fat) 421
baked, without bone and skin, 8.1 oz.
(yield from 1 lb. raw with fat) 495
baked, without bone and skin, 4 oz. 246
baked, chopped or diced, 1 cup 304
baked, ground, 1 cup 239
light-cured, lean with fat:
raw, with bone and skin, 1 lb. 1,100
baked, with bone and skin, 11.3 oz. (yield from 1 lb. raw) .. 925
raw, without bone and skin, 1 lb. 1,279
baked, without bone and skin, 13.1 oz. (yield from 1 lb. raw) .1,075
baked, without bone and skin, 4 oz. 328
baked, chopped or diced, 1 cup 405
baked, ground, 1 cup 318
light-cured, lean only (trimmed of fat):
baked, with bone and skin, 8.7 oz.
(yield from 1 lb. raw with fat) 460
baked, without bone and skin, 10.2 oz.
(yield from 1 lb. raw with fat) 539
baked, without bone and skin, 4 oz. 212
baked, chopped or diced, 1 cup 262
baked, ground, 1 cup 206
long-cured, dry, unbaked:
medium-fat, lean with fat, with bone and skin, 4 oz. 384
relatively lean, lean with fat, with bone and skin, 4 oz. 302
picnic, see **Pork**
Ham, boiled:
packaged, 8 oz. (about 8 slices) 531
packaged, 1 slice (6¼" x 4" x 1/16"; about 1 oz.) 66
Ham, canned:
cured, boneless, 16-oz. can 875
cured, boneless, 4 oz. 219
Ham, deviled, canned:
2½-oz. can 225
1 cup 790
1 oz. 100
1 tbsp. 46

Ham, minced:

4 oz. 259

Ham, spiced, canned:

7-oz. can 582

1 slice (3″ x 2″ x ½″; ⅓ of 7-oz. can) 176

Hamburger, see Beef, ground

Ham croquettes, home recipe:

pan-fried, 1 croquette (1″ in diam., 3″ thick) 163

Hazelnuts, see Filberts

Head cheese:

packaged, 8 oz. (about 8 slices) 608

packaged, 1 slice (4″ x 4″ x 3/32″; about 1 oz.) 76

Hearts, fresh:

beef, lean only, raw, 8 oz. 245

beef, lean only, braised, 4 oz. 213

beef, lean only, braised, chopped or diced, 1 cup 273

calf, raw, 8 oz. 281

calf, braised, 4 oz. 236

calf, braised, chopped or diced, 1 cup 302

chicken, raw, 8 oz. 304

chicken, simmered, 4 oz. 196

chicken, simmered, chopped or diced, 1 cup 251

hog, raw, 8 oz. 257

hog, braised, 4 oz. 221

hog, braised, chopped or diced, 1 cup 283

lamb, raw, 8 oz. 368

lamb, braised, 4 oz. 295

lamb, braised, chopped or diced, 1 cup 377

turkey, raw, 8 oz. 388

turkey, simmered, 4 oz. 245

turkey, simmered, chopped or diced, 1 cup 313

Herring:

fresh, Atlantic, raw, whole, 1 lb. 407

fresh, Atlantic, raw, meat only, 4 oz. 200

fresh, Pacific, raw, meat only, 4 oz. 111

canned, plain, with liquid, 15-oz. can 884

canned, plain, with liquid, 4 oz. 236

canned, in tomato sauce, 4 oz. 200

canned, in tomato sauce, 1 tbsp. sauce, 1 herring

(4¾″ x 1⅛″ x ⅝″) 97

pickled, Bismarck or marinated, 4 oz. 253

pickled, Bismarck, 1 herring (7" x 1½" x ½")	112
pickled, marinated pieces, 1 piece (1¾" x ⅞" x ½")	33
salted or brined, 4 oz.	247
smoked, bloaters, 4 oz.	222
smoked, hard, 4 oz.	340
smoked, kippered, 4 oz.	239
smoked, kippered, canned, drained, 4 oz.	244
smoked, kippered, canned, drained, 1 fillet (7" x 2¼" x ¼")	137
smoked, kippered, canned, drained, 1 fillet (4⅜" x 1¾" x ¼")	84
smoked, kippered, canned, drained, 1 fillet (2⅜" x 1⅜" x ¼")	42

Herring, lake, see **Lake herring**

Hickory nuts:

in shell, 4 oz.	267
shelled, 4 oz.	763

Hominy grits, see **Corn grits**

Honey:

strained or extracted, 4 oz.	345
strained or extracted, 1 cup	1,031
strained or extracted, 1 tbsp.	64
strained or extracted, 1 packet (½ oz.)	43

Honeydew melon, fresh:

whole, with rind and seeds, 1 lb.	94
1 wedge (2" x 7")	49
cubed or diced, 1 cup	56

Horseradish:

raw, whole, 1 lb.	288
raw, pared, 1 oz.	25
prepared, 1 oz.	11
prepared, 1 tbsp.	6
prepared, 1 tsp.	2

Hot dogs, see **Frankfurters**

Hyacinth beans, raw:

young pods, untrimmed, 1 lb.	140
young pods, cuts (½" pieces), 1 cup	32
mature seeds, dry, 4 oz.	383

I

Ice cream:
hardened, 10% fat, 1 cup 257
hardened, 12% fat, 1 cup 275
hardened, rich, 16% fat, 1 cup 329
soft-serve (frozen custard), 1 cup 334
Ice-cream cone:
1 oz. 107
1 average 19
rolled sugar, 1 average 37
Ice milk:
hardened, 5.1% fat, 1 cup 199
soft-serve, 5.1% fat, 1 cup 266
Ices, water:
lime, 1 cup 247
Icings, cake, home recipe:
caramel, ½ cup 612
chocolate, ½ cup 517
coconut, ½ cup 302
white, uncooked, ½ cup 600
white, boiled, ½ cup 149
Icings, cake, prepared from mix:
chocolate fudge, ½ cup 586
creamy fudge, made with water, ½ cup 416
creamy fudge, made with water and table fat, ½ cup 469
Inconnu (sheefish), raw:
whole, 1 lb. 417
meat only, 4 oz. 166

J

Jack fruit, fresh:
whole, 1 lb. 124
peeled and seeded, 4 oz. 111

Jack mackerel, raw:
meat only, 4 oz. 162
Jams and preserves, commercial:
all flavors, 1 oz. 77
all flavors, 1 tbsp. 54
all flavors, 1 packet (½ oz.) 38
Jellies, commercial:
all flavors, 1 oz. 70
all flavors, 1 tbsp. 49
all flavors, 1 packet (½ oz.) 38
Jerusalem artichokes, fresh:
whole, with skin, 1 lb. 207
pared, 4 oz. 75
Juices, see individual listings
Jujubes (Chinese dates):
fresh, whole, 1 lb. 443
fresh, seeded, 4 oz. 119
dried, whole, with seeds, 1 lb. 1,159
dried, seeded, 4 oz. 325

K

food and measure	calories

Kale, fresh:
raw, whole, with stems, 1 lb. 128
raw, whole, without stems, 1 lb. 154
raw, trimmed, leaves only, 4 oz. 80
boiled, drained, with stems, 1 cup 31
boiled, drained, leaves only, 1 cup 43
Kale, frozen:
unthawed, 10-oz. pkg. 91
boiled, drained, 7.7 oz. (yield from 10-oz. pkg.) 68
boiled, drained, 1 cup 40
Kidneys, fresh:
beef, raw, 8 oz. 294
beef, braised, 4 oz. 286
beef, braised, pieces (½" x ½" x ¼"), 1 cup 353

calf, raw, 8 oz.	256
hog, raw, 8 oz.	240
lamb, raw, 8 oz.	238

Kingfish, fresh:

raw, whole, 1 lb.	210
raw, meat only, 4 oz.	119

Kippers, see Herring

Knockwurst:

packaged, 12-oz. pkg. (about 5 links)	945
packaged, 1 link (4″ long, 1⅛″ in diam.)	189

Kohlrabi, fresh:

raw, whole, without leaves, 1 lb.	96
raw, pared, 4 oz.	33
raw, pared, diced, 1 cup	41
boiled, drained, 4 oz.	27
boiled, drained, diced, 1 cup	40

Kumquats, fresh:

whole, with seeds, 1 lb.	274
with seeds, trimmed, 4 oz.	74
1 medium	12

L

food and measure	calories

Lake herring (cisco), raw:

whole, 1 lb.	226
meat only, 4 oz.	109

Lake trout, raw:

drawn, 1 lb.	282
meat only, 4 oz.	191

Lake trout (siscowet), raw:

under 6.5 lb., whole, 1 lb.	404
under 6.5 lb., meat only, 4 oz.	273
over 6.5 lb., whole, 1 lb.	856
over 6.5 lb., meat only, 4 oz.	594

Lamb, retail cuts:

  leg, lean with fat:

    raw, with bone, 1 lb. 845

    roasted, with bone, 9.4 oz. (yield from 1 lb. raw) 745

    raw, boneless, 1 lb. 1,007

    roasted, boneless, 11.2 oz. (yield from 1 lb. raw) 887

    roasted, boneless, 4 oz. 317

    roasted, chopped or diced, 1 cup 391

  leg, lean only (trimmed of fat):

    roasted, with bone, 7.8 oz. (yield from 1 lb. raw with fat) ... 411

    roasted, boneless, 9.3 oz. (yield from 1 lb. raw with fat) ... 491

    roasted, boneless, 4 oz. 211

    roasted, chopped or diced, 1 cup 260

  loin chops, with bone, lean with fat:

    raw, 1 lb. 1,146

    broiled, 10.1 oz. (yield from 1 lb. raw) 1,023

    broiled, 4 oz. 407

    broiled, 1 chop, 3.4 oz. (3 chops per lb.) 341

    broiled, 1 chop, 2.5 oz. (4 chops per lb.) 255

  loin chops, with bone, lean only (trimmed of fat):

    broiled, 6.9 oz. (yield from 1 lb. raw with fat) 368

    broiled, 4 oz. 213

    broiled, 1 chop, 2.3 oz. (3 chops per lb.) 122

    broiled, 1 chop, 1.7 oz. (4 chops per lb.) 92

  rib chops, with bone, lean with fat:

    raw, 1 lb. 1,229

    broiled, 9.5 oz. (yield from 1 lb. raw) 1,091

    broiled, 4 oz. 462

    broiled, 1 chop, 3.1 oz. (3 chops per lb.) 362

    broiled, 1 chop, 2.4 oz. (4 chops per lb.) 273

  rib chops, with bone, lean only (trimmed of fat):

    broiled, 6 oz. (yield from 1 lb. raw with fat) 361

    broiled, 4 oz. 239

    broiled, 1 chop, 2 oz. (3 chops per lb.) 120

    broiled, 1 chop, 1.5 oz. (4 chops per lb.) 91

  shoulder, lean with fat:

    raw, with bone, 1 lb. 1,082

    roasted, with bone, 9.5 oz. (yield from 1 lb. raw) 913

    raw, boneless, 1 lb. 1,275

    roasted, boneless, 11.2 oz. (yield from 1 lb. raw) 1,075

roasted, boneless, 4 oz.	383
roasted, chopped or diced, 1 cup	473
shoulder, lean only (trimmed of fat):	
roasted, with bone, 7 oz. (yield from 1 lb. raw with fat)	410
roasted, boneless, 8.3 oz. (yield from 1 lb. raw with fat)	482
roasted, boneless, 4 oz.	233
roasted, chopped or diced, 1 cup	287

Lamb's-quarters:

raw, trimmed, 1 lb.	195
boiled, drained, 4 oz.	36
boiled, drained, 1 cup	64

Lard:

8 oz.	2,045
1 cup	1,849
1 tbsp.	117

Leeks:

raw, untrimmed, 1 lb.	123
raw, bulb and lower leaf, 4 oz.	59
raw, 3 average	52

Lemonade, frozen:

undiluted, 6-fl.-oz. can	427
diluted with 4⅓ parts water, 1 cup	107

Lemon juice, fresh:

1 cup	61
1 tbsp.	4

Lemon juice, canned or bottled, unsweetened:

6-fl.-oz. can	42
1 cup	56
1 tbsp.	3

Lemon juice, frozen, unsweetened:

single-strength, 6-fl.-oz. can	40
single-strength, 1 tbsp.	3

Lemon peel, candied:

1 oz.	90

Lemons, fresh:

whole, 1 lb.	90
pulp only, 1 large (2⅜" in diam.)	29
pulp only, 1 medium (2⅛" in diam.)	20
1 slice (3/16" thick)	2
1 wedge, ¼ of large lemon	7

1 wedge, 1/6 of large lemon	5
1 wedge, ¼ of medium lemon	5
1 wedge, 1/6 of medium lemon	3

Lentils:

whole, dry, 8 oz.	771
whole, dry, 1 cup	646
whole, cooked, 1 cup	212
split, without seed coat, dry, 8 oz.	783
split, without seed coat, dry, 1 cup	656

Lettuce, fresh:

Boston or bibb, untrimmed, 1 lb.	47
Boston or bibb, 1 head (5" in diam.)	23
Boston or bibb, 1 large, 2 medium, or 3 small leaves	2
Boston or bibb, chopped or shredded, 1 cup	8
iceberg, untrimmed, 1 lb.	56
iceberg, 1 head trimmed (6" in diam.)	70
iceberg, 1 leaf (5" x 4½")	3
iceberg, 1 wedge (¼ of 6" head)	18
iceberg, 1 wedge (1/6 of 6" head)	12
iceberg, small chunks, 1 cup	10
iceberg, chopped or shredded, 1 cup	7
loose leaf, untrimmed, 1 lb.	52
loose leaf, 2 large leaves	9
loose leaf, chopped or shredded, 1 cup	10
romaine or cos, untrimmed, 1 lb.	52
romaine or cos, 3 leaves (8" long)	5
romaine or cos, chopped or shredded, 1 cup	10

Lichee nuts:

raw, in shell, 1 lb.	174
raw, shelled, 4 oz.	73
raw, 6 average nuts	41
dry, in shell, 1 lb.	578
dry, shelled, 4 oz.	316

Lima beans, see Beans, lima

Limeade, frozen:

undiluted, 6-fl.-oz. can	408
diluted with 4⅓ parts water, 1 cup	102

Lime juice, fresh:

1 cup	64
1 tbsp.	4

Lime juice, canned or bottled, unsweetened:

1 cup 64

1 tbsp. 4

Limes, fresh:

whole, 1 lb. 107

pulp only, 1 lime (2" in diam.) 19

Ling cod, raw:

whole, 1 lb. 130

meat only, 4 oz. 95

Liquor, see **Alcoholic beverages**

Liver, fresh:

beef, raw, 1 lb. 635

beef, fried, 4 oz. 260

beef, fried, 1 slice (6½" x 2⅜" x ⅜") 195

calves', raw, 1 lb. 635

calves', fried, 4 oz. 296

calves', fried, 1 slice (6½" x 2⅜" x ⅜") 222

chicken, raw, 1 lb. 585

chicken, simmered, 4 oz. 187

chicken, simmered, 1 liver (2" x 2" x ⅝") 41

chicken, simmered, chopped, 1 cup 231

goose, raw, 1 lb. 826

hog, raw, 1 lb. 594

hog, fried, 4 oz. 273

hog, fried, 1 slice (6½" x 2⅜" x ⅜") 205

lamb, raw, 1 lb. 617

lamb, broiled, 4 oz. 296

lamb, broiled, 1 slice (3½" x 2" x ⅜") 117

turkey, raw, 1 lb. 626

turkey, simmered, 4 oz. 197

turkey, simmered, 1 liver from 20–25-lb. turkey 212

turkey, simmered, 1 liver from 17-lb. turkey 191

turkey, simmered, 1 liver from 12–13-lb. turkey 131

turkey, simmered, chopped, 1 cup 244

Liver paste, see **Pâté de foie gras**

Liverwurst:

fresh, 4 oz. 348

smoked, see **Braunschweiger**

Lobster, northern:

raw, in shell, 1 lb. 107

cooked, in shell, 1 lb. 112

cooked or canned, meat only, 4 oz.	108
cooked or canned, meat only, cubed (½" pieces), 1 cup	138

Lobster Newburg, home recipe:
made with butter, egg yolks, sherry, cream, 1 cup	485

Lobster paste, canned:
1 oz.	51
1 tsp.	13

Loganberries, fresh:
untrimmed, 1 lb.	267
trimmed, 4 oz.	71
trimmed, 1 cup	89

Loganberries, canned:
in water, with liquid, 8 oz.	90
in heavy syrup, with liquid, 8 oz.	202

Longans:
fresh, in shell, 1 lb.	147
fresh, shelled and seeded, 4 oz.	69
dried, in shell, 1 lb.	467
dried, shelled and seeded, 4 oz.	326

Loquats, fresh:
whole, 1 lb.	168
seeded, 4 oz.	54
seeded, 10 fruits	59

Luncheon meat, see individual listings
Lychees, see **Lichee nuts**

M

food and measure	calories

Macadamia nuts:
in shell, 1 lb.	972
shelled, 4 oz.	784
6 average nuts	104

Macaroni:
dry, 8-oz. pkg.	838
dry, 1 cup	502
cooked, firm stage (8–10 minutes), hot, 1 cup	192

Macaroni, continued

cooked, tender stage (14–20 minutes), hot, 1 cup	155
cooked, tender stage (14–20 minutes), cold, 1 cup	117

Macaroni and cheese, home recipe:

baked, 8 oz.	488
baked, 1 cup	430

Macaroni and cheese, canned:

8 oz.	215
1 cup	228

Mackerel, Atlantic, fresh:

raw, whole, 1 lb.	468
raw, fillets, 1 lb.	866
fillets, broiled with butter, 12⅞ oz. (yield from 1 lb. raw)	861
fillets, broiled with butter, 4 oz.	268
fillets, broiled with butter, 1 fillet (8½" x 2½" x ½")	248

Mackerel, Atlantic, canned:

with liquid, 8 oz.	416

Mackerel, jack, see Jack mackerel

Mackerel, Pacific, fresh:

raw, dressed, 1 lb.	519
raw, meat only, 4 oz.	181

Mackerel, Pacific, canned:

drained, 15-oz. can	765
drained, 4 oz.	204

Mackerel, salted:

fillets, 4 oz.	345
fillets, 1 piece (7¾" x 2½" x ½")	342

Mackerel, smoked:

meat only, 4 oz.	248

Malt:

dry, 1 oz.	104

Malt extract:

dry, 1 oz.	104

Mandarin oranges, see Tangerines

Mangoes, fresh:

whole, 1 lb.	201
whole, 1 average (about 10.6 oz.)	152
diced or sliced, 1 cup	109

Maple syrup, see Syrups

Margarine, regular:

1 cup or 8 oz.	1,634

1 stick or 4 oz.	816
1 tbsp.	102
1 tsp.	34
1 pat (1" x ⅓"; 90 pats per lb.)	36

Margarine, whipped:

8-oz. container	1,634
1 cup	1,087
1 stick or ½ cup	544
1 tbsp.	68
1 tsp.	23
1 pat (1¼" x ⅓"; 120 pats per lb.)	27

Marmalade, citrus:

1 oz.	73
1 tbsp.	51
1 packet (½ oz.)	36

Marmalade plums, see Sapotes

Marshmallows, see Candy

Matai, see Water chestnuts, Chinese

Mayonnaise, see Salad dressings

Meat, see individual listings

Meat, potted, see individual listings

Meat loaf (luncheon meat):

4 oz.	227

Melon, see individual listings

Melon balls (cantaloupe and honeydew), frozen:

in syrup, unthawed, 12-oz. pkg.	211
in syrup, unthawed, 1 cup	143

Milk, canned:

condensed, sweetened, 1 cup	982
condensed, sweetened, 1 fl. oz.	123
evaporated, unsweetened, 1 cup	345
evaporated, unsweetened, 1 fl. oz.	43

Milk, chocolate, canned or dairy-packed:

made with skim milk, 1 cup	190
made with whole milk (3.5% fat), 1 cup	213

Milk, cow's, fluid:

whole, 3.5% fat, 1 cup	159
whole, 3.7% fat, 1 cup	161
buttermilk, cultured, made from skim milk, 1 cup	88
half and half, see Cream	

Milk, cow's, fluid, continued

skim, 1 cup 88
skim, partially (with 2% nonfat solids added), 1 cup 145

Milk, dry (dry form):

whole, regular, dry, 1 cup 643
whole, regular, dry, 1 tbsp. 35
whole, instant, low-density (4¼ oz. to 3⅔ cups water), 1 cup . 351
whole, instant, high-density (¼ cup to 1 cup water), 1 cup ... 527
nonfat, regular, dry, 1 cup 436
nonfat, instant, 1 envelope (3.2 oz.) 327
nonfat, instant, low-density (3.2 oz. yields 1⅓ cups), 1 cup .. 244
nonfat, instant, high-density (3.2 oz. yields ⅞ cup), 1 cup 373
buttermilk, cultured, 1 cup 464
buttermilk, cultured, 1 tbsp. 25

Milk, goat's:

whole, 1 cup 163

Milk, malted:

dry powder, 3 heaping tsp. (1 oz.) 116
beverage, 1 cup 244

Milk, reindeer:

1 cup 580

Millet:

whole-grain, 4 oz. 371

Mince pie, see Pies

Mints, see Candy

Miso, see Soybeans, fermented

Molasses:

first extraction (light), 1 cup 827
first extraction (light), 1 tbsp. 50
first extraction (light), 1 fl. oz. 103
second extraction (medium), 1 cup 761
second extraction (medium), 1 tbsp. 46
second extraction (medium), 1 fl. oz. 95
third extraction (blackstrap), 1 cup 699
third extraction (blackstrap), 1 tbsp. 43
third extraction (blackstrap), 1 fl. oz. 87
Barbados, 1 cup 889
Barbados, 1 tbsp. 54
Barbados, 1 fl. oz. 111

Mortadella:

4 oz.	357
1 slice (4⅞" in diam., 3/32" thick)	79

Muffins, baked from home recipe:

plain, 4 oz.	334
plain, 1 muffin (about 1.4 oz.)	118
blueberry, 4 oz.	319
blueberry, 1 muffin (about 1.4 oz.)	112
bran, 4 oz.	296
bran, 1 muffin (about 1.4 oz.)	104
corn, made from degermed corn meal, 4 oz.	358
corn, made from degermed corn meal, 1 muffin (about 1.4 oz.)	126
corn, made from whole-ground corn meal, 4 oz.	327
corn, made from whole-ground corn meal, 1 muffin (about 1.4 oz.)	115

Muffins, baked from mix:

corn, made with egg and milk, 4 oz.	368
corn, made with egg and milk, 1 muffin (about 1.4 oz.)	130

Mullet, raw:

whole, 1 lb.	351
meat only, 4 oz.	166

Mung beans, see Beans, mung and Bean sprouts, mung

Mushrooms, fresh (commercial variety):

raw, untrimmed, 1 lb.	123
raw, sliced, chopped, or diced, 1 cup	20

Mushrooms, canned:

with liquid, 8 oz.	38
with liquid, 1 cup	41

Muskellunge, raw:

whole, 1 lb.	242
meat only, 4 oz.	124

Muskmelon, see Cantaloupe, Casaba melon, and Honeydew melon

Muskrat:

roasted, 4 oz.	174

Mussels, Atlantic and Pacific, fresh:

raw, in shell, 1 lb.	153
raw, meat only, 4 oz.	108

Mussels, canned:

meat only, drained, 4 oz.	130

Mustard, prepared:

brown, 1 cup	228
brown, 1 oz.	26

brown, 1 tsp. or 1 serving packet	5
yellow, 1 cup	188
yellow, 1 oz.	21
yellow, 1 tsp. or 1 serving packet	4
Mustard greens, fresh:	
raw, untrimmed, 1 lb.	98
raw, trimmed, 4 oz.	35
leaves, boiled, drained, 8 oz.	52
leaves, boiled, drained, 1 cup	32
Mustard greens, frozen:	
chopped, unthawed, 10-oz. pkg.	57
chopped, boiled, drained, 7.5 oz. (yield from 10-oz. pkg.)	42
chopped, boiled, drained, 1 cup	30
Mustard spinach (tendergreens), fresh:	
raw, 1 lb.	100
boiled, drained, 8 oz.	37
boiled, drained, 1 cup	29

N

food and measure	calories

Natal plums, see Carissas	
Natto, see Soybeans, fermented	
Nectarines, fresh:	
whole, 1 lb.	267
whole, 1 nectarine (2½″ in diam.)	88
pitted, 4 oz.	73
New Zealand spinach, fresh:	
raw, 1 lb.	86
boiled, drained, 8 oz.	30
boiled, drained, 1 cup	23
Noodles, chow mein, canned:	
5-oz. can	694
1 cup	220
Noodles, egg:	
dry, 8-oz. pkg.	881
cooked, 1 cup	200
Nuts, see individual listings	

O

Oats or oatmeal, see Cereals
Ocean perch, Atlantic (redfish), fresh:
    raw, whole, 1 lb. 124
    raw, meat only, 4 oz. 100
    breaded, fried, 4 oz. 258
Ocean perch, Atlantic (redfish), frozen:
    fillets, breaded, fried, reheated, 4 oz. 382
    fillets, breaded, fried, reheated, 1 fillet (6¾″ x 1¾″ x ⅝″) .. 281
Ocean perch, Pacific, fresh:
    raw, whole, 1 lb. 116
    raw, meat only, 4 oz. 108
Octopus:
    raw, 4 oz. 83
Oils, cooking or salad:
    corn, cottonseed, safflower, sesame, or soybean, 1 cup 1,927
    corn, cottonseed, safflower, sesame, or soybean, 1 tbsp. 120
    olive or peanut, 1 cup 1,909
    olive or peanut, 1 tbsp. 119
Okra, fresh:
    raw, untrimmed, 1 lb. 140
    raw, fully trimmed, 4 oz. 41
    raw, crosscut slices, 1 cup 36
    boiled, drained, crosscut slices, 1 cup 46
    boiled, drained, 10 pods (3″ x ⅝″) 31
    boiled, drained, 4 oz. 33
Okra, frozen:
    cuts and pods, unthawed, 10-oz. pkg. 111
    cuts and pods, boiled, drained, 9 oz. (yield from 10-oz. pkg.) .. 97
    cuts, boiled, drained, 1 cup 70
Oleomargarine, see Margarine
Olive oil, see Oils
Olives, pickled, canned or bottled, drained:
    green, 2 oz. 66
    green, 10 giant (⅞″ in diam., 1⅛″ long) 76
    green, 10 large (¾″ in diam., 15/16″ long) 45

green, 10 small (⅝" in diam., 13/16" long)	33
ripe, Ascolano, pitted, 2 oz.	73
ripe, Ascolano, pitted, sliced, 1 cup	174
ripe, Ascolano, 10 jumbo (15/16" in diam., 1 3/16" long)	105
ripe, Ascolano, 10 giant (13/16" in diam., 1⅛" long)	89
ripe, Ascolano, 10 mammoth (13/16" in diam., 1 1/16" long)	72
ripe, Ascolano, 10 extra large (¾" in diam., 1" long)	61
ripe, Manzanilla, pitted, 2 oz.	73
ripe, Manzanilla, pitted, sliced, 1 cup	174
ripe, Manzanilla, 10 extra large (¾" in diam., 1" long)	61
ripe, Manzanilla, 10 large (¾" in diam., 15/16" long)	51
ripe, Manzanilla, 10 medium (11/16" in diam., ⅞" long)	44
ripe, Manzanilla, 10 small (⅝" in diam., 13/16" long)	38
ripe, Mission, pitted, 2 oz.	105
ripe, Mission, pitted, sliced, 1 cup	248
ripe, Mission, 10 extra large (¾" in diam., 1" long)	87
ripe, Mission, 10 large (¾" in diam., 15/16" long)	73
ripe, Mission, 10 medium (11/16" in diam., ⅞" long)	63
ripe, Mission, 10 small (⅝" in diam., 13/16" long)	54
ripe, Sevillano, pitted, 2 oz.	53
ripe, Sevillano, pitted, sliced, 1 cup	126
ripe, Sevillano, 10 supercolossal (1 1/16" in diam., 1⅜" long)	114
ripe, Sevillano, 10 colossal (1" in diam., 1¼" long)	95
ripe, Sevillano, 10 jumbo (15/16" in diam., 1 3/16" long)	76
ripe, Sevillano, 10 giant (13/16" in diam., 1⅛" long)	64
ripe, salt-cured, Greek-style, pitted, 2 oz.	193
ripe, salt-cured, Greek-style, 10 extra large (137 per lb.)	89
ripe, salt-cured, Greek-style, 10 medium (188 per lb.)	65

Onions, dehydrated:

flakes, 1 cup	224

Onions, mature, fresh:

raw, untrimmed, 1 lb.	157
raw, trimmed, 4 oz.	43
raw, 1 medium onion (2½" in diam.)	40
raw, chopped, 1 cup	65
raw, chopped or minced, 1 tbsp.	4
raw, grated or ground, 1 cup	89
raw, sliced, 1 cup	44
large, boiled, drained, halves, 1 cup	52

large, boiled, drained, whole, 1 cup 61
pearl, boiled, drained, whole, 1 cup 54
Onions, young green, fresh:
bulb and entire top, untrimmed, 1 lb. 157
bulb and entire top, trimmed, 1 lb. 163
bulb and entire top, chopped or sliced, 1 cup 36
bulb and entire top, chopped, 1 tbsp. 2
bulb and white portion of top, 2 medium (4½″ long) 14
bulb and white portion of top, chopped or sliced, 1 cup 45
bulb and white portion of top, chopped, 1 tbsp. 3
tops only (green portion), chopped, 1 cup 27
tops only (green portion), chopped, 1 tbsp. 2
Onions, Welsh:
raw, untrimmed, 1 lb. 100
raw, trimmed, 4 oz. 39
Opossum:
roasted, meat only, 4 oz. 252
Orange-apricot juice drink, canned:
1 cup 125
Orange-cranberry relish, see **Cranberry-orange relish**
Orange-grapefruit juice, canned:
unsweetened, 6-fl.-oz. can 80
unsweetened, 1 cup 106
sweetened, 6-fl.-oz. can 93
sweetened, 1 cup 125
Orange-grapefruit juice concentrate, frozen:
unsweetened, undiluted, 6-fl.-oz. can 330
unsweetened, diluted with 3 parts water, 1 cup 109
Orange juice, fresh:
all commercial varieties, 1 cup 112
California, navels (winter oranges):
1 cup 120
juice from 1 large orange (3 1/16″ in diam.) 50
juice from 1 medium orange (2⅞″ in diam.) 41
juice from 1 small orange (2⅜″ in diam.) 26
California, Valencias (summer oranges):
1 cup 117
juice from 1 large orange (3 1/16″ in diam.) 58
juice from 1 medium orange (2⅝″ in diam.) 37
juice from 1 small orange (2⅜″ in diam.) 30
Florida, all commercial varieties, 1 cup 106

Florida, early and midseason (Hamlin, parson Brown, etc.)

1 cup 98
juice from 1 large orange (2 15/16″ in diam.) 49
juice from 1 medium orange (2 11/16″ in diam.) 39
juice from 1 small orange (2½″ in diam.) 31

Florida, late season (Valencias):

1 cup 112
juice from 1 large orange (2 15/16″ in diam.) 60
juice from 1 medium orange (2 11/16″ in diam.) 48
juice from 1 small orange (2½″ in diam.) 38

Florida, temple:

1 cup 134
juice from 1 large orange (3⅛″ in diam.) 87
juice from 1 medium orange (2⅞″ in diam.) 65
juice from 1 small orange (2 9/16″ in diam.) 48

Orange juice, canned:

unsweetened, 6-fl.-oz. can 89
unsweetened, 1 cup 120
sweetened, 6-fl.-oz. can 97
sweetened, 1 cup 130

Orange juice concentrate, canned:

unsweetened, undiluted, 1 fl. oz. 84
unsweetened, diluted with 5 parts water, 1 cup 114

Orange juice concentrate, frozen:

unsweetened, undiluted, 6-fl.-oz. can 362
unsweetened, diluted with 3 parts water, 1 cup 112

Orange juice, dehydrated:

crystals, dry, 1 oz. 108
crystals, prepared with water, 1 cup 114

Orange peel, candied:

1 oz. 90

Orange-pineapple juice drink, see **Pineapple-orange juice drink**

Oranges, fresh:

all commercial varieties:

whole, 1 lb. 162
whole, 1 orange (2⅝″ in diam.) 64
sections, without membranes, 1 cup 88
bite-size pieces, 1 cup 81
diced, 1 cup 103

California, navels (winter oranges):
- whole, 1 lb. 157
- whole, 1 large orange (3 1/16" in diam.) 87
- whole, 1 medium orange (2⅞" in diam.) 71
- whole, 1 small orange (2⅜" in diam.) 45
- sections, with membranes, 1 cup 77
- sections, without membranes, 1 cup 84
- bite-size pieces, peeled, with membranes, 1 cup 77
- bite-size pieces, pared, without membranes, 1 cup 82
- diced, 1 cup 107
- sliced, peeled, 1 slice (2½" in diam., ¼" thick) 11
- sliced, peeled, 1 slice (2¼" in diam., ¼" thick) 9
- wedge, ¼ of medium orange 18
- wedge, 1/6 of medium orange 12

California, Valencias (summer oranges):
- whole, 1 lb. 174
- whole, 1 large orange (3 1/16" in diam.) 96
- whole, 1 medium orange (2⅝" in diam.) 62
- whole, 1 small orange (2⅜" in diam.) 50
- sections, without membranes, 1 cup 92
- bite-size pieces, peeled, with membranes, 1 cup 79
- bite-size pieces, pared, without membranes, 1 cup 84
- diced, 1 cup 107
- sliced, peeled, 1 slice (2⅜" in diam., ¼" thick) 10
- sliced, peeled, 1 slice (2" in diam., ¼" thick) 8
- wedge, ¼ of medium orange 15
- wedge, 1/6 of medium orange 10

Florida, all commercial varieties:
- whole, 1 lb. 158
- whole, 1 large orange (2 15/16" in diam.) 89
- whole, 1 medium orange (2 11/16" in diam.) 71
- whole, 1 small orange (2½" in diam.) 57
- sections, without membranes, 1 cup 87
- bite-size pieces, 1 cup 78
- diced, 1 cup 99
- sliced, peeled, 1 slice (2½" in diam., ¼" thick) 10
- sliced, peeled, 1 slice (2" in diam., ¼" thick) 7
- wedge, ¼ of medium orange 18
- wedge, 1/6 of medium orange 12

Oyster plant, see Salsify

Oysters, raw:
eastern, in shell, 1 lb. 30
eastern, meat only, 8 oz. 150
eastern, meat only, 1 cup (13–19 medium or 19–31
   small oysters) 158
eastern, meat only, 1 oz. (2 medium or 3 small oysters) 19
eastern, canned, drained, 12-fl.-oz. can 224
Pacific and western, meat only, 8 oz. 207
Pacific, meat only, 1 cup (4–6 medium or 6–9 small oysters) .. 218
Pacific, canned, drained, 12-fl.-oz. can 309
Oysters, cooked:
breaded, fried, 4 oz. 272
breaded, fried, 4 medium (select) oysters 108
Oyster stew, home recipe (see also **Soups, frozen**):
1 part oysters to 1 part milk, 1 cup 245
1 part oysters to 2 parts milk, 1 cup 233
1 part oysters to 3 parts milk, 1 cup 206

P

food and measure	calories

Pancakes, made from home recipe:
1 pancake (6″ in diam., ½″ thick) 169
1 pancake (4″ in diam., ⅜″ thick) 62
Pancakes, made from mix:
plain and buttermilk:
   dry form, 1 cup loosely packed 481
   dry form, 1 cup packed 523
   baked, made with egg and milk, 1 pancake
     (6″ in diam., ½″ thick) 164
   baked, made with egg and milk, 1 pancake
     (4″ in diam., ⅜″ thick) 61
buckwheat and other cereal flours:
   dry form, 1 cup loosely packed 426
   dry form, 1 cup packed 443
   baked, made with egg and milk, 1 pancake
     (6″ in diam., ½″ thick) 146

baked, made with egg and milk, 1 pancake
(4" in diam., ⅜" thick) 54
Pancake syrup, see **Syrups**
Pancreas, raw:
  beef, fat, 4 oz. 358
  beef, medium fat, 4 oz. 321
  beef, lean, 4 oz. 160
  calf, 4 oz. 183
  hog (hog sweetbreads), 4 oz. 274
Papaw, North American-type, fresh:
  whole, 1 lb. 289
  whole, 1 papaw (3¾" long, 2" in diam.) 83
  peeled and seeded, 4 oz. 96
  peeled and seeded, mashed, 1 cup 213
Papayas, fresh:
  whole, 1 lb. 119
  whole, 1 papaya (5⅛" long, 3½" in diam.) 119
  peeled and seeded, 4 oz. 44
  peeled and seeded, mashed, 1 cup 90
  peeled and seeded, cubed (½" pieces), 1 cup 55
Parsley, fresh:
  whole, 1 lb. 200
  chopped, 1 cup 26
  chopped, 1 tbsp. 2
  1 sprig (about 2½" long) 4
Parsnips, fresh:
  raw, whole, 1 lb. 293
  whole, boiled, drained, 1 large (9" long, 2¼" in diam.) ... 106
  whole, boiled, drained, 1 small (6" long, 1⅛" in diam.) ... 23
  boiled, drained, diced (2" lengths), 1 cup 102
  boiled, drained, mashed, 1 cup 139
Passion fruit, see **Granadillas**
Pastini, dry:
  carrot, 8 oz. 840
  egg, 8 oz. 800
  egg, 1 cup 651
  spinach, 8 oz. 836
Pastry, see individual listings
Pastry shell, see **Pie crust**
Pâté de foie gras, canned:
  1 oz. 131

1 tbsp.	60
1 tsp.	18

Peach nectar, canned:

5½-fl.-oz. can	82
1 cup	120

Peach pie, see Pies

Peaches, fresh:

whole, 1 lb.	150
peeled, 1 peach (2¾″ in diam.; about 2½ peaches per lb.) ...	58
peeled, 1 peach (2½″ in diam.; about 4 peaches per lb.)	38
pared, 1 peach (2¾″ in diam.; about 2½ peaches per lb.)	51
pared, 1 peach (2½″ in diam.; about 4 peaches per lb.)	33
pared, diced, 1 cup	70
pared, sliced, 1 cup	65

Peaches, canned:

in water, with liquid, 8 oz.	70
in water, with liquid, halves or slices, 1 cup	76
in water, 1 peach half and 2 tbsp. liquid	28
in juice, with liquid, 8 oz.	102
in juice, 2 peach halves and 2 tbsp. juice	45
in heavy syrup, with liquid, 8 oz.	177
in heavy syrup, with liquid, halves, slices, or chunks, 1 cup ..	200
in heavy syrup, 1 peach half and 2½ tbsp. liquid	85

Peaches, dehydrated (nuggets):

uncooked, 8 oz.	771
uncooked, 1 cup	340
cooked, sweetened, with liquid, 8 oz.	275
cooked, sweetened, with liquid, 1 cup	351

Peaches, dried (halves):

uncooked, 8 oz.	594
uncooked, 1 cup	419
uncooked, 10 large halves	380
uncooked, 10 medium halves	341
cooked, unsweetened, with liquid, 8 oz.	186
cooked, unsweetened, with liquid, 1 cup	205
cooked, sweetened, with liquid, 8 oz.	270
cooked, sweetened, with liquid, 1 cup	321

Peaches, frozen:

sliced, sweetened, unthawed, 10-oz. pkg.	250
sliced, sweetened, thawed, 1 cup	220

Peanut butter, commercial variety:

4 oz.	1,336
1 cup	1,520
1 tbsp.	94

Peanut flour, defatted:

8 oz.	842
1 cup	223

Peanut oil, see Oils

Peanuts:

raw, in shell, 1 lb.	1,868
raw, shelled, 4 oz.	640
roasted, in shell, 1 lb.	1,769
roasted, in shell, 10 peanuts	105
roasted, shelled, 4 oz.	660
roasted, shelled, halves, 1 cup	842
roasted, shelled, chopped, 1 cup	838
roasted, shelled, chopped, 1 tbsp.	52
chocolate-coated, see Candy	

Peanut spread:

4 oz.	685
1 tbsp.	84

Pear nectar, canned:

5½-fl.-oz. can	89
1 cup	130

Pears, fresh:

whole, 1 lb.	252
Bartlett, whole, 1 pear (3½" long, 2½" in diam.; about 2½ per lb.)	100
bosc, whole, 1 pear (3¼" long, 2½" in diam.; about 3 per lb.)	86
D'Anjou, whole, 1 pear (3" long, 3" in diam.; about 2 per lb.)	122
sliced or cubed, 1 cup	101

Pears, canned:

in water, with liquid, 8 oz.	73
in water, with liquid, 1 cup	78
in water, 1 pear half and 1 tbsp. liquid	14
in water, 1 pear half and 2 tbsp. liquid	29
in juice, with liquid, 8 oz.	105
in heavy syrup, with liquid, 8 oz.	173
in heavy syrup, with liquid, 1 cup	194

  in heavy syrup, 1 pear half and 1 tbsp. liquid 36
  in heavy syrup, 1 pear half and 2 tbsp. liquid 71

Pears, dried (halves):
  uncooked, 8 oz. 608
  uncooked, 1 cup 482
  uncooked, 10 pear halves 469
  cooked, unsweetened, with liquid, 8 oz. 286
  cooked, unsweetened, with liquid, 1 cup 321
  cooked, sweetened, 8 oz. 343
  cooked, sweetened, 1 cup 423

Pears, candied:
  1 oz. 86

Pears, prickly, see **Prickly pears**

Peas, black-eyed, see **Cowpeas**

Peas, green, immature, fresh:
  raw, in pods, 1 lb. 145
  raw, shelled, 8 oz. 191
  raw, shelled, 1 cup 122
  boiled, drained, 8 oz. 160
  boiled, drained, 1 cup 114

Peas, green, immature, canned:
  Alaska (early or June peas):
    with liquid, 8 oz. 150
    with liquid, 1 cup 164
    drained, 8 oz. 200
    drained, 1 cup 150
    dietary (low-sodium) pack, with liquid, 8 oz. 125
    dietary (low-sodium) pack, with liquid, 1 cup 137
    dietary (low-sodium) pack, drained, 8 oz. 177
    dietary (low-sodium) pack, drained, 1 cup 133
  sweet (sweet wrinkled or sugar peas):
    with liquid, 8 oz. 130
    with liquid, 1 cup 142
    drained, 8 oz. 182
    drained, 1 cup 136
    dietary (low-sodium) pack, with liquid, 8 oz. 107
    dietary (low-sodium) pack, with liquid, 1 cup 117
    dietary (low-sodium) pack, drained, 8 oz. 164
    dietary (low-sodium) pack, drained, 1 cup 122

Peas, green, immature, frozen:
unthawed, 10-oz. pkg. 207
unthawed, 1 cup 106
boiled, drained, 8.9 oz. (yield from 10-oz. pkg.) 172
boiled, drained, 1 cup 109

Peas, mature seeds, dry:
whole, uncooked, 0 oz. 771
whole, uncooked, 1 cup 680
split, without seed coat, uncooked, 8 oz. 790
split, without seed coat, uncooked, 1 cup 696
split, without seed coat, cooked, 8 oz. 261
split, without seed coat, cooked, 1 cup 230

Peas and carrots, frozen:
unthawed, 10-oz. pkg. 156
unthawed, 1 cup 77
boiled, drained, 9.8 oz. (yield from 10-oz. pkg.) 147
boiled, drained, 1 cup 85

Pecan pie, see Pies

Pecans:
in shell, 1 lb. 1,652
in shell, 10 oversize nuts (55 or less per lb.) 299
in shell, 10 extra large nuts (56–63 per lb.) 277
in shell, 10 large nuts (64–77 per lb.) 236
shelled, 1 lb. 3,116
shelled, 1 oz. 195
shelled, 1 cup 742
shelled, 10 mammoth nuts (250 or less per lb.) 124
shelled, 10 jumbo nuts (301–350 per lb.) 96
shelled, 10 large nuts (451–550 per lb.) 62
shelled, chopped, 1 cup 811
shelled, chopped, 1 tbsp. 52
shelled, ground, 1 cup 653

Pepper, black:
½ tsp. 2

Pepper, hot chili, green (immature):
raw, whole, 1 lb. 123
raw, seeded, 4 oz. 42
pods, canned, with liquid, 4 oz. 28
chili sauce, canned, 4 oz. 23
chili sauce, canned, 1 cup 49

Pepper, hot chili, red (mature):
raw, whole, 1 lb. 405
raw, pods with seeds, 4 oz. 105
raw, pods, seeded, 4 oz. 74
chili sauce, canned, 4 oz. 24
chili sauce, canned, 1 cup 51
dried pods, 1 oz. 91
dried pods, 1 tbsp. 26
dried, powder, see **Chili powder**

Peppers, sweet, green (immature):
raw, whole, 1 lb. 82
raw, cored and seeded, 4 oz. 25
raw, 1 pepper fancy grade (3¾" long, 3" in diam.; 2¼ per lb.) 36
raw, 1 pepper No. 1 grade (2¾" long, 2½" in diam.; 5 per lb.) 16
raw, chopped or diced, 1 cup 33
raw, cut in strips, 1 cup 22
raw, sliced, 1 cup 18
raw, 1 ring (3" in diam., ¼" thick) 2
boiled, drained, 1 pepper fancy grade (3¾" long, 3" in diam.) 29
boiled, drained, 1 pepper No. 1 grade (2¾" long, 2½" in diam.) 13
boiled, drained, strips, 1 cup 24
boiled, drained, 4 oz. 21

Peppers, sweet, red (mature):
raw, whole, 1 lb. 112
raw, cored and seeded, 4 oz. 35
raw, 1 pepper fancy grade (3¾" long, 3" in diam.; 2¼ per lb.) 51
raw, 1 pepper No. 1 grade (2¾" long, 2½" in diam.; 5 per lb.) 23
raw, chopped or diced, 1 cup 47
raw, cut in strips, 1 cup 31
raw, sliced, 1 cup 25
raw, 1 ring (3" in diam., ¼" thick) 3
canned, see **Pimientos**

Perch, raw:
white, whole, 1 lb. 193
white, meat only, 4 oz. 134
yellow, whole, 1 lb. 161
yellow, meat only, 4 oz. 103

Perch, ocean, see **Ocean perch**

Persimmons, fresh:
Japanese or kaki, with seeds, 1 lb. 286
Japanese or kaki, seedless, whole, 1 lb. 293

Japanese or kaki, seedless, trimmed, 4 oz. 87
Japanese or kaki, seedless, 1 average (3" long, 2½" in diam.) 129
native, whole, 1 lb. 472
native, trimmed and seeded, 4 oz. 144
native, 1 average 31

Pheasant, raw:
ready-to-cook, whole, 1 lb. 596
meat only, 4 oz. 184

Pickerel, chain, raw:
whole, 1 lb. 194
meat only, 4 oz. 95

Pickle relish:
sour, 4 oz. 22
sour, 1 tbsp. 3
sweet, 4 oz. 132
sweet, 1 cup 338
sweet, 1 tbsp. 21

Pickles, chowchow (with cauliflower):
sour, 4 oz. 33
sour, 1 cup 70
sweet, 4 oz. 132
sweet, 1 cup 284

Pickles, cucumber:
dill, 8 oz. 25
dill, 1 large (4" long, 1¾" in diam.) 15
dill, 1 medium (3¾" long, 1¼" in diam.) 7
dill, sliced lengthwise, 1 spear (6" long) 3
dill, 2 crosscut slices (1½" in diam., ¼" thick) 1
dill, crosscut slices, 1 cup (about 23 slices) 17
fresh, bread-and-butter, 8 oz. 166
fresh, bread-and-butter, 2 crosscut slices
    (1½" in diam., ¼" thick) 11
fresh, bread-and-butter, crosscut slices, 1 cup (about 23 slices) 124
sour, 8 oz. 23
sour, 1 large (4" long, 1¾" in diam.) 14
sour, 1 medium (3¾" long, 1¼" in diam.) 7
sweet, 8 oz. 331
sweet, gherkins, 1 large (3" long, 1" in diam.) 51
sweet, gherkins, 1 small (2½" long, ¾" in diam.) 22
sweet, gherkins, 1 midget (2⅛" long, ⅜" in diam.) 9
sweet, sliced lengthwise, 1 spear (4¼" long) 29

sweet, chopped (¼″ cubes), 1 cup 234
sweet, chopped, 1 tbsp. 14

Pie crust, baked from home recipe:

1 pie shell (9″) 900

Pie crust, baked from mix:

made with water, 11.3 oz. (yield from 10-oz. pkg. mix) 1,485
made with water, 9″ shell 675

Pies, baked from home recipe:

apple, 1 whole pie (9″ in diam.) 2,419
apple, 4¾″ arc (1/6 of 9″ pie) 404
apple, 3½″ arc (⅛ of 9″ pie) 302
banana custard, 1 whole pie (9″ in diam.) 2,011
banana custard, 4¾″ arc (1/6 of 9″ pie) 336
banana custard, 3½″ arc (⅛ of 9″ pie) 252
blackberry, 1 whole pie (9″ in diam.) 2,296
blackberry, 4¾″ arc (1/6 of 9″ pie) 384
blackberry, 3½″ arc (⅛ of 9″ pie) 287
blueberry, 1 whole pie (9″ in diam.) 2,287
blueberry, 4¾″ arc (1/6 of 9″ pie) 382
blueberry, 3½″ arc (⅛ of 9″ pie) 287
Boston cream, 1 whole pie (8″ in diam., 3⅓″ high) 2,492
Boston cream, 3⅛″ arc (⅛ of 8″ pie) 311
butterscotch, 1 whole pie (9″ in diam.) 2,430
butterscotch, 4¾″ arc (1/6 of 9″ pie) 406
butterscotch, 3½″ arc (⅛ of 9″ pie) 304
cherry, 1 whole pie (9″ in diam.) 2,466
cherry, 4¾″ arc (1/6 of 9″ pie) 412
cherry, 3½″ arc (⅛ of 9″ pie) 308
chocolate chiffon, 1 whole pie (9″ in diam.) 2,125
chocolate chiffon, 4¾″ arc (1/6 of 9″ pie) 354
chocolate chiffon, 3½″ arc (⅛ of 9″ pie) 266
chocolate meringue, 1 whole pie (9″ in diam.) 2,293
chocolate meringue, 4¾″ arc (1/6 of 9″ pie) 383
chocolate meringue, 3½″ arc (⅛ of 9″ pie) 287
coconut custard, 1 whole pie (9″ in diam.) 2,139
coconut custard, 4¾″ arc (1/6 of 9″ pie) 357
coconut custard, 3½″ arc (⅛ of 9″ pie) 268
custard, 1 whole pie (9″ in diam.) 1,984
custard, 4¾″ arc (1/6 of 9″ pie) 331

Pies, baked from mix:
  coconut custard, made with egg yolks and milk:
    1 whole pie (8″ in diam.) 1,618
    4⅛″ arc (1/6 of 8″ pie) 270
    3⅛″ arc (⅛ of 8″ pie) 203
Pies, frozen:
  apple, baked, 1 whole pie (8″ in diam.) 1,386
  apple, baked, 4⅛″ arc (1/6 of 8″ pie) 231
  apple, baked, 3⅛″ arc (⅛ of 8″ pie) 173
  cherry, baked, 1 whole pie (8″ in diam.) 1,690
  cherry, baked, 4⅛″ arc (1/6 of 8″ pie) 282
  cherry, baked, 3⅛″ arc (⅛ of 8″ pie) 211
  coconut custard, baked, 1 whole pie (8″ in diam.) 1,494
  coconut custard, baked, 4⅛″ arc (1/6 of 8″ pie) 249
  coconut custard, baked, 3⅛″ arc (⅛ of 8″ pie) 187
Pigeon peas:
  raw, immature seeds in pods, 1 lb. 207
  dry, 4 oz. 388
Pignolias, see Pine nuts
Pigs' feet, pickled:
  4 oz. 227
Pike, raw:
  blue, whole, 1 lb. 180
  blue, meat only, 4 oz. 102
  northern, whole, 1 lb. 104
  northern, meat only, 4 oz. 100
  walleye, whole, 1 lb. 240
  walleye, meat only, 4 oz. 106
Pili nuts:
  in shell, 1 lb. 546
  shelled, 4 oz. 763
Pimientos, canned:
  with liquid, 4-oz. can or jar 31
  drained, 1 average 10
Pineapple, fresh:
  whole, 1 lb. 123
  trimmed, 4 oz. 59
  diced, 1 cup 81
  sliced, 1 slice (3½″ in diam., ¾″ thick) 44
Pineapple, candied:
  4-oz. container (2 slices or ⅓ cup chunks) 357

Pistachio nuts, continued

shelled, 1 cup 743
shelled, chopped, 1 tbsp. 53

Pitangas (Surinam cherries), raw:

whole. 1 lb. 187
whole, 2 average 5
pitted, 1 cup 87

Pizza baked from home recipe:

cheese topping, 1 whole pizza (13¾″ in diam.) 1,227
cheese topping, 1 sector, 5⅓″ arc (⅛ of 13¾″ pizza) 153
sausage topping, 1 whole pizza (13¾″ in diam.) 1,252
sausage topping, 1 sector, 5⅓″ arc (⅛ of 13¾″ pizza) 157

Pizza, chilled. commercial:

cheese, baked, 1 whole pizza (12″ in diam.) 1,179
cheese, baked, 1 sector, 4¾″ arc (⅛ of 12″ pizza) 147

Pizza, frozen, commercial:

cheese, baked, 1 whole pizza (10″ in diam.) 973
cheese, baked, 1 sector, 4½″ arc (1/7 of 10″ pizza) 139
cheese, baked, 1 whole small pizza (5¼″ in diam.) 179

Plantains (baking bananas), raw:

whole, with skin, 1 lb. 389
peeled, 4 oz. 135
1 banana (11″ long, 1⅞″ in diam.) 313

Plate dinners, frozen, commercial:

beef pot roast, oven-browned potatoes, peas, and corn, 1 lb. .. 481
fried chicken, mashed potatoes. and mixed vegetables, 1 lb. .. 736
meat loaf with tomato sauce, mashed potatoes, and peas, 1 lb. . 594
sliced turkey, mashed potatoes, and peas, 1 lb. 508

Plums, fresh:

damson, whole, 1 lb. 272
damson, whole, 10 plums (1″ in diam.) 66
damson, with pits, 1 cup 87
damson, pitted, 4 oz. 75
damson, pitted, halves, 1 cup 112
Japanese or hybrid, whole, 1 lb. 205
Japanese or hybrid, whole, 1 plum (2⅛″ in diam.) 32
Japanese or hybrid, pitted, 4 oz. 55
Japanese or hybrid, pitted, halves, 1 cup 89
Japanese or hybrid, pitted, sliced or diced, 1 cup 79
prune-type, whole, 1 lb. 320
prune-type, whole, 1 plum (1½″ in diam.) 21

prune-type, pitted, 4 oz. 85
prune-type, pitted, halves, 1 cup 124
Plums, canned:
greengage, in water, with liquid, 8 oz. 72
purple, in water, with liquid, 8 oz. 99
purple, in water, with liquid, 1 cup 114
purple, in water, 3 plums and 2 tbsp. liquid 44
purple, in heavy syrup, with liquid, 8 oz. 179
purple, in heavy syrup, with liquid, 1 cup 214
purple, in heavy syrup, 3 plums and 2¾ tbsp. liquid 110
purple, in extra heavy syrup, with liquid, 8 oz. 222
Pohas, see Ground cherries
Poke shoots (pokeberry):
raw, 1 lb. 104
boiled, drained, 8 oz. 46
boiled, drained, 1 cup 33
Pollack:
raw, drawn, 1 lb. 194
raw, fillets, 1 lb. 431
cooked, creamed with flour, butter, and milk, 8 oz. 201
cooked, creamed with flour, butter, and milk, 1 cup 320
Pomegranates, fresh:
whole, 1 lb. 160
whole, 1 average (3⅜″ in diam., 2¾″ high) 97
Pompano, raw:
whole, 1 lb. 422
meat only, 4 oz. 188
Popcorn:
unpopped, 4 oz. 411
unpopped, 1 cup 742
popped, plain, 2 oz. 219
popped, plain, large-kernel, 1 cup 23
popped, with oil and salt added, 2 oz. 259
popped, with oil and salt added, large-kernel, 1 cup 41
popped, sugar coated, 2 oz. 217
popped, sugar-coated, 1 cup 104
Popovers, baked from home recipe:
1 popover (4″ high; about 1.4 oz.) 90
Porgy, raw:
whole, 1 lb. 208
meat only, 4 oz. 127

Pork, fresh, retail cuts (see also Ham and Pork, cured):

Boston butt (shoulder), with bone and skin, lean with fat:
- raw, 1 lb. **1,220**
- roasted, 10.2 oz. (yield from 1 lb. raw) **1,024**

Boston butt (shoulder), without bone and skin, lean with fat:
- raw, 1 lb. **1,302**
- roasted, 10.9 oz. (yield from 1 lb. raw) **1,087**
- roasted, 3 pieces (2½" x 2½" x ¼") 300
- roasted, chopped, or diced, 1 cup loosely packed 494
- roasted, ground, 1 cup loosely packed 388

Boston butt (shoulder), with bone and skin, lean only (trimmed of fat):
- roasted, 8.1 oz. (yield from 1 lb. raw with fat) 559

Boston butt (shoulder), without bone and skin, lean only (trimmed of fat):
- roasted, 8.6 oz. (yield from 1 lb. raw with fat) 595
- roasted, chopped or diced, 1 cup loosely packed 342
- roasted, ground, 1 cup loosely packed 268

loin chops, with bone, lean with fat:
- raw, 1 lb. **1,065**
- broiled, 8.2 oz. (yield from 1 lb. raw) 911
- broiled, 1 chop (2.7 oz.; 3 chops per lb. raw) 305
- broiled, 1 chop (2 oz.; 4 chops per lb. raw) 227

loin chops, without bone, lean with fat:
- raw, 1 lb. **1,352**
- broiled, 10.4 oz. (yield from 1 lb. raw) **1,153**
- broiled, 4 oz. 411

loin chops, with bone, lean only (trimmed of fat):
- broiled, 5.9 oz. (yield from 1 lb. raw with fat) 454
- broiled, 1 chop (2 oz.; 3 chops per lb. raw with fat) 151
- broiled, 1 chop (1.5 oz.; 4 chops per lb. raw with fat) 113

loin chops, without bone, lean only (trimmed of fat):
- broiled, 7.5 oz. (yield from 1 lb. raw with fat) 572
- broiled, 4 oz. 288

loin roast, with bone, lean with fat:
- raw, 1 lb. **1,065**
- baked or roasted, 8.6 oz. (yield from 1 lb. raw) 883

loin roast, without bone, lean with fat:
- raw, 1 lb. **1,352**
- baked or roasted, 10.9 oz. (yield from 1 lb. raw) **1,115**
- baked or roasted, 4 oz. 411

baked or roasted, 1 piece (2½" x 2½" x ¾") 308
baked or roasted, chopped or diced, 1 cup loosely packed .. 507
loin roast, with bone, lean only (trimmed of fat):
baked or roasted, 6.9 oz. (yield from 1 lb. raw with fat) 495
baked or roasted, 1 piece (2½" x 2½" x ¾") 216
baked or roasted, chopped or diced, 1 cup loosely packed .. 356
loin roast, without bone, lean only (trimmed of fat):
baked or roasted, 8.7 oz. (yield from 1 lb. raw with fat) 627
baked or roasted, 4 oz. 288
baked or roasted, chopped or diced, 1 cup loosely packed .. 356
picnic (shoulder), with bone and skin, lean with fat:
raw, 1 lb. 1,083
simmered, 8.4 oz. (yield from 1 lb. raw) 890
picnic (shoulder), without bone and skin, lean with fat:
raw, 1 lb. 1,315
simmered, 10.2 oz. (yield from 1 lb. raw) 1,085
simmered, 4 oz. 424
simmered, 3 pieces (2½" x 2½" x ¼") 318
simmered, chopped or diced, 1 cup loosely packed 524
picnic (shoulder), with bone and skin, lean only (trimmed of fat):
simmered, 6.2 oz. (yield from 1 lb. raw with fat) 373
picnic (shoulder), without bone and skin, lean only
(trimmed of fat):
simmered, 7.6 oz. (yield from 1 lb. raw with fat) 456
simmered, 4 oz. 241
simmered, 3 pieces (2½" x 2½" x ¼") 180
simmered, chopped or diced, 1 cup loosely packed 297
spareribs, with bone, lean with fat:
raw, 1 lb. 976
braised, 6.3 oz. (yield from 1 lb. raw) 792
braised, 4 oz. 499
Pork, cured, retail shoulder cuts (see also Bacon and Ham).
Boston butt, with bone and skin, lean with fat:
unbaked, 1 lb. 1,227
baked or roasted, 11 oz. (yield from 1 lb. unbaked) 1,030
Boston butt, without bone and skin, lean with fat:
unbaked, 1 lb. 1,320
baked or roasted, 11.8 oz. (yield from 1 lb. unbaked) 1,109
baked or roasted, 4 oz. 374
baked or roasted, 3 pieces (2½" x 2½" x ¼") 281

Pork, cured, continued

baked or roasted, chopped or diced, 1 cup loosely packed .. 462
baked or roasted, ground, 1 cup loosely packed 363
Boston butt, with bone and skin, lean only (trimmed of fat):
baked or roasted, 9.1 oz. (yield from 1 lb. unbaked with fat) 629
Boston butt, without bone and skin, lean only (trimmed of fat):
baked or roasted, 9.8 oz. (yield from 1 lb. unbaked with fat) 678
baked or roasted, 4 oz. 276
baked or roasted, 3 pieces (2½" x 2½" x ¼") 207
baked or roasted, chopped or diced, 1 cup loosely packed .. 340
baked or roasted, ground, 1 cup loosely packed 267
picnic, with bone and skin, lean with fat:
unbaked, 1 lb. 1,060
baked or roasted, 9.7 oz. (yield from 1 lb. unbaked) 888
picnic, without bone and skin, lean with fat:
unbaked, 1 lb. 1,293
baked or roasted, 11.8 oz. (yield from 1 lb. unbaked) 1,085
baked or roasted, 4 oz. 366
baked or roasted, 3 pieces (2½" x 2½" x ¼") 275
baked or roasted, chopped or diced, 1 cup loosely packed .. 452
baked or roasted, ground, 1 cup loosely packed 355
picnic, with bone and skin, lean only (trimmed of fat):
baked or roasted, 6.8 oz. (yield from 1 lb. unbaked with fat) 405
picnic, without bone and skin, lean only (trimmed of fat):
baked or roasted, 8.3 oz. (yield from 1 lb. unbaked with fat) 496
baked or roasted, 4 oz. 239
baked or roasted, 3 pieces (2½" x 2½" x ¼") 179
baked or roasted, chopped or diced, 1 cup loosely packed .. 295
baked or roasted, ground, 1 cup loosely packed 232

Pork, cured, canned, see **Ham**

Pork, salt, see **Salt pork**

Pork and beans, see **Beans, baked**

Pork and gravy, canned:
8 oz. 581

Pork sausage, see **Sausages**

Potato chips:
smooth or corrugated surface, 2 oz. 324
smooth or corrugated surface, 10 chips (1/16" x 1¾" x 2½") 114

Potatoes, fresh:
raw, whole, 1 lb. 279
raw, peeled, chopped, diced, or sliced, 1 cup 114

baked in skin, 4 oz.	81
baked in skin, 1 long (4¾" long, 2⅓" in diam.)	145
boiled in skin, 4 oz.	79
boiled in skin, 1 long (4¾" long, 2⅓" in diam.)	173
boiled in skin, 1 round (2½" in diam.)	104
boiled in skin, diced or sliced, 1 cup	118
boiled, peeled, 4 oz.	74
boiled, peeled (split-knife peeler), 1 long	
(4¾" long, 2⅓" in diam.)	146
boiled, peeled (split-knife peeler), 1 round (2½" in diam.)	88
boiled, peeled, diced or sliced, 1 cup	101
French-fried, 4 oz.	311
French-fried, 10 strips, 3½"–4" long)	214
French-fried, 10 strips (2"–3½" long)	137
French-fried, 10 strips (1"–2" long)	96
fried, 4 oz.	304
fried, 1 cup	456
hash brown, 4 oz.	260
hash brown, 1 cup	355
mashed, with milk, 4 oz.	74
mashed, with milk, 1 cup	137
mashed, with milk and butter, 4 oz.	107
mashed, with milk and butter, 1 cup	197
scalloped or au gratin, with cheese, 4 oz.	165
scalloped or au gratin, with cheese, 1 cup	355
scalloped or au gratin, without cheese, 4 oz.	118
scalloped or au gratin, without cheese, 1 cup	255
Potatoes, canned:	
with liquid, 8 oz.	100
with liquid, 1 cup	110
Potatoes, dehydrated:	
flakes, dry form, 4 oz.	418
flakes, dry form, 1 cup	164
flakes, prepared with water, milk, butter, 4 oz.	106
flakes, prepared with water, milk, butter, 1 cup	195
granules without milk, dry form, 4 oz.	399
granules without milk, dry form, 1 cup	704
granules without milk, prepared with water, milk, butter, 4 oz.	109
granules without milk, prepared with water, milk, butter, 1 cup	202
granules with milk, dry form, 4 oz.	406
granules with milk, dry form, 1 cup	716

granules with milk, prepared with water, milk, butter, 4 oz. ... 89
granules with milk, prepared with water, milk, butter, 1 cup ... 166

Potatoes, frozen:
diced, shredded, or crinkle-cut for hash browning:
    unthawed, 12-oz. pkg. 248
    unthawed, crinkle-cut, 1 cup 80
    unthawed, diced or shredded, 1 cup 102
    cooked (hash brown), 1 cup 347
French-fried, straight and crinkle-cut strips (½" in diam.):
    unthawed, 9 oz. pkg. 434
    unthawed, 10 strips (3½"–4" long) 170
    unthawed, 10 strips (2"–3½" long) 111
    unthawed, 10 strips (1"–2" long) 77
    oven heated, 7 oz. (yield from 9 oz. pkg.) 434
    oven heated, 10 strips (3½"–4" long unheated) 172
    oven heated, 10 strips (2"–3½" long unheated) 110
    oven heated, 10 strips (1"–2" long) 77

Potatoes, sweet, see **Sweet potatoes**

Potato flour:
4 oz. 400

Potato salad, home recipe:
made with cooked salad dressing, seasonings:
    8 oz. 225
    1 cup 248
made with mayonnaise and French dressing, hard-cooked eggs,
    seasonings:
    8 oz. 329
    1 cup 363

Potato sticks:
2 oz. 310
1 cup 190

Poultry, see individual listings

Preserves, see **Jams and preserves**

Pretzels, commercial varieties:
all varieties, 2 oz. 221
logs, 10 pretzels (3" long, ½" in diam.) 195
rods, 1 pretzel (7½"–7¾" long, ½" in diam.) 55
sticks, 10 pretzels (3⅛" long, ⅛" in diam.) 23
sticks, 10 pretzels (2¼" long, ⅛" in diam.) 12
twisted, Dutch, 1 pretzel (2¾" x 2⅝" x ⅝") 62

twisted, rings (1-ring), 10 pretzels (1½" in diam., 1"-diam. hole) 78
twisted, rings (3-ring), 10 pretzels (1⅞" x 1¾" x ¼") 117
twisted, thins, 10 pretzels (3¼" x 2¼" x ¼") 234

Prickly pears:
raw, whole, 1 lb. 84
peeled and seeded, 4 oz. 48

Prune juice, canned or bottled:
4-fl.-oz. bottle 99
1 cup 197

Prune whip, home recipe:
baked, served hot, 1 cup 140
baked, served cold, 1 cup 203

Prunes, dehydrated (nugget type):
uncooked, 8 oz. 780
uncooked, 1 cup 344
cooked, sweetened, with liquid, 8 oz. 408
cooked, sweetened, with liquid, 1 cup 504

Prunes, dried, "softenized":
uncooked, whole, with pits:
   extra large size (up to 43 per lb.), 8 oz. 509
   extra large size (up to 43 per lb.), 10 prunes 274
   large size (up to 53 per lb.), 8 oz. 501
   large size (up to 53 per lb.), 10 prunes 215
   medium size (up to 67 per lb.), 8 oz. 498
   medium size (up to 67 per lb.), 10 prunes 164
uncooked, whole, pitted, 8 oz. 579
uncooked, whole, pitted, 1 cup 459
uncooked, whole, pitted, 10 prunes 260
uncooked, chopped or ground, 1 cup loosely packed 408
uncooked, chopped or ground, 1 cup packed 663
cooked, with pits, unsweetened, with liquid, cold, 8 oz. 230
cooked, with pits, unsweetened, with liquid, cold, 1 cup 253
cooked, with pits, sweetened, with liquid, cold, 8 oz. 332
cooked, with pits, sweetened, with liquid, cold, 1 cup 409

Pudding, rennin, see Rennin dessert

Pudding, vegetable gum base, mix:
custard, cooked with milk, 1 cup 380

Puddings, starch base, home recipe:
chocolate, prepared, 1 cup 385
vanilla (blancmange), prepared, 1 cup 283

Puddings, starch base, mix:
    chocolate, dry form, 4-oz. pkg. 408
    chocolate, cooked with milk, 1 cup 322
    chocolate, instant, dry form, 4½-oz. pkg. 457
    chocolate, instant no-cook, prepared with milk, 1 cup 325
Pumpkin, fresh:
    raw, whole, 1 lb. 83
    raw, pulp only, 4 oz. 30
Pumpkin, canned:
    8 oz. 75
    1 cup 81
Pumpkin pie, see Pies
Pumpkinseed kernels, dry:
    hulled, 4 oz. 627
    hulled, 1 cup 774
    whole, weighed in hull, 4 oz. 464
Purslane leaves, fresh:
    raw, whole, with stems, 1 lb. 95
    boiled, drained, 1 cup 27

Q

food and measure	calories

Quail, raw:
    whole, ready-to-cook, 1 lb. 686
    meat and skin only, 4 oz. 196
    giblets, 2 oz. 100
Quinces, fresh:
    whole, 1 lb. 158
    peeled and seeded, 4 oz. 65

R

food and measure	calories

Rabbit, domesticated:
    raw, whole, ready-to-cook, 1 lb. 581
    raw, meat only, 4 oz. 184

stewed, whole, 8.6 oz. (yield from 1 lb. raw, ready-to-cook) ...	529
stewed, meat only, 4 oz.	245
stewed, chopped or diced, 1 cup	302
stewed, ground, 1 cup	238

Rabbit, wild, raw:

whole, ready-to-cook, 1 lb.	490
meat only, 4 oz.	153

Raccoon, roasted:

meat only, 4 oz.	290

Radishes, raw:

with tops, 1 lb.	49
without tops, prepackaged, 6-oz. pkg.	26
whole, 10 large radishes (over 1"–1¼" in diam.)	14
whole, 10 medium radishes (¾"–1" in diam.)	8
sliced, 1 cup	20

Radishes, Oriental, raw:

with tops, 1 lb.	57
without tops, 1 lb.	67
pared, 4 oz.	22

Raisin pie, see Pies

Raisins, natural (unbleached), seedless:

uncooked, 8 oz.	656
uncooked, 1½-oz. pkg.	124
uncooked, ½-oz. pkg.	40
uncooked, whole, 1 cup loosely packed	419
uncooked, whole, 1 cup packed	477
uncooked, whole, 1 tbsp.	26
uncooked, chopped, 1 cup loosely packed	390
uncooked, chopped, 1 cup packed	549
uncooked, ground, 1 cup loosely packed	578
uncooked, ground, 1 cup packed	780
cooked, sweetened, with liquid, 8 oz.	484
cooked, sweetened, with liquid, 1 cup	628

Raspberries, fresh:

black, 1 lb.	331
black, 1 cup	98
red, 1 lb.	259
red, 1 pint	185
red, 1 cup	70

Raspberries, canned:

black, in water, with liquid, 8 oz.	116

    red, in water, with liquid, 8 oz. 80
    red, in water, with liquid, 1 cup 85
Raspberries, frozen:
    red, sweetened, unthawed, 10-oz. pkg. 278
    red, sweetened, unthawed, 1 cup 245
Red and gray snapper, raw:
    whole, 1 lb. 219
    meat only, 4 oz. 106
Redfish, see **Drum, red** and **Ocean perch, Atlantic**
Red horse, silver, raw:
    drawn, 1 lb. 204
    meat only, 4 oz. 111
Reindeer, raw:
    lean meat only, 4 oz. 144
Relish, see **Pickle relish**
Rennin dessert, mix:
    chocolate, dry form, 2-oz. pkg. 221
    chocolate, prepared with milk, 1 cup 260
    vanilla, caramel, or fruit flavor, dry form, 1½-oz. pkg. 165
    vanilla, caramel, or fruit flavor, prepared with milk, 1 cup ... 238
Rhubarb, fresh:
    raw, with leaves, 1 lb. 33
    raw, well trimmed, 1 lb. 62
    raw, diced, 1 cup 20
    cooked, sweetened, 1 cup 381
Rhubarb, frozen:
    sweetened, unthawed, 10-oz. pkg. 213
    sweetened, cooked with added sugar, 1 cup 386
Rhubarb pie, see **Pies**
Rice, brown:
    raw, long-grain, 1 cup 666
    raw, short-grain, 1 cup 720
    cooked, long-grain, 1 cup hot rice 232
    cooked, long-grain, 1 cup cold rice 173
Rice, Spanish, see **Spanish rice**
Rice, white:
    raw, long-grain, 1 cup 672
    raw, medium-grain, 1 cup 708
    raw, short-grain, 1 cup 726
    cooked, long-grain, 1 cup hot rice 223

Rolls and buns, commercial, continued

frankfurter or hot-dog, 1.4-oz. roll (6″ x 2″ x 1½″) 119
hamburger, 1.4-oz. roll (3½″ in diam., 1½″ high) 119
hard, round or kaiser, 1¾-oz. roll (3¾″ in diam., 2″ high) .. 156
hard, rectangular, ⅞-oz. roll (3¾″ x 2½″ x 1¾″) 78
hoagie or submarine, see **Breads, French** or **Vienna**
plain (pan rolls), 1-oz. roll (2″ square, 2″ high) 83
raisin, 1-oz. roll 78
sweet, 1-oz. roll 89
whole-wheat, 1-oz. roll 73
partially baked (brown-and-serve):
cloverleaf, pan or dinner rolls, 1-oz. roll 84
Romaine, see **Lettuce**
Root beer, see **Soft drinks**
Rose apples, raw:
whole, 1 lb. 170
trimmed and seeded, 4 oz. 64
Rum, see **Alcoholic beverages**
Rusks, see **Crackers**
Rutabagas, fresh:
raw, without tops, 1 lb. 177
raw, trimmed, 4 oz. 52
raw, diced, 1 cup 64
boiled, drained, cubes or slices, 1 cup 60
boiled, drained, mashed, 1 cup 84
Rye, see **Flour**
Rye wafers, see **Crackers**

S

food and measure	calories

Sablefish, raw:
whole, 1 lb. 362
meat only, 4 oz. 216
Safflower oil, see **Oils**
Safflower seed kernels:
dry, 1 oz. 174

Safflower seed meal:
  partially defatted, 4 oz. 405
St.-John's-bread flour, see Flour, carob
Salad dressings, made from home recipe:
  French, 1 cup 1,390
  French, 1 tbsp. 88
  cooked, 1 cup 418
  cooked, 1 tbsp. 26
Salad dressings, commercial (see also **Salad dressings, dietary**):
  blue cheese, 1 cup 1,235
  blue cheese, 1 tbsp. 76
  French, 1 cup 1,025
  French, 1 tbsp. 66
  Italian, 1 cup 1,297
  Italian, 1 tbsp. 83
  mayonnaise, 1 cup 1,580
  mayonnaise, 1 tbsp. 101
  Roquefort cheese, 1 cup 1,235
  Roquefort cheese, 1 tbsp. 76
  Russian, 1 cup 1,210
  Russian, 1 tbsp. 74
  salad dressing (mayonnaise-type), 1 cup 1,022
  salad dressing (mayonnaise-type), 1 tbsp. 65
  Thousand Island, 1 cup 1,255
  Thousand Island, 1 tbsp. 80
Salad dressings, dietary (low-calorie), commercial:
  blue cheese (about 5 calories per tsp.), 1 cup 194
  blue cheese (about 5 calories per tsp.), 1 tbsp. 12
  blue cheese (about 1 calorie per tsp.), 1 cup 47
  blue cheese (about 1 calorie per tsp.), 1 tbsp. 3
  French (about 5 calories per tsp.), 1 cup 250
  French (about 5 calories per tsp.), 1 tbsp. 15
  Italian (about 2 calories per tsp.), 1 cup 120
  Italian (about 2 calories per tsp.), 1 tbsp. 8
  mayonnaise-type (about 8 calories per tsp.), 1 cup 340
  mayonnaise-type (about 8 calories per tsp.), 1 tbsp. 22
  Roquefort cheese (about 5 calories per tsp.), 1 cup 194
  Roquefort cheese (about 5 calories per tsp.), 1 tbsp. 12
  Roquefort cheese (about 1 calorie per tsp.), 1 cup 47
  Roquefort cheese (about 1 calorie per tsp.), 1 tbsp. 3

Thousand Island (about 10 calories per tsp.), 1 cup 441
Thousand Island (about 10 calories per tsp.), 1 tbsp. 27
Salad oil, see Oils
Salami:
  dry, roll, 8¼-oz. roll 1,053
  dry, roll, 1 slice (1¾" in diam., ⅛" thick) 23
  dry, sliced, 4-oz. pkg. 509
  dry, sliced, 1 slice (3⅛" in diam., 1/16" thick) 45
  cooked, 8-oz. pkg. 706
  cooked, 1 slice (4½" in diam.; about 1 oz.) 88
  cooked, 1 slice (4" in diam.; about ¾ oz.) 68
Salmon, fresh:
  Atlantic, raw, whole, 1 lb. 640
  Atlantic, raw, meat only, 4 oz. 246
  chinook (king), raw, steak, 1 lb. 886
  chinook (king), raw, meat only, 4 oz. 252
  pink (humpback), raw, steak, 1 lb. 475
  pink (humpback), raw, meat only, 4 oz. 135
  broiled or baked with butter, meat only, 4 oz. 207
  broiled or baked with butter, 1 steak (6¾" x 2½") 232
Salmon, canned, with liquid:
  Atlantic, 7¾-oz. can 447
  Atlantic, 4 oz. 230
  chinook (king), 7¾-oz. can 462
  chinook (king), 4 oz. 238
  chum, 7¾-oz. can 306
  chum, 4 oz. 158
  coho (silver), 7¾-oz. can 337
  coho (silver), 4 oz. 174
  pink (humpback), 7¾-oz. can 310
  pink (humpback), 4 oz. 160
  sockeye (red), 7¾-oz. can 376
  sockeye (red), 4 oz. 194
Salmon, smoked:
  4 oz. 200
Salmon rice loaf, home recipe:
  1 whole loaf (7½" x 7½" x 1½") 1,275
  1 piece (3¾" x 2½" x 1¼"; 1/6 of whole loaf) 212
Salsify, fresh:
  freshly harvested, raw, without tops, 1 lb. 51

stored, raw, without tops, 1 lb.	324
freshly harvested, boiled, drained, cubed, 1 cup	16
stored, boiled, drained, cubed, 1 cup	94

Salt, table:

| 1 lb. | 0 |
| 1 cup | 0 |

Salt pork, raw:

| with skin, 1 lb. | 3,410 |
| without skin, 1 oz. | 222 |

Salt sticks, see **Bread sticks**

Sand dab, raw:

| whole, 1 lb. | 118 |
| meat only, 4 oz. | 89 |

Sandwich spread, with chopped pickle:

regular, 1 cup	929
regular, 1 tbsp.	57
dietary (about 5 calories per tsp.), 1 tbsp.	17

Sapodillas:

| whole, 1 lb. | 323 |
| peeled and seeded, 4 oz. | 101 |

Sapotes (marmalade plums):

| whole, 1 lb. | 431 |
| peeled and seeded, 4 oz. | 143 |

Sardines, Atlantic:

canned in oil, 4 oz.	353
canned in oil, with liquid, 3¾-oz. can	330
canned in oil, drained, 3¼ oz. (yield from 3¾-oz. can with oil)	187
canned in oil, 1 fish (3½" long, 1½" wide; 5 fish per can)	41
canned in oil, 1 fish (3" long, ½" wide; 8 fish per can)	24
canned in oil, 1 fish (2⅔" long, ½" wide; 16–20 fish per can)	10

Sardines, Pacific:

raw, meat only, 4 oz.	181
canned in brine or mustard, 4 oz.	223
canned in tomato sauce, 4 oz.	225

Sauces, see individual listings

Sauerkraut, canned:

| with liquid, 8 oz. | 41 |
| with liquid, 1 cup | 42 |

Sauerkraut juice, canned:

| 15-fl.-oz. can | 45 |
| 1 cup | 24 |

Sauger, raw:
  whole, 1 lb. 133
  meat only, 4 oz. 95
Sausages (see also individual listings):
  blood (pudding), 4 oz. 447
  blood (pudding), 1 slice (2¼" in diam., ⅛" thick) 32
  brown-and-serve, before browning:
    8-oz. pkg. (8–9 patties or 10–11 links) 892
    1 link (3⅞" long, ⅝" in diam.) 83
    1 patty (2⅜" x 1⅛" x ½") 111
  brown-and-serve, browned:
    6.3 oz. (yield from 8-oz. pkg. before browning) 760
    1 link (3⅞" long, ⅝" in diam. before browning) 72
    1 patty (2⅜" x 1⅛" x ½" before browning) 97
    4 oz. 479
  country-style, 4 oz. 391
  Polish, 4 oz. 345
  Polish, 8-oz. sausage (10" long, 1¼" in diam.) 690
  Polish, 2.7 oz. sausage (5⅜" long, 1" in diam.) 231
  pork, raw, 8-oz. pkg. (4 patties or 8 links) 1,130
  pork, raw, 2.4-oz. piece (3" long, 1¼" in diam.) 339
  pork, raw, 2-oz. patty (3⅞" in diam., ¼" thick) 284
  pork, raw, 1-oz. link (4" long, ⅞" in diam.) 141
  pork, cooked, 3.8 oz. (yield from 8-oz. pkg. raw) 509
  pork, cooked, 1 piece (yield from 2.4-oz. piece raw) 152
  pork, cooked, 1 patty (yield from 2-oz. patty raw) 129
  pork, cooked, 1 link (yield from 1-oz. link raw) 62
  pork, cooked, 4 oz. 543
  pork, canned, with liquid, 8-oz. can (about 14 links) 942
  pork, canned, drained, 5.7 oz. (yield from 8-oz. can with liquid) 617
  pork, canned, drained, 1 link (3" long, ½" in diam.) 46
  pork and beef, chopped, 4 oz. 383
  pork, smoked, see Sausages, country-style
  scrapple, 16-oz. loaf (4½" x 2¾" x 2⅛") 975
  scrapple, 1 slice (2¾" x 2⅛" x ¼"; 1/18 of 16-oz. loaf) 54
  scrapple, 4 oz. 244
  souse, 6-oz. pkg. (about 6 slices) 308
  souse, 1 slice (1 oz.) 51
  souse, 4 oz. 205
  summer sausage, see Thuringer cervelat

110

Shrimp, fresh:

raw, whole, in shell, 1 lb. 285

raw, shelled and cleaned, 4 oz. 103

breaded, French-fried, 4 oz. 255

Shrimp, canned:

with liquid, 8 oz. 182

drained or dry pack, 8 oz. 263

drained, 1 cup (22 large, 40 medium, or 76 small shrimp) 148

drained, 10 large shrimp (about 3¼″ long) 67

drained, 10 medium shrimp (about 2½″ long) 37

drained, 10 small shrimp (about 2″ long) 17

Shrimp, frozen:

breaded, fried, 4 oz. 158

Shrimp paste, canned:

1 oz. 51

1 tsp. 13

Siscowet, see Lake trout

Skate (Raja fish), raw:

meat only, 4 oz. 111

Smelt, Atlantic, jack or bay, raw:

whole, 1 lb. 244

meat only, 4 oz. 111

Smelt, eulachon, see Eulachon

Smelt, canned:

with liquid, 8 oz. 454

Snails, raw:

meat only, 4 oz. 103

giant African, meat only, 4 oz. 83

Snapper, see Red and gray snapper

Soft drinks, carbonated:

club soda, 12-fl.-oz. can or bottle 0

club soda, 1 cup 0

cola-type, 12-fl.-oz. can or bottle 144

cola-type, 1 cup 96

cream soda, 12-fl.-oz. can or bottle 160

cream soda, 1 cup 105

fruit flavor (citrus, cherry, grape, etc.), 12-fl.-oz. can or bottle . 171

fruit flavor (citrus, cherry, grape, etc.), 1 cup 113

ginger ale, pale dry or golden, 12-fl.-oz. can or bottle 113

ginger ale, pale dry or golden, 1 cup 76

quinine water (tonic), 12-fl.-oz. can or bottle 113

quinine water (tonic), 1 cup	76
root beer, 12-fl.-oz. can or bottle	152
root beer, 1 cup	100
Tom Collins mixer, 12-fl.-oz. can or bottle	171
Tom Collins mixer, 1 cup	113

Sole, raw:

whole, 1 lb.	118
meat only (fillets), 4 oz.	80

Sorghum grain:

4 oz.	378

Sorghum syrup, see Syrups
Sorrel, see Dock
Soups, canned:

asparagus, cream of:

condensed, 10½-oz. can	161
diluted with equal part water, 1 cup	65
diluted with equal part whole milk, 1 cup	147

bean with pork:

condensed, 11½-oz. can	437
diluted with equal part water, 1 cup	168

beef broth, bouillon, or consommé:

condensed, 10½-oz. can	77
diluted with equal part water, 1 cup	31

beef noodle:

condensed, 10½-oz. can	170
diluted with equal part water, 1 cup	67

borscht, ready-to-serve, 1 cup	73

celery, cream of:

condensed, 10½-oz. can	215
diluted with equal part water, 1 cup	86
diluted with equal part whole milk, 1 cup	169

chicken consommé:

condensed, 10½-oz. can	54
diluted with equal part water, 1 cup	22

chicken, cream of:

condensed, 10½-oz. can	235
diluted with equal part water, 1 cup	94
diluted with equal part whole milk, 1 cup	179

chicken gumbo:

condensed, 10½-oz. can	137
diluted with equal part water, 1 cup	55

vegetable with beef broth:

  condensed, 10¾-oz. can 195

  diluted with equal part water, 1 cup 78

vegetarian vegetable:

  condensed, 10¾-oz. can 195

  diluted with equal part water, 1 cup 78

Soups, dehydrated.

beef noodle:

  mix, dry form, 2-oz. pkg. 221

  prepared (2 oz. mix with 3 cups water), 1 cup 67

chicken noodle:

  mix, dry form, 2-oz. pkg. 218

  prepared (2 oz. mix with 4 cups water), 1 cup 53

chicken rice:

  mix, dry form, 1½-oz. pkg. 152

  prepared (1½ oz. mix with 3 cups water), 1 cup 48

onion:

  mix, dry form, 1½-oz. pkg. 150

  prepared (1½ oz. mix with 4 cups water), 1 cup 36

pea, green:

  mix, dry form, 4-oz. pkg. 409

  prepared (4 oz. mix with 3 cups water), 1 cup 123

tomato vegetable with noodles:

  mix, dry form, 2½-oz. pkg. 247

  prepared (2½ oz. mix with 4 cups water), 1 cup 65

Soups, frozen:

clam chowder, New England:

  condensed, 8 oz. 243

  diluted with equal part water, 1 cup 127

  diluted with equal part whole milk, 1 cup 202

oyster stew:

  condensed, 8 oz. 232

  diluted with equal part water, 1 cup 120

  diluted with equal part whole milk, 1 cup 197

pea, green, with ham:

  condensed, 8 oz. 257

  diluted with equal part water, 1 cup 134

potato, cream of:

  condensed, 8 oz. 197

  diluted with equal part water, 1 cup 103

  diluted with equal part whole milk, 1 cup 179

   shrimp, cream of:

      condensed, 8 oz. 302

      diluted with equal part water, 1 cup 155

      diluted with equal part whole milk, 1 cup 233

   vegetable with beef:

      condensed, 8 oz. 159

      diluted with equal part water, 1 cup 82

Sour cream, see **Cream, sour**

Soursop, raw:

   whole, 1 lb. 200

   peeled and seeded, 4 oz. 74

   puréed, 1 cup 146

Souse, see **Sausages**

Soybean curd (tofu):

   4 oz. 82

   1 piece (2½" x 2¾" x 1") 86

Soybean flour, see **Flour**

Soybean milk:

   fluid, 4 oz. 37

   powder, 4 oz. 486

Soybean oil, see **Oils**

Soybean protein:

   4 oz. 365

Soybean proteinate:

   4 oz. 354

Soybean seeds, immature:

   raw, in pods, 1 lb. 322

   raw, shelled, 1 lb. 608

   boiled, drained, 4 oz. 135

   canned, with liquid, 8 oz. 170

   canned, drained, 8 oz. 234

Soybean seeds, mature, dry:

   uncooked, 8 oz. 914

   uncooked, 1 cup 846

   cooked, 8 oz. 295

   cooked, 1 cup 234

Soybean sprouts, see **Bean sprouts**

Soybeans, fermented:

   natto, 4 oz. 190

   miso (with cereal), 4 oz. 194

Soy sauce:

1 cup 197
1 tbsp. 12

Spaghetti, plain:

dry form, 8-oz. pkg. 838
cooked, firm stage (8–10 minutes), 1 cup 192
cooked, tender stage (14–20 minutes), 1 cup 155

Spaghetti, with meatballs and tomato sauce:

home recipe, 8 oz. 304
home recipe, 1 cup 332
canned, 8 oz. 235
canned, 1 cup 258

Spaghetti, in tomato sauce, with cheese:

home recipe, 8 oz. 236
home recipe, 1 cup 260
canned, 8 oz. 173
canned, 1 cup 190

Spanish mackerel, raw:

whole, 1 lb. 490
meat only, 4 oz. 202

Spanish rice, home recipe:

8 oz. 197
1 cup 213

Spinach, fresh:

raw, whole, 1 lb. 85
raw, trimmed, packaged, 1 lb. 118
raw, trimmed, leaves, 1 cup 9
raw, trimmed, chopped, 1 cup 14
boiled, drained, leaves, 1 cup 41

Spinach, canned:

with liquid, 8 oz. 43
with liquid, 1 cup 44
drained, 8 oz. 55
drained, 1 cup 49
dietary (low-sodium) pack, with liquid, 8 oz. 48
dietary (low-sodium) pack, with liquid, 1 cup 49
dietary (low-sodium) pack, drained, 8 oz. 59
dietary (low-sodium) pack, drained, 1 cup 53

Spinach, frozen:

chopped, unthawed, 10-oz. pkg. 68
chopped, boiled, drained, 7¾ oz. (yield from 10-oz. pkg.) 51

chopped, boiled, drained, 1 cup	47
leaf, unthawed, 10-oz. pkg.	71
leaf, boiled, drained, 7¾ oz. (yield from 10-oz. pkg.)	53
leaf, boiled, drained, 1 cup	46

Spinach, New Zealand, see **New Zealand spinach**

Spiny lobster, see **Crayfish**

Spleen, raw:

beef or calf, 4 oz.	118
hog, 4 oz.	122
lamb, 4 oz.	131

Spot, fresh:

raw, fillets, 4 oz.	248
baked, fillets, 4 oz.	335

Squab (pigeon), raw:

whole, dressed, 1 lb.	569
meat only, 4 oz.	162
light meat only, 4 oz.	143

Squash, summer, fresh:

white and pale green, scallop varieties:

raw, whole, 1 lb.	93
raw, trimmed, 8 oz.	48
raw, cubed, diced, or sliced, 1 cup	27
boiled, drained, 8 oz.	37
boiled, drained, sliced, 1 cup	29
boiled, drained, cubed or diced, 1 cup	34
boiled, drained, mashed, 1 cup	38

yellow, crookneck or straightneck:

raw, whole, 1 lb.	89
raw, trimmed, 8 oz.	46
raw, cubed, diced, or sliced, 1 cup	26
boiled, drained, 8 oz.	34
boiled, drained, sliced, 1 cup	27
boiled, drained, cubed or diced, 1 cup	32
boiled, drained, mashed, 1 cup	36

zucchini or cocozelle (Italian marrow-type), green:

raw, whole, 1 lb.	73
raw, trimmed, 8 oz.	39
raw, cubed, diced, or sliced, 1 cup	22
boiled, drained, 8 oz.	27
boiled, drained, sliced, 1 cup	22

```
   boiled, drained, cubed or diced, 1 cup ...................   25
   boiled, drained, mashed, 1 cup ..........................   29
```

Squash, summer, frozen:
```
   yellow crookneck, unthawed, 12-oz. pkg. .................   71
   yellow crookneck, boiled, drained, 8 oz. ................   48
```

Squash, winter, fresh:
```
   acorn, raw, whole, 1 lb. ................................  152
   acorn, raw, whole, 1 squash (4⅓" long., 4" in diam; 1¼ lbs.) ..  190
   acorn, raw, cavity cleaned, ½ squash ....................   97
   acorn, baked, 8 oz. .....................................  125
   acorn, baked, ½ squash ..................................   86
   acorn, baked, mashed, 1 cup .............................  113
   acorn, boiled, 8 oz. ....................................   77
   acorn, boiled, mashed, 1 cup ............................   83
   butternut, raw, whole, 1 lb. ............................  171
   butternut, baked, 8 oz. .................................  154
   butternut, baked, mashed, 1 cup .........................  139
   butternut, boiled, 8 oz. ................................   93
   butternut, boiled, mashed, 1 cup ........................  100
   hubbard, raw, whole, 1 lb. ..............................  117
   hubbard, baked, 8 oz. ...................................  114
   hubbard, baked, mashed, 1 cup ...........................  103
   hubbard, boiled, 8 oz. ..................................   68
   hubbard, boiled, cubed or diced, 1 cup ..................   71
   hubbard, boiled, mashed, 1 cup ..........................   74
```

Squash, winter, frozen:
```
   unthawed, 12-oz. pkg. ...................................  129
   heated, 8 oz. ...........................................   86
   heated, 1 cup ...........................................   91
```

Squash seed kernels:
```
   dry, 4 oz. ..............................................  630
```

Squid, raw:
```
   meat only, 4 oz. ........................................   95
```

Starch, see **Cornstarch**

Stomach, pork:
```
   scalded, 4 oz. ..........................................  173
```

Strawberries, fresh:
```
   whole, with caps and stems, 1 lb. .......................  161
   whole, capped, trimmed, 1 lb. ...........................  168
   whole, 1 cup ............................................   55
```

Strawberries, canned:
in water, with liquid, 8 oz. 50
in water, with liquid, 1 cup 53
Strawberries, frozen:
sweetened, whole, 16-oz. pkg. 417
sweetened, whole, 1 cup 235
sweetened, sliced, 10-oz. pkg. 310
sweetened, sliced, 1 cup 278
Strawberry pie, see **Pies**
Sturgeon, fresh:
raw, meat only, 4 oz. 107
steamed, meat only, 4 oz. 181
Sturgeon, smoked:
4 oz. 169
Succotash (corn and lima beans), frozen:
unthawed, 10-oz. pkg. 275
unthawed, 1 cup 150
boiled, drained, 8 oz. 211
boiled, drained, 1 cup 158
Sucker, carp, raw:
whole, 1 lb. 196
meat only, 4 oz. 126
Sucker, white and mullet, raw:
whole, 1 lb. 203
meat only (fillets), 4 oz. 118
Suet (beef kidney fat), raw:
1 oz. 242
Sugar, beet or cane:
brown, 1 lb. 1,692
brown, 1 cup loosely packed 541
brown, 1 cup firm packed 821
brown, 1 tbsp. firm packed 52
granulated, 1 lb. 1,746
granulated, 1 cup 770
granulated, 1 tbsp. 46
granulated, 1 tsp. 15
granulated, 1 cube (½") 10
granulated, 1 lump (1⅛" x ¾" x 5/16") 19
granulated, 1 packet 23
powdered (confectioners'), 1 lb. 1,746
powdered (confectioners'), unsifted, 1 cup 462

Sweet potatoes, fresh, continued
boiled in skin, 1 potato (5″ long, 2″ in diam.)	172
boiled in skin, sliced, 1 cup	181
boiled in skin, mashed, 1 cup	291

Sweet potatoes, candied:
4 oz.	191
1 piece (2½″ long, 2″ in diam.)	176

Sweet potatoes, canned:
liquid pack, with liquid, 8 oz.	259
vacuum pack, 8 oz.	245
vacuum pack, 1 piece (2¾″ long, 1″ in diam.)	43
vacuum pack, pieces, 1 cup	216
vacuum pack, mashed, 1 cup	275
dietary pack, with liquid, 8 oz.	104

Sweet potatoes, dehydrated:
flakes, dry form, 4 oz.	432
flakes, dry form, 1 cup	455
flakes, prepared with water, 8 oz.	216
flakes, prepared with water, 1 cup	242

Sweetsop, see Sugar apples
Swiss chard, see Chard, Swiss
Swordfish, fresh:
raw, meat only 1 lb.	535
broiled with butter, 10.1 oz. (yield from 1 lb. raw)	499
broiled with butter, 4 oz.	186
broiled with butter, 1 piece (4½″ x 2⅛″ x ⅞″)	237

Swordfish, canned:
with liquid, 8 oz.	116

Syrups (see also individual listings):
cane, 1 cup	828
cane, 1 tbsp.	53
maple, 1 cup	794
maple, 1 tbsp.	50
sorghum, 1 cup	848
sorghum, 1 tbsp.	53
table blend (chiefly corn, light and dark), 1 cup	951
table blend (chiefly corn, light and dark), 1 tbsp.	59
table blend (cane and maple), 1 cup	794
table blend (cane and maple), 1 tbsp.	50

T

Tamarinds, fresh:
whole, 1 lb.	520
shelled and seeded, 4 oz.	271

Tangelo juice, fresh:
1 cup	101
juice from 1 large tangelo (2¾″ in diam.)	47
juice from 1 medium tangelo (2 9/16″ in diam.)	39
juice from 1 small tangelo (2¼″ in diam.)	28

Tangerine juice, fresh:
1 cup	106

Tangerine juice, canned:
unsweetened, 6-fl.-oz. can	80
unsweetened, 1 cup	106
sweetened, 6-fl.-oz. can	94
sweetened, 1 cup	125

Tangerine juice concentrate, frozen:
unsweetened, undiluted, 6-fl.-oz. can	342
unsweetened, diluted with 3 parts water, 1 cup	114

Tangerines, fresh (Dancy variety):
whole, 1 lb.	154
whole, 1 large tangerine (2½″ in diam.)	46
whole, 1 medium tangerine (2⅜″ in diam.)	39
whole, 1 small tangerine (2¼″ in diam.)	33
sections, without membranes, 1 cup	90

Tapioca, dry form:
8-oz. pkg.	799
1 cup	535
1 tbsp.	30

Tapioca pudding, home recipe:
apple, 1 cup	293
cream, 1 cup	221

Taro:
corms and tubers, whole, 1 lb.	373
corms and tubers, without skin, 4 oz.	111
leaves and stems, 1 lb.	181

123

Tartar sauce:
- 1 cup 1,221
- 1 tbsp. 74
- dietary pack, 1 tbsp. 31

Tautog (blackfish), raw:
- whole, 1 lb. 149
- meat only, 4 oz. 101

Tea, instant:
- dry form, 1 oz. 83
- dry form, 1 tsp. 1

Tendergreens, see Mustard spinach

Terrapin (diamondback), raw:
- in shell, 1 lb. 106
- meat only, 4 oz. 126

Thuringer cervelat (summer sausage):
- 8-oz. pkg. 697
- 1 slice (4⅜″ in diam., ⅛″ thick; 1 oz.) 87
- 1 slice (4⅛″ in diam., ⅛″ thick; ¾ oz.) 68
- 1 slice (2⅞″ in diam., 1/16″ thick; ¼ oz.) 23

Tilefish:
- raw, whole, 1 lb. 183
- raw, meat only, 4 oz. 90
- baked, meat only, 4 oz. 156

Tofu, see Soybean curd

Tomato catsup, see Catsup

Tomato chili sauce, see Chili sauce

Tomato juice, canned or bottled:
- 5½-fl.-oz. can 32
- 1 cup 46
- dietary (low-sodium) pack, 12-fl.-oz. can 69
- dietary (low-sodium) pack, 1 cup 46

Tomato juice, dehydrated:
- crystals, dry form, 1 oz. 86
- crystals, prepared with water, 1 cup 49

Tomato juice cocktail, canned or bottled:
- 1 cup 51

Tomato paste, canned:
- 8 oz. 186
- 6-oz. can 139
- 1 cup 215

124

Tomato purée, canned:
8 oz. 89
1 cup 98
dietary (low-sodium) pack, 8 oz. 89
Tomato soup, see Soups
Tomatoes, green, fresh:
whole, 1 lb. 99
Tomatoes, ripe, fresh:
raw, whole, 1 lb. 100
raw, whole, 1 tomato (about 2⅗″ in diam.) 27
raw, whole, 1 tomato (about 2⅖″ in diam.) 20
raw, whole, peeled, 1 tomato (2⅖″ in diam.) 19
raw, sliced, 1 cup 40
boiled, 1 cup 63
Tomatoes, ripe, canned:
with liquid, 8 oz. 48
with liquid, 1 cup 51
dietary (low-sodium) pack, with liquid, 8 oz. 46
dietary (low-sodium) pack, with liquid, 1 cup 48
Tomcod, Atlantic, raw:
whole, 1 lb. 136
meat only, 4 oz. 88
Tom Collins mix, see Soft drinks
Tongue, fresh:
beef, very fat, raw, trimmed, 8 oz. 615
beef, fat, raw, trimmed, 8 oz. 524
beef, medium-fat, raw, trimmed, 8 oz. 470
beef, medium-fat, braised, 4 oz. 277
beef, medium-fat, braised, 1 slice (3″ long, 2″ wide, ⅛″ thick) 49
calf, raw, trimmed, 8 oz. 295
calf, braised, 4 oz. 181
calf, braised, 1 slice (3″ long, 2″ wide, ⅛″ thick) 32
hog, raw, trimmed, 8 oz. 488
hog, braised, 4 oz. 287
hog, braised, 1 slice (3″ long, 2″ wide, ⅛″ thick) 51
lamb, raw, trimmed, 8 oz. 452
lamb, braised, 4 oz. 288
lamb, braised, 1 slice (3″ long, 2″ wide, ⅛″ thick) 51
sheep, raw, trimmed, 8 oz. 602
sheep, braised, 4 oz. 366
sheep, braised, 1 slice (3″ long, 2″ wide, ⅛″ thick) 65

Tongue, canned or cured:
    canned or pickled, 4 oz. 303
    potted or deviled, 4 oz. 329
Towel gourd:
    whole, 1 lb. 69
    pared, 4 oz. 20
Tripe, beef:
    commercial, 4 oz. 113
    pickled, 4 oz. 70
Trout, brook, raw:
    whole, 1 lb. 224
    meat only, 4 oz. 115
Trout, lake, see Lake trout
Trout, rainbow, fresh:
    raw, meat with skin, 4 oz. 221
Trout, rainbow, canned:
    4 oz. 237
Tuna, raw:
    bluefin, meat only, 4 oz. 165
    yellowfin, meat only, 4 oz. 151
Tuna, canned:
    in oil, all styles, with liquid, 8 oz. 653
    in oil, solid pack with liquid, 7-oz. can 570
    in oil, chunk-style, with liquid, 6½-oz. can 530
    in oil, flake- or grated-style, with liquid, 6–6¼-oz. can 501
    in oil, solid pack or chunk-style, drained, 8 oz. 447
    in oil, solid pack or chunk-style, drained, 1 cup 315
    in oil, solid pack, drained, 6 oz. (yield from 7-oz. can) 333
    in oil, chunk-style, drained, 5½ oz. (yield from 6½-oz. can) .. 309
    in water, all styles, with liquid, 8 oz. 288
    in water, solid pack, with liquid, 7-oz. can 251
    in water, solid pack, with liquid, 3½-oz. can 126
    in water, chunk-style, with liquid, 6½-oz. can 234
    in water, chunk-style, with liquid, 3½-oz. can 117
Tuna salad, home recipe:
    with celery, mayonnaise, pickle, onion, and eggs, 8 oz. 386
    with celery, mayonnaise, pickle, onion, and eggs, 1 cup 349
Turbot, Greenland, raw:
    whole, 1 lb. 344
    meat only, 4 oz. 166

Turkey, fresh (all classes):

raw, whole, ready-to-cook, 1 lb.	722
roasted, whole, with giblets and skin, 8.6 oz. (yield from 1 lb. raw)	644

roasted, dark meat without skin:

4 oz.	230
4 pieces (2½″ x 1⅝″ x ¼″)	173
chopped or diced, 1 cup	264
ground, 1 cup	223

roasted, light meat without skin:

4 oz.	200
4 pieces (2½″ x 1⅝″ x ¼″)	150
chopped or diced, 1 cup	246
ground, 1 cup	194
roasted, skin only, 1 oz.	256

Turkey, boned, canned:

5½-oz. can	315
4 oz.	229
1 cup	414

Turkey, potted, canned:

5½-oz. can	387
1 cup	558
1 tbsp.	32
1 oz.	70

Turkey giblets (some gizzard fat):

raw, 8 oz.	340
simmered, 4 oz.	264
simmered, chopped or diced, 1 cup	338

Turkey pot pie, home recipe:

baked, 1 whole pie (9″ in diam.)	1,654
baked, ⅓ of 9″ pie	550
baked, 8 oz.	538

Turkey pot pie, frozen:

8-oz. pie	447

Turkey soup, see Soups

Turnip greens, fresh:

raw, whole, 1 lb.	107
raw, trimmed, 1 lb.	127
boiled in small amount water, short time, drained, 8 oz.	46
boiled in small amount water, short time, drained, 1 cup	29

127

boiled in large amount water, long time, drained, 8 oz.	43
boiled in large amount water, long time, drained, 1 cup	28
Turnip greens, canned:	
with liquid, 8 oz.	41
with liquid, 1 cup	42
Turnip greens, frozen:	
chopped, unthawed, 10-oz. pkg.	65
chopped, boiled, drained, 7¾ oz. (yield from 10-oz. pkg.)	51
chopped, boiled, drained, 1 cup	38
Turnips, fresh:	
raw, without tops, untrimmed, 1 lb.	117
raw, cubed or sliced, 1 cup	39
boiled, drained, 8 oz.	52
boiled, drained, cubed, 1 cup	36
boiled, drained, mashed, 1 cup	53
Turtle, green, raw:	
in shell, 1 lb.	97
meat only, 4 oz.	101
Turtle, green, canned:	
4 oz.	120

V

food and measure	calories

Veal, fresh, retail cuts:	
chuck cuts and boneless for stew, lean with fat:	
raw, with bone, 1 lb.	628
stewed, with bone, 8.4 oz. (yield from 1 lb. raw)	564
raw, without bone, 1 lb.	785
stewed, without bone, 10.6 oz. (yield from 1 lb. raw)	703
stewed, without bone, 4 oz.	267
stewed, without bone, 1 piece (2½" x 2½" x ¾")	200
stewed, chopped or diced, 1 cup	329
loin cuts, lean with fat:	
raw, with bone, 1 lb.	681
braised or broiled, with bone, 9.5 oz. (yield from 1 lb. raw)	629

raw, without bone, 1 lb. 821
braised or broiled, without bone, 11.4 oz.
  (yield from 1 lb. raw) 758
braised or broiled, without bone, 4 oz. 245
braised or broiled, without bone, 1 piece (2½" x 2½" x ¾") 199
braised or broiled, chopped or diced, 1 cup 328
plate (breast of veal), lean with fat:
raw, with bone, 1 lb. 628
braised or stewed, with bone, 8.3 oz. (yield from 1 lb. raw) 718
raw, without bone, 1 lb. 1,048
braised or stewed, without bone, 10.6 oz.
  (yield from 1 lb. raw) 906
braised or stewed, without bone, 4 oz. 344
rib roast, lean with fat:
raw, with bone, 1 lb. 723
roasted, with bone, 8.5 oz. (yield from 1 lb. raw) 648
raw, without bone, 1 lb. 939
roasted, without bone, 11 oz. (yield from 1 lb. raw) 842
roasted, without bone, 4 oz. 305
roasted, without bone, 2 pieces (4⅛" x 2¼" x ¼") 229
roasted, chopped or diced, 1 cup 377
roasted, ground, 1 cup 296
round with rump (roasts and leg cutlets), lean with fat:
raw, with bone, 1 lb. 573
braised or broiled, with bone, 8.7 oz. (yield from 1 lb. raw) 534
raw, without bone, 1 lb. 744
braised or broiled, without bone, 11.3 oz.
  (yield from 1 lb. raw) 693
braised or broiled, without bone, 4 oz. 245
braised or broiled, without bone, 1 piece (4⅛" x 2¼" x ½") 184
braised or broiled, chopped or diced, 1 cup 302

Vegetable fat, see Fats, cooking

Vegetable juice cocktail, canned:
6-fl.-oz. can 31
1 cup 41

Vegetable oil, see Oils

Vegetable-oyster, see Salsify

Vegetables, see individual listings

Vegetables, mixed, frozen:
unthawed, 10-oz. pkg. 185

Vegetables, mixed, continued
   boiled, drained, 9.7 oz. (yield from 10-oz. pkg.) 176
   boiled, drained, 1 cup 116
Vegetable soup, see **Soups**
Venison, raw:
   lean meat only, 4 oz. 143
Vienna sausage, see **Sausages**
Vinegar, cider:
   1 cup 34
   1 tbsp. 2
Vinegar, distilled:
   1 cup 29
   1 tbsp. 2
Vine spinach (Basella), **raw:**
   4 oz. 22
Vodka, see **Alcoholic beverages**

W

food and measure	calories

Waffles, baked from home recipe:
   1 round waffle (7″ in diam., ⅝″ thick) 209
   1 square waffle (9″ x 9″ x ⅝″) 558
   1 square piece (4½″ x 4½″ x ⅝″) 140
Waffles, baked with mix:
   made with egg and milk, 1 round waffle (7″ in diam., ⅝″ thick) 206
   made with egg and milk, 1 square waffle (9″ x 9″ x ⅝″) 550
   made with egg and milk, 1 square piece (4½″ x 4½″ x ⅝″) .. 138
Waffles, frozen:
   prebaked, unheated, 1 waffle (4⅝″ x 3¾″ x ⅝″) 86
   prebaked, unheated, 1 waffle (3½″ x 2¾″ x ⅝″) 56
Waffle syrup, see **Syrups**
Walnuts, black:
   in shell, 1 lb. 627
   shelled, 4 oz. 712
   shelled, chopped or broken kernels, 1 cup 785
   shelled, chopped or broken kernels, 1 tbsp. 50
   shelled, finely ground, 1 cup 502

Walnuts, English or Persian:
  in shell, 1 lb. 1,329
  in shell, 10 large nuts 322
  shelled, 4 oz. 738
  shelled, 14 halves (1 oz.) 185
  shelled, halves, 1 cup 651
  shelled, chopped, 1 cup 781
  shelled, chopped, 1 tbsp. 52

Water chestnuts, Chinese, raw:
  whole, 1 lb. 276
  whole, 10–14 corms (1¼″–2″ in diam.; 8 oz.) 138
  peeled, 4 oz. 90

Watercress, fresh:
  whole, with stems, 1 lb. 79
  whole, with stems, 1 cup (about 10 sprigs) 7
  finely chopped, 1 cup 24

Water ice, see Ices, water

Watermelon, fresh:
  whole, with rind, 1 lb. 54
  1 wedge (4″ x 8″; about 2 lbs. with rind) 111
  diced, 8 oz. 59
  diced, 1 cup 42

Weakfish, fresh:
  raw, whole, 1 lb. 263
  raw, meat only, 4 oz. 138
  broiled with butter, 4 oz. 236

Welsh rarebit, home recipe:
  8 oz. 406
  1 cup 415

West Indian cherries, see Acerolas

Whale, raw:
  meat only, 4 oz. 177

Wheat, parboiled, see Bulgur

Wheat, whole-grain:
  durum, 4 oz. 376
  hard red spring, 4 oz. 374
  hard red winter, 4 oz. 374
  soft red winter, 4 oz. 370
  white, 4 oz. 380

Wheat bran:
  commercially milled, 4 oz. 242

food and measure	calories

Yam beans, tuber, raw:
whole, with skin, 1 lb. 225
pared, 4 oz. 62
Yams, canned, see **Sweet potatoes**
Yams, tuber, raw:
whole, with skin, 1 lb. 394
pared, 4 oz. 115
Yeast, baker's:
compressed, 1 oz. 24
compressed, 1 cake 19
dry (active), 1 oz. 80
dry (active), 1 pkg. (¼ oz.) or 1 tbsp. 20
Yeast, brewer's:
dry, 1 oz. 80
dry, 1 tbsp. 23
Yellowtail, raw:
meat only, 4 oz. 157
Yogurt, plain:
partially skim milk, 8-oz. container 113
partially skim milk, 1 cup 123
whole milk, 8-oz. container 140
whole milk, 1 cup 152
Youngberries, see **Blackberries**

food and measure	calories

Zucchini, see **Squash, summer**
Zwiebacks, see **Crackers**

METRIC
HOUSEHOLD
MEASURES

As the use of the metric system becomes more and more widespread in this country, you will probably find yourself referring to this section of the book with greater frequency. Even today, metric measures of weight, volume, and length are a meaningful part of our language—Did you ever use 35-millimeter film? Or smoke a 100-millimeter cigarette? Or diet by counting carbohydrate grams? (It is important to remember that the grams given as household measures for the foods in this section designate the *weight* of the entire food, as do the more familiar *ounces*. These are *not* carbohydrate grams, which measure only the carbohydrate content of a food. So don't attempt to utilize this counter for low-carbohydrate dieting. The information presented here is inappropriate for such use.)

Metric basics are simple, straightforward, and actually easier to understand than our own system because the language is more logical. The measures you should know are:

the *gram*, a measurement of weight, abbreviated *g*.
the *meter*, a measurement of length, abbreviated *m*.
the *liter*, a measurement of volume, abbreviated *l*.

Prefixes are commonly tagged onto these terms to identify larger and smaller units of the basic measures, the identical prefixes applying to all types of measurement. You should familiarize yourself with these prefixes:

milli = a thousand times smaller, abbreviated *m*.
centi = a hundred times smaller, abbreviated *c*.
kilo = a thousand times greater, abbreviated *k*.

Thus, one milliliter is one-thousandth (1/1000) of a liter and one centimeter is one-hundredth (1/100) of a meter. Milliliter is abbreviated *ml.* (*milli* + liter = ml.) and centimeter, *cm.* (*centi* + meter = cm.).

For the sake of convenience, most listings are given in rounded metric measures that are equivalent to the amounts in which particular foods are usually purchased—for example, 500 grams or 250 milliliters, and *not* 454 grams (the standard one pound) or 236 milliliters (the standard eight-fluid-ounce cup). Metric measuring utensils are geared to whole numbers. Therefore, measures expressed in metric quantities that approximate standard measures are utterly useless to the person who attempts to use the metric system for dieting and food preparation. Other counters have done this, but they are merely translating standard measures into metric measures and thereby avoid having to change the calorie content. You will find that the listings in this counter are ones you can actually utilize for planning meals and menus—and for shopping metric as well.

Until you gain a working knowledge of the metric system, you will want to refer often to this list of metric equivalents of familiar standard units:

EQUIVALENTS BY CAPACITY
(all measurements level)

1 quart = .95 liter	1 fluid ounce = 29.57 milliliters
1 cup = .24 liter	1 tablespoon = 15 milliliters
1 pint = .17 liter	1 teaspoon = 5 milliliters

EQUIVALENTS BY WEIGHT

1 pound = .45 kilogram   1 ounce = 28.35 grams

EQUIVALENTS BY LENGTH
1 inch = 2.54 centimeters

ABBREVIATIONS USED IN THIS SECTION

cm.	centimeter	kg.	kilogram
diam.	diameter	ml.	milliliter
g.	gram	pkg.	package

CALORIE COUNTER:
METRIC
HOUSEHOLD
MEASURES

A

food and measure	calories

Abalone, raw:

in shell, 500 g.	206
meat only, 125 g.	122

Abalone, canned:

125 g.	100

Acerola juice, fresh:

250 ml.	59
juice from 500 g. cherries	78

Acerolas (West Indian cherries), fresh:

whole, with pits, 500 g.	115
pitted, 125 g.	35
10 cherries, with pits (2.54 cm. in diam.; about 100 g.)	23

Alcoholic beverages:

beer, 4.5% alcohol, 360-ml. can or bottle	151
beer, 4.5% alcohol, 250 ml.	107
pure distilled liquor (gin, rum, whiskey, vodka, etc.):	
80 proof, 45-ml. jigger	97
86 proof, 45-ml. jigger	105
90 proof, 45-ml. jigger	110

94 proof, 45-ml. jigger	116
100 proof, 45-ml. jigger	124
wine, dessert, 18.8% alcohol, 105-ml. glass	141
wine, table or dry, 12.2% alcohol, 105-ml. glass	87

Alewife, raw:

whole, 500 g.	311
meat only, 125 g.	159

Alewife, canned:

with liquid, 125 g.	352

Almond meal:

partially defatted, 25 g.	102

Almonds, dried:

in shell, 500 g.	1,523
in shell, 250 ml.	199
in shell, 10 nuts	60
shelled, 125 g.	748
shelled, 25 g.	150
shelled, whole, 250 ml.	900
shelled, chopped, 250 ml.	824
shelled, chopped, 15 ml.	48
shelled, slivered, 250 ml. loosely packed	729

Almonds, roasted and salted:

roasted in oil, 125 g.	784
roasted in oil, 25 g.	157
roasted in oil, 250 ml.	1,043

Almonds, sugar- or chocolate coated, see Candy

Amaranth, fresh:

whole, with stems, 500 g.	113
leaves, 500 g.	180

Anchovies, canned:

flat or rolled, 57-g. can drained	79
flat, 5 average anchovies	35

Anchovy paste:

15 ml.	42

Apple brown Betty, home recipe:

250 g.	377
250 ml.	344

Apple butter, commercial:

340-g. jar	632
25 g.	47

Apple butter, continued

250 ml.	556
15 ml.	33

Apple drink, canned:

250 ml.	123

Apple juice, canned or bottled:

163-ml. can	80
250 ml.	124

Apple pie, see **Pies**

Apples, commercial varieties:

freshly harvested and stored:

with skin, 500 g.	266
with skin, 1 apple (8.26 cm. in diam.; 230 g.)	123
with skin, 1 apple (7.62 cm. in diam.; 180 g.)	96
with skin, 1 apple (7 cm. in diam.; 150 g.)	80
with skin, 1 apple (6.35 cm. in diam.; 115 g.)	61
with skin, quarters or finely chopped pieces, 250 ml.	77
with skin, sliced (.64 cm. thick) or diced, 250 ml.	68
pared, 1 apple (8.26 cm. in diam.; 230 g. whole)	107
pared, 1 apple (7.62 cm. in diam.; 180 g. whole)	84
pared, 1 apple (7 cm. in diam.; 150 g. whole)	70
pared, 1 apple (6.35 cm. in diam.; 115 g. whole)	53
pared, quarters or finely chopped pieces, 250 ml.	72
pared, sliced (.64 cm. thick) or diced, 250 ml.	62

Apples, canned, see **Applesauce**

Apples, dehydrated:

uncooked, 250 g.	883
uncooked, 250 ml.	374
cooked, sweetened, 250 g.	190
cooked, sweetened, 250 ml.	206

Apples, dried:

uncooked, 250 g.	688
uncooked, 250 ml.	248
cooked, unsweetened, 250 g.	195
cooked, unsweetened, 250 ml.	211
cooked, sweetened, 250 g.	280
cooked, sweetened, 250 ml.	333

Apples, frozen:

sliced, sweetened, 250 g.	233

Applesauce, canned:

unsweetened, 250 g.	103

unsweetened, 250 ml. 106
sweetened, 250 g. 228
sweetened, 250 ml. 246

Apricot nectar, canned or bottled:
163-ml. can 99
250 ml. 151

Apricot-orange juice drink, see Orange-apricot juice drink

Apricots, fresh:
whole, 500 g. 239
whole, 3 apricots (114 g.) 55
pitted, halves, 500 g. 254
pitted, halves, 250 ml. 84

Apricots, candied:
25 g. 85

Apricots, canned:
in water, with liquid, 250 g. 95
in water, with liquid, halves, 250 ml. 99
in water, 3 halves and 1¾ tbsp. liquid 32
in juice, with liquid, 250 g. 135
in heavy syrup, whole, with liquid, 250 g. 202
in heavy syrup, halves with liquid, 250 g. 215
in heavy syrup, whole or halves, with liquid, 250 ml. ... 235
in heavy syrup, 2 whole apricots and 2 tbsp. liquid 78
in heavy syrup, 3 halves and 1¾ tbsp. liquid 73

Apricots, dehydrated (nugget type):
uncooked, 250 g. 830
uncooked, 250 ml. 352
cooked, sweetened, 250 g. 298
cooked, sweetened, 250 ml. 357

Apricots, dried (halves):
uncooked, 250 g. 650
uncooked, 250 ml. 358
uncooked, 10 large halves 126
uncooked, 10 medium halves 91
cooked, unsweetened, with liquid, 250 g. 213
cooked, unsweetened, with liquid, 250 ml. 226
cooked, sweetened, 250 g. 305
cooked, sweetened, 250 ml. 349

Apricots, frozen:
sweetened, 250 g. 245
sweetened, 250 ml. 271

Artichoke hearts, frozen:

3 average 22

Artichokes, globe or French, fresh:

raw, whole, 500 g. 94

stored, boiled, drained, 1 whole bud (about 380 g.) 67

Artichokes, Jerusalem, see **Jerusalem artichokes**

Asparagus spears, fresh:

raw, whole spears, 500 g. 73

raw, cut spears, 250 ml. 37

boiled, drained, 4 large spears (1.91-cm. base) 20

boiled, drained, 4 medium spears (1.27-cm. base) 12

boiled, drained, 4 small spears (.95-cm. base) 8

boiled, drained, cut spears, 250 ml. 31

Asparagus spears, canned (green or white):

with liquid, 250 g. 45

with liquid, 250 ml. 47

cut spears, with liquid, 250 g. 45

cut spears, with liquid, 250 ml. 46

drained, 250 g. 53

drained, 250 ml. 54

cut spears, drained, 250 ml. 52

dietary (low-sodium) pack, with liquid, 250 g. 40

dietary (low-sodium) pack, cut spears, with liquid, 250 ml. 40

dietary (low-sodium) pack, drained, 250 g. 50

dietary (low-sodium) pack, cut spears, drained, 250 ml. 50

Asparagus spears, frozen:

unthawed, 284-g. pkg. 68

boiled, drained, 250 g. 58

boiled, drained, 250 ml. 47

boiled, drained, 4 large spears (1.91-cm. base) 18

boiled, drained, 4 medium spears (1.27-cm. base) 14

boiled, drained, 4 small spears (.95-cm. base) 9

cuts and tips, unthawed, 284-g. pkg. 65

cuts and tips, boiled, drained, 250 g. 55

cuts and tips, boiled, drained, 250 ml. 42

Avocados, California, fresh:

whole, with peel and pit, 500 g. 649

peeled and pitted, 1 average half (7.94 cm. in diam.) 185

cubed (1.27-cm. pieces), 250 ml. 272

mashed, 250 ml. 417

Avocados, Florida, fresh:

whole, with peel and pit, 500 g.	428
peeled and pitted, 1 average half (9.21 cm. in diam.)	196
cubed (1.27-cm. pieces), 250 ml.	204
mashed, 250 ml.	312

B

food and measure	calories

Bacon, Canadian-style:

unheated, 454 g.	980
fried, drained, about 336 g. (yield from 454 g. raw)	921
fried, drained, 125 g.	346
fried, drained, 1 slice (8.57 cm. in diam.)	58

Bacon, cured, sliced:

raw, 454 g.	3,016
fried, drained, about 145 g. (yield from 454 g. raw)	860
fried, drained, 2 thick slices (12 slices per 454 g. raw)	143
fried, drained, 2 medium slices (20 slices per 454 g. raw)	86
fried, drained, 2 thin slices (28 slices per 454 g. raw)	61
canned, 454-g. can (17–18 slices)	3,107

Bagels, egg or water:

1 medium (7.62 cm. in diam.)	165

Baking powder:

SAS, 15 ml.	14
SAS, 5 ml.	4
phosphate, 15 ml.	15
phosphate, 5 ml.	5
tartrate, 15 ml.	7
tartrate, 5 ml.	2
low-sodium, commercial, 15 ml.	23
low-sodium, commercial, 5 ml.	7

Bamboo shoots, raw:

250 g.	68
cuts (2.54-cm. pieces), 250 ml.	43

Banana custard pie, see Pies
Bananas, baking-type, see Plantains

Bananas, common varieties, fresh:
whole, with skin, 500 g. 288
whole, 1 large (24.77 cm. long) 116
whole, 1 medium (22.23 cm. long) 101
whole, 1 small (19.69 cm. long) 81
sliced, 250 ml. 144
mashed, 250 ml. 202

Bananas, dehydrated:
flakes, 125 g. 425
flakes, 25 g. 85
flakes, 250 ml. 360
flakes, 15 ml. 21

Bananas, red, fresh:
whole, with skin, 500 g. 306
whole, 1 average (18.42 cm. long) 118
sliced, 250 ml. 143

Barbados cherries, see Acerolas

Barbecue sauce:
250 g. 228
250 ml. 242

Barley, pearled:
light, uncooked, 250 g. 873
light, uncooked, 250 ml. 740
pot or Scotch, uncooked, 250 g. 870
pot or Scotch, uncooked, 250 ml. 738

Barracuda, Pacific, raw:
meat only, 125 g. 141

Basella, see Vine spinach

Bass, black sea:
raw, whole, 500 g. 182
raw, meat only, 125 g. 116
baked fillets, stuffed with bacon, butter, celery, and bread cubes:
  125 g. 324
  1 piece (8.89 x 11.43 x 3.81 cm.) 531

Bass, smallmouth and largemouth, raw:
whole, 500 g. 160
meat only, 125 g. 130

Bass, striped:
raw, whole, 500 g. 226
raw, meat only, 125 g. 131
oven-fried fillets, prepared with milk, bread crumbs, and butter:

125 g.	245
1 piece (22.23 x 11.43 x 1.59 cm.)	392

Bean curd, see Soybean curd

Bean flour (lima):

250 g.	858
sifted and spooned into cup, 250 ml.	458

Bean soup, see Soups

Bean sprouts, mung:

uncooked, 250 g.	88
uncooked, 250 ml.	39
boiled, drained, 250 g.	70
boiled, drained, 250 ml.	37

Bean sprouts, soy:

uncooked, 250 g.	115
uncooked, 250 ml.	51
boiled, drained, 250 g.	95
boiled, drained, 250 ml.	51

Beans, baked, canned, solids and liquid:

in tomato sauce, meatless, 250 g.	300
in tomato sauce, meatless, 250 ml.	324
with pork, in molasses sauce, 250 g.	375
with pork, in molasses sauce, 250 ml.	406
with pork, in tomato sauce, 250 g.	305
with pork, in tomato sauce, 250 ml.	330
with sliced frankfurters, 250 g.	360
with sliced frankfurters, 250 ml.	389

Beans, black, dry:

uncooked, 250 g.	848

Beans, broad, see Broad beans

Beans, great northern, dry:

uncooked, 250 g.	850
uncooked, 250 ml.	649
cooked, 250 g.	295
cooked, 250 ml.	226

Beans, green or snap, fresh:

raw, whole, 500 g.	141
raw, trimmed, 500 g.	160
raw, cuts (2.54–5.08 cm. lengths), 250 ml.	36
boiled, drained, cuts or French-style, 250 ml.	33

Beans, green or snap, canned:

with liquid, 250 g.	45

Beans, green or snap, canned, continued

with liquid, 250 ml.	46
drained, 250 g.	60
drained, cuts, 250 ml.	34
drained, French-style, 250 ml.	33
dietary (low-sodium) pack, with liquid, 250 g.	40
dietary (low-sodium) pack, with liquid, 250 ml.	40
dietary (low-sodium) pack, drained, 250 g.	55
dietary (low-sodium) pack, drained, 250 ml.	32

Beans, green or snap, frozen:

cuts, unthawed, 284-g. pkg.	74
cuts, boiled, drained, 260 g. (yield from 284-g. pkg.)	65
cuts, boiled, drained, 250 ml.	36
French-style, unthawed, 284-g. pkg.	77
French-style, boiled, drained, 250 g. (yield from 284-g. pkg.)	65
French-style, boiled, drained, 250 ml.	36

Beans, lima, immature seeds, fresh:

in pods, raw, 500 g.	246
shelled, raw, 250 g.	308
shelled, raw, 250 ml.	202
boiled, drained, 250 g.	278
boiled, drained, 250 ml.	200

Beans, lima, immature seeds, canned:

with liquid, 250 g.	176
with liquid, 250 ml.	187
drained, 250 g.	240
drained, 250 ml.	173
dietary (low-sodium) pack, with liquid, 250 g.	175
dietary (low-sodium) pack, with liquid, 250 ml.	184
dietary (low-sodium) pack, drained, 250 g.	238
dietary (low-sodium) pack, drained, 250 ml.	172

Beans, lima, immature seeds, frozen:

Fordhook, unthawed, 284-g. pkg.	290
Fordhook, boiled, drained, 295 g. (yield from 284-g. pkg.)	283
Fordhook, boiled, drained, 250 ml.	178
baby, unthawed, 284-g. pkg.	346
baby, boiled, drained, 315 g. (yield from 284-g. pkg.)	339
baby, boiled, drained, 250 ml.	225

Beans, lima, mature seeds, dry:

uncooked, 250 g.	863
uncooked, Fordhook (large-seeded), 250 ml.	658

uncooked, baby (small-seeded), 250 ml. 695
cooked, 250 g. 345
cooked, 250 ml. 278
Beans, mung, dry:
uncooked, 250 g. 850
uncooked, 250 ml. 757
Beans, pea or navy, dry:
uncooked, 250 g. 850
uncooked, 250 ml. 739
cooked, 250 ml. 237
Beans, pinto or red Mexican, dry:
uncooked, 250 g. 873
uncooked, 250 ml. 703
Beans, red kidney:
dry, uncooked, 250 g. 858
dry, uncooked, 250 ml. 673
dry, cooked, 250 ml. 231
canned, with liquid, 250 g. 225
canned, with liquid, 250 ml. 244
Beans, wax or yellow, fresh:
raw, 500 g. 134
raw, cuts (2.54–5.08 cm. pieces), 250 ml. 32
boiled, drained, whole or cuts, 250 g. 55
boiled, drained, cuts (2.54–5.08 cm. pieces), 250 ml. ... 30
Beans, wax or yellow, canned:
with liquid, 250 g. 48
with liquid, 250 ml. 48
drained, 250 g. 60
drained, cuts, 250 ml. 34
drained, French-style, 250 ml. 33
dietary (low-sodium) pack, with liquid, 250 g. 38
dietary (low-sodium) pack, with liquid, 250 ml. 38
dietary (low-sodium) pack, drained, 250 g. 53
dietary (low-sodium) pack, drained, 250 ml. 30
Beans, wax or yellow, frozen:
cuts, unthawed, 255-g. pkg. 71
cuts, boiled, drained, 235 g. (yield from 255-g. pkg.) ... 63
cuts, boiled, drained, 250 ml. 38
Beans, white, dry:
uncooked, 250 g. 850
cooked, 250 ml. 237

Beaver:
  roasted, meat only, 250 g. 620
Beechnuts:
  in shell, 500 g. 1,729
  shelled, 125 g. 710
Beef, choice-grade, retail trim:
  chuck, arm, roast or steak, boneless, lean with fat:
    raw, 500 g. 1,113
    braised, drained, 334 g. (yield from 500 g. raw) 967
    braised, drained, 125 g. 361
    braised, drained, chopped or diced, 250 ml. 429
    braised, drained, ground, 250 ml. 337
  chuck, arm, roast or steak, boneless, lean only (trimmed of fat):
    braised, drained, 284 g. (yield from 500 g. raw with fat) 548
    braised, drained, 125 g. 241
    braised, drained, chopped or diced, 250 ml. 286
    braised, drained, ground, 250 ml. 225
  chuck, rib, roast or steak, boneless, lean with fat:
    raw, 500 g. 1,757
    braised, drained, 334 g. (yield from 500 g. raw) 1,428
    braised, drained, 125 g. 533
    braised, drained, chopped or diced, 250 ml. 634
    braised, drained, ground, 250 ml. 498
  chuck, rib, roast or steak, boneless, lean only (trimmed of fat):
    braised, drained, 231 g. (yield from 500 g. raw with fat) 575
    braised, drained, 125 g. 311
    braised, drained, chopped or diced, 250 ml. 370
    braised, drained, ground, 250 ml. 290
  chuck, stewing, boneless, lean with fat:
    raw, 500 g. 1,283
    stewed, drained, 334 g. (yield from 500 g. raw) 1,093
    stewed, drained, 125 g. 409
    stewed, drained, chopped or diced, 250 ml. 485
  chuck, stewing, boneless, lean only (trimmed of fat):
    raw, 500 g. 789
    stewed, drained, 334 g. (yield from 500 g. raw) 716
    stewed, drained, 125 g. 268
    stewed, drained, chopped or diced, 250 ml. 318
  club steak, with bone, lean with fat:
    raw, 500 g. 1,587

broiled, 306 g. (yield from 500 g. raw) 1,388
broiled, 125 g. without bone 568
club steak, with bone, lean only (trimmed of fat):
broiled, 177 g. (yield from 500 g. raw with fat) 432
broiled, 125 g. without bone 305
flank steak, boneless, all lean:
raw, 500 g. 718
braised, drained, 334 g. (yield from 500 g. raw) 656
braised, drained, 125 g. 245
braised, drained, 1 piece (6.35 x 6.35 x 1.91 cm.) 167
ground, lean with 10% fat:
raw, 500 g. 893
broiled well-done, 374 g. (yield from 500 g. raw) 820
raw, 114-g. patty 202
broiled well-done, 85-g. patty (yield from 114 g. raw) 186
ground, lean with 21% fat:
raw, 500 g. 1,337
broiled rare to medium, 359 g. (yield from 500 g. raw) 1,025
raw, 114-g. patty 303
broiled rare to medium, 82-g. patty (yield from 114 g. raw) .. 235
plate, boneless, lean with fat:
raw, 500 g. 1,777
simmered, drained, 334 g. (yield from 500 g. raw) 1,444
simmered, drained, 125 g. 540
plate, boneless, lean only (trimmed of fat):
simmered, drained, 204 g. (yield from 500 g. raw with fat) .. 405
simmered, drained, 125 g. 248
porterhouse steak, with bone, lean with fat:
raw, 500 g. 1,763
broiled, 331 g. (yield from 500 g. raw) 1,540
broiled, 125 g. without bone 580
porterhouse steak, with bone, lean only (trimmed of fat):
broiled, 189 g. (yield from 500 g. raw with fat) 424
broiled, 125 g. without bone 280
rib roast, boneless, lean with fat:
raw, 500 g. 2,001
roasted, 364 g. (yield from 500 g. raw) 1,602
roasted, 125 g. 550
roasted, chopped or diced, 250 ml. 653
roasted, ground, 250 ml. 513

147

rib roast, boneless, lean only (trimmed of fat):
    roasted, 233 g. (yield from 500 g. raw with fat) 562
    roasted, 125 g. 300
    roasted, chopped or diced, 250 ml. 357
    roasted, ground, 250 ml. 281
round steak, boneless, lean with fat:
    raw, 500 g. 983
    braised or broiled, 345 g. (yield from 500 g. raw) 902
    braised or broiled, 125 g. 326
round steak, boneless, lean only (trimmed of fat):
    braised or broiled, 295 g. (yield from 500 g. raw with fat) .. 558
    braised or broiled, 125 g. 235
rump roast, boneless, lean with fat:
    raw, 500 g. 1,511
    roasted, 364 g. (yield from 500 g. raw) 1,264
    roasted, 125 g. 433
    roasted, chopped or diced, 250 ml. 515
    roasted, ground, 250 ml. 405
rump roast, boneless, lean only (trimmed of fat):
    roasted, 273 g. (yield from 500 g. raw with fat) 568
    roasted, 125 g. 260
    roasted, chopped or diced, 250 ml. 308
    roasted, ground, 250 ml. 243
sirloin steak, double-bone, 18% bone, lean with fat:
    raw, 500 g. 1,364
    broiled, 300 g. (yield from 500 g. raw) 1,221
    broiled, 125 g. without bone 509
sirloin steak, double-bone, 18% bone, lean only (trimmed of fat):
    broiled, 197 g. (yield from 500 g. raw with fat) 426
    broiled, 125 g. without bone 270
sirloin steak, hip-bone, 15% bone, lean with fat:
    raw, 500 g. 1,744
    broiled, 309 g. (yield from 500 g. raw) 1,505
    broiled, 125 g. without bone 607
sirloin steak, hip-bone, 15% bone, lean only (trimmed of fat):
    broiled, 170 g. (yield from 500 g. raw with fat) 409
    broiled, 125 g. without bone 299
sirloin steak, round-bone, 7% bone, lean with fat:
    raw, 500 g. 1,448
    broiled, 339 g. (yield from 500 g. raw) 1,311

broiled, 125 g. without bone 483
sirloin steak, round-bone, 7% bone, lean only (trimmed of fat):
   broiled, 223 g. (yield from 500 g. raw with fat) 462
   broiled, 125 g. without bone 259
T-bone steak, 11% bone, lean with fat:
   raw, 500 g. 1,756
   broiled, 325 g. (yield from 500 g. raw) 1,535
   broiled, 125 g. without bone 591
T-bone steak, 11% bone, lean only (trimmed of fat):
   broiled, 182 g. (yield from 500 g. raw with fat) 405
   broiled, 125 g. without bone 278
Beef, corned, hash (with potatoes), canned:
   439-g. can 795
   250 g. 451
   250 ml. 422
Beef, corned, medium-fat:
   raw, 500 g. 1,462
   cooked, 334 g. (yield from 500 g. raw) 1,244
   cooked, 125 g. 464
   canned, 340-g. can 734
   canned, 125 g. 270
   canned, 1 slice (7.62 x 5.08 x .95 cm.) 86
Beef, dried (chipped), commercial:
   uncooked, 71-g. jar 144
   uncooked, 142-g. jar. 288
Beef, dried, cooked (creamed), home recipe:
   250 g. 385
   250 ml. 400
Beef, potted, canned:
   156-g. can 387
   25 g. 63
   250 ml. 591
   15 ml. 32
Beef, roast, canned (see also Beef, rib roast or rump roast):
   250 g. 559
Beef heart, see **Hearts**
Beef kidney, see **Kidneys**
Beef liver, see **Liver**
Beef pot pie, home recipe:
   baked, 1 whole pie (22.86 cm. in diam.) 1,550

Beef pot pie, home recipe, continued
  baked, ⅓ of 22.86-cm. pie 517
  baked, 250 g. 614
Beef pot pie, frozen:
  227-g. pie 436
Beef soup, see Soups
Beef tongue, see Tongue
Beef-vegetable stew, home recipe:
  cooked with lean chuck, 250 g. 222
  cooked with lean chuck, 250 ml. 231
Beef-vegetable stew, canned:
  425-g. can 336
  250 g. 197
  250 ml. 206
Beer, see Alcoholic beverages
Beet greens, fresh:
  raw, trimmed, 500 g. 67
  boiled, drained, 250 g. 45
  boiled, drained, 250 ml. 28
Beets, fresh:
  raw, trimmed, 500 g. 151
  raw, whole, 1 medium beet (5.08 cm. in diam.) 21
  raw, diced, 250 ml. 61
  boiled, drained, whole, 2 medium beets (5.08 cm. in diam.) 32
  boiled, drained, diced, 250 ml. 61
  boiled, drained, sliced, 250 ml. 70
Beets, canned:
  with liquid, 250 g. 85
  with liquid, 250 ml. 89
  drained, 250 g. 92
  drained, whole, small, 250 ml. 63
  drained, diced, 250 ml. 64
  drained, sliced, 250 ml. 69
  dietary (low-sodium) pack, with liquid, 250 g. 80
  dietary (low-sodium) pack, with liquid, 250 ml. 84
  dietary (low-sodium) pack, drained, 250 g. 92
  dietary (low-sodium) pack, drained, whole, small, 250 ml. 63
  dietary (low-sodium) pack, drained, diced or sliced, 250 ml. ... 67
  Harvard, with liquid, 250 ml. 117
  pickled, with liquid, 250 ml. 159
Beverages, see individual listings

Biscuit dough, canned:
chilled, 125 g. 350
frozen, 125 g. 289
Biscuit mix, baked:
made with milk, 28-g. biscuit (5.08 cm. in diam., 3.18 cm. high)   91
Biscuits, baking-powder, home recipe:
baked, 28-g. biscuit (5.08 cm. in diam., 3.18 cm. high) 103
Blackberries, fresh:
500 g. 275
250 ml. 89
Blackberries, canned:
in water, with liquid, 250 g. 100
in water, with liquid, 250 ml. 104
in heavy syrup, with liquid, 250 g. 228
in heavy syrup, with liquid, 250 ml. 247
Blackberries, frozen, see Boysenberries, frozen
Blackberry juice, canned:
unsweetened, 250 ml. 96
Blackberry pie, see Pies
Black-eyed peas, see Cowpeas
Blackfish, see Tautog
Blueberries, fresh:
500 g. 285
250 ml. 95
Blueberries, canned:
in water, with liquid, 250 g. 98
in heavy syrup, with liquid, 250 g. 253
in heavy syrup, with liquid, 250 ml. 268
Blueberries, frozen:
unsweetened, 284-g. pkg. 156
unsweetened, 250 ml. 96
sweetened, 284-g. pkg. 298
sweetened, 250 ml. 257
Blueberry pie, see Pies
Bluefish, fillets:
raw, meat only, 500 g. 584
broiled with butter, 402 g. (yield from 500 g. raw) 638
broiled with butter, 125 g. 198
fried with egg, milk, bread crumbs, 424 g.
(yield from 500 g. raw) 868
fried, with egg, milk, bread crumbs, 125 g. 255

Blood sausage (pudding), see Sausages
Bockwurst:
  454-g. pkg. (about 7 links) 1,198
  1 link (about 65 g.) 172
Bologna:
  without binders, chub, 1 slice (7.62 cm. in diam., .32 cm. thick) 36
  without binders, ring, 340-g. ring
    (38.10 cm. long, 3.49 cm. in diam.) 942
  without binders, sliced, 227-g. pkg. 629
  without binders, sliced, 170-g. pkg. 471
  without binders, sliced, 28-g. slice
    (11.43 cm. in diam., .32 cm. thick) 79
  without binders, sliced, 21-g. slice
    (10.16 cm. in diam., .32 cm. thick) 61
  with cereal, chub, 1 slice (7.62 cm. in diam., .32 cm. thick) .. 34
  with cereal, ring, 340-g. ring
    (38.10 cm. long, 3.49 cm. in diam.) 891
  with cereal, sliced, 227-g. pkg. 595
  with cereal, sliced, 170-g. pkg. 445
  with cereal, sliced, 28-g. slice
    (11.43 cm. in diam., .32 cm. thick) 74
  with cereal, sliced, 21-g. slice
    (10.16 cm. in diam., .32 cm. thick) 58
Bonito, raw:
  meat only, 125 g. 210
Borscht, see Soups
Boston cream pie, see Pies
Bouillon, dry form:
  cubes, 1.27-cm. cube 5
  powder (instant), 25 g. 30
  powder (instant), 1 packet 6
  powder (instant), 5 ml. 2
Boysenberries, fresh, see Blackberries, fresh
Boysenberries, canned:
  in water, with liquid, 250 g. 90
  in water, with liquid, 250 ml. 93
Boysenberries, frozen:
  unsweetened, 284-g. pkg. 136
  unsweetened, 250 ml. 64
  sweetened, 284-g. pkg. 272
  sweetened, 250 ml. 145

Brains, fresh (all types):
   raw, 250 g. 312
Bran, wheat, see **Wheat bran**
Bran flakes, see **Cereals, ready-to-eat**
Braunschweiger (smoked liverwurst):
   rolls, 227-g. roll (13.97 cm. long, 5.08 cm. in diam.) 724
   rolls, 1 slice (5.08 cm. in diam., .04 cm. think) 32
   slices, 170-g. pkg. (6 slices) 542
   slices, 1 slice (7.94 cm. in diam., .64 cm. thick) 90
Brazil nuts:
   in shell, 500 g. 1,566
   in shell, 250 ml. 406
   in shell, 3 large or 3½ medium nuts (28 g.) 89
   shelled, 125 g. 815
   shelled, 250 ml. 971
   shelled, 6 large or 8 medium nuts (28 g.) 185
Bread crumbs:
   dry, grated, 250 ml. 416
   dry, grated, 25 g. 100
   soft, 250 ml. 129
Bread cubes, white bread:
   firm-crumb type, 250 ml. 88
   soft-crumb type, 250 ml. 86
Breadfruit, fresh:
   raw, untrimmed, 500 g. 396
   raw, trimmed, peeled, 125 g. 129
Breads, commercial:
   Boston brown, 1 slice (7.62 x 1.91 cm.) 101
   corn, see **Cornbread**
   cracked-wheat, 454-g. loaf 1,193
   cracked-wheat, 1 slice (18 slices per loaf) 66
   cracked-wheat, 1 slice (20 slices per loaf) 60
   French, 454-g. loaf 1,316
   French, 1 slice (6.35 x 5.08 x 1.27 cm.) 44
   French, 1 slice (12.70 x 6.35 x 2.54 cm.) 102
   Italian, 454-g. loaf 1,252
   Italian, 1 slice (11.43 x 8.26 x 1.91 cm.) 83
   Italian, 1 slice (8.26 x 6.35 x 1.27 cm.) 28
   pumpernickel, 454-g. loaf 1,117
   pumpernickel, 1 slice (12.70 x 10.16 x .95 cm.) 79
   pumpernickel, snack size, 227-g. loaf 558

pumpernickel, snack size, 1 slice (6.35 x 5.08 x .64 cm.) 17
raisin, 454-g. loaf 1,188
raisin, 1 slice (18 slices per loaf) 66
raisin, 1 slice (20 slices per loaf) 60
rye, light, 454-g. loaf 1,102
rye, light, 1 slice (12.07 x 9.53 x 1.12 cm.) 61
rye, light, 1 slice (20 slices per loaf) 56
rye, light, snack size, 227-g. loaf 552
rye, light, snack size, 1 slice (6.35 x 5.08 x .64 cm.) 17
Vienna, 454-g. loaf 1,316
Vienna, 1 slice (12.07 x 10.16 x 1.27 cm.) 73
white, firm-crumb type, 454-g. loaf 1,247
white, firm-crumb type, 1 slice (20 slices per loaf) 63
white, firm-crumb type, 1 slice (30 slices per loaf) 41
white, soft-crumb type, 454-g. loaf 1,225
white, soft-crumb type, 1 slice (18 slices per loaf) 68
white, soft-crumb type, 1 slice (22 slices per loaf) 54
whole-wheat, firm-crumb type, 454-g. loaf 1,102
whole-wheat, firm-crumb type, 1 slice (18 slices per loaf) 61
whole-wheat, firm-crumb type, 1 slice (20 slices per loaf) 56
whole-wheat, soft-crumb type, 454-g. loaf 1,093
whole-wheat, soft-crumb type, 1 slice (16 slices per loaf) 67

Bread sticks:
regular, 25 g. 96
regular, 1 stick (11.43 cm. long, 1.27 cm. in diam.) 38
Vienna, 25 g. 76
Vienna, 1 stick (16.51 cm. long, 3.18 cm. in diam.) 106

Bread stuffing, mix:
dry form, 227-g. pkg. 842
dry form, coarse crumbs, 250 ml. 276
dry form, cubes, 250 ml. 118
prepared with butter and water, 250 g. 893
prepared with butter and water, 250 ml. 531
moist, prepared with egg, butter, and water, 250 g. 519
moist, prepared with egg, butter, and water, 250 ml. 441

Broad beans, raw:
immature seeds, 250 g. 262
mature seeds, 250 g. 844

Broccoli, fresh:
raw, untrimmed, 500 g. 98

154

raw, trimmed, 500 g.	160
boiled, drained, 250 g.	65
boiled, drained, 1 large spear (280 g.)	73
boiled, drained, 1 medium spear (180 g.)	47
boiled, drained, 1 small spear (140 g.)	36
boiled, drained, cuts (1.27-cm. pieces), 250 ml.	42

Broccoli, frozen:

spears, unthawed, 284-g. pkg.	80
spears, boiled, drained, 250 g. (yield from 284-g. pkg.)	65
spears, boiled, drained, 1 average spear (11.43–12.70 cm. long)	8
chopped, unthawed, 284-g. pkg.	82
chopped, boiled, drained, 250 g. (yield from 284-g. pkg.)	65
chopped, boiled, drained, 250 ml.	51

Brownies, see Cookies

Brown-and-serve sausages, see Sausages

Brussels sprouts, fresh:

raw, whole, 500 g. (about 26½ medium sprouts, about 3.5 cm. in diam.)	224
raw, trimmed, 500 g.	207
boiled, drained, 250 g. (about 11½ medium sprouts)	90
boiled, drained, 250 ml. (about 8 medium sprouts)	59
boiled, drained, 4 medium sprouts	30

Brussels sprouts, frozen:

unthawed, 284-g. pkg.	102
boiled, drained, 284 g. (yield from 284-g. pkg.)	94
boiled, drained, 250 ml.	54

Buckwheat flour, see Flour

Bulgur (parboiled wheat):

club wheat, dry, 250 g.	895
club wheat, dry, 250 ml.	666
hard red winter wheat, dry, 250 g.	882
hard red winter wheat, dry, 250 ml.	639
white wheat, dry, 250 g.	890
white wheat, dry, 250 ml.	586
canned, hard red winter wheat, unseasoned, 250 g.	420
canned, hard red winter wheat, unseasoned, 250 ml.	241
canned, hard red winter wheat, seasoned, 250 g.	453
canned, hard red winter wheat, seasoned, 250 ml.	261

Buns, see Rolls and buns

Butter, regular:

250 g.	1,790

250 ml.	1,723
1 stick (114 g.)	812
15 ml.	102
5 ml.	34
1 pat (2.54 x .85 cm.; 100 pats per 500 g.)	36

Butter, whipped:

250 g.	1,790
250 ml.	1,146
1 stick (75 g.)	812
15 ml.	67
5 ml.	23
1 pat (3.18 x .85 cm.; 132 pats per 500 g.)	27

Butterfish, raw:

gulf, meat only, 125 g.	119
northern, meat only, 125 g.	211

Buttermilk, see **Milk**

Butternuts:

in shell, 125 g.	110
shelled, 125 g.	784
4–5 nuts	94

Butter oil:

15 ml.	123

Butterscotch, see **Candy**

Butterscotch pie, see **Pies**

C

food and measure	calories

Cabbage, Chinese (celery cabbage), fresh:

raw, 500 g.	68
raw, trimmed, 500 g.	70
raw, cuts (2.54-cm. pieces), 250 ml.	12
raw, strips, 250 ml.	8

Cabbage, common varieties, fresh:

raw, whole, 500 g.	108
raw, trimmed, 500 g.	120

chocolate, milk, sugar-coated, 25 g. 116
chocolate, milk, sugar-coated, discs (1.27 cm. in diam.) 125 ml. 487
chocolate, semisweet, 25 g. 127
chocolate, sweet, 25 g. 130
chocolate fudge, chocolate-coated, 25 g. 108
chocolate fudge, with nuts, chocolate-coated, 25 g. 113
coconut, chocolate-coated, 25 g. 109
fondant, uncoated, 25 g. 91
fondant, chocolate-coated, 25 g. 102
fondant, mint, chocolate-coated, 25 g. 102
fondant, mint, chocolate-coated, 1 large (6.35 cm. in diam.) .. 144
fondant, mint, chocolate-coated, 1 small (3.49 cm. in diam.) .. 45
fondant, mint, chocolate-coated, 1 miniature (1.91 cm. in diam.) 10
fudge, chocolate, 25 g. 100
fudge, chocolate, 1 piece (2.54-cm. cube) 89
fudge, chocolate, with nuts, 25 g. 107
fudge, chocolate, with nuts, 1 piece (2.54-cm. cube) 89
fudge, vanilla, 25 g. 100
fudge, vanilla, 1 piece (2.54-cm. cube) 84
fudge, vanilla, with nuts, 25 g. 106
fudge, vanilla, with nuts, 1 piece (2.54-cm. cube) 89
fudge, with caramel and nuts, chocolate-coated, 25 g. 108
fudge, with nuts and caramel, chocolate-coated, 25 g. 115
gumdrops, 25 g. 86
hard candy, 25 g. 96
honey with peanut butter, chocolate-coated, 25 g. 116
jellybeans, 25 g. 92
jellybeans, 125 ml. 428
marshmallow, 25 g. 79
marshmallow, regular, 1 average (2.86 x 1.91 cm.) 23
marshmallow, soft, 1 average (2.86 x 1.91 cm.) 19
marshmallow, miniature, 125 ml. loosely packed 156
mints, uncoated, 25 g. 91
mints, chocolate-coated, see **Candy, fondant**
nougat and caramel, chocolate-coated, 25 g. 104
peanut bar, 25 g. 129
peanut brittle, 25 g. 105
peanuts, chocolate-coated, 25 g. 140
peanuts, whole, chocolate-coated, 125 ml. 506
raisins, chocolate-coated, 25 g. 106

Candy, continued

raisins, whole, chocolate-coated, 125 ml.	428
vanilla creams, chocolate-coated, 25 g.	108

Cantaloupe, fresh:

½ melon (12.70 cm. in diam.)	58
cubed or diced, 250 ml.	51

Cape gooseberries, see Ground cherries

Capers, in jars:

15 ml.	6

Capicola:

128-g. pkg. (about 6 slices)	639
1 slice (10.80 x 10.80 x .16 cm.)	105
25 g.	124

Carambolas, fresh:

raw, whole, 500 g.	164
raw, peeled and seeded, 125 g.	44

Carissas (natal plums), fresh:

raw, whole, 500 g.	300
raw, peeled and seeded, 125 g.	87
raw, sliced (.32 cm. thick), 250 ml.	111

Carob flour, see Flour

Carrots, fresh:

raw, whole, with tops, 500 g.	123
raw, whole, without tops, packaged, 500 g.	172
raw, whole, trimmed and scraped, 250 g.	105
raw, whole, 1 medium (13.97 x 2.54 cm.)	21
raw, chunks, 250 ml.	61
raw, diced, 250 ml.	64
raw, grated or shredded, 250 ml.	49
raw, slices, 250 ml.	56
raw, strips, 250 ml.	52
raw, strips, 6 strips (.64 x 7.62 cm.)	12
boiled, drained, chunks, 250 ml.	54
boiled, drained, diced, 250 ml.	46
boiled, drained, slices, 250 ml.	50

Carrots, canned:

with liquid, 250 g.	70
with liquid, 250 ml.	73
drained, 250 g.	75
drained, diced, 250 ml.	47
drained, slices, 250 ml.	50

dietary (low-sodium) pack, with liquid, 250 g. 55
dietary (low-sodium) pack, with liquid, 250 ml. 57
dietary (low-sodium) pack, drained, 250 g. 63
dietary (low-sodium) pack, drained, slices, 250 ml. 41

Carrots, dehydrated:
25 g. 86

Casaba melon, fresh:
whole, with rind, 500 g. 07
wedge (19.69 x 5.08 cm.) 22
cubed or diced, 250 ml. 49

Cashew nuts, shelled, roasted in oil:
125 g. 703
250 ml. 832
25 g. (about 12 large, 16 medium, or 23 small nuts) 140
dry-roasted, 25 g. 153

Catfish, freshwater:
raw, fillets, 125 g. 129

Catsup, tomato, canned or bottled:
250 g. 265
250 ml. 306
15 ml. 16
1 packet (14 g.) 15

Cauliflower, fresh:
raw, whole, 500 g. 53
raw, flowerets, 500 g. 134
raw, flowerets, whole, 250 ml. 29
raw, flowerets, chopped, 250 ml. 33
raw, flowerets, sliced, 250 ml. 24
boiled, drained, flowerets, 250 ml. 30

Cauliflower, frozen:
unthawed, 284-g. pkg. 62
boiled, drained, 270 g. (yield from 284-g. pkg.) 49
boiled, drained, 250 ml. (about 7½ flowerets) 34

Caviar, sturgeon:
granular, 25 g. 65
granular, 15 ml. 42
pressed, 25 g. 79
pressed, 15 ml. 54

Celeriac root, raw:
whole, with skin, 500 g. 172

161

pared, 125 g.	50
pared, 4–6 roots	40

Celery, fresh:

raw, untrimmed, with leaves, 500 g.	64
raw, trimmed, packaged, 500 g. (about 7½ stalks)	67
raw, 1 large outer stalk (20.32 cm. long)	7
raw, 3 small inner stalks (12.70 cm. long)	9
raw, chopped or diced, 250 ml.	21
raw, sliced, 250 ml.	19
boiled, drained, diced, 250 ml.	22
boiled, drained, sliced, 250 ml.	25

Celery cabbage, see Cabbage, Chinese

Cereals, cooking-type:

farina, regular, dry, 250 ml.	708
farina, regular, cooked 15 minutes, 250 ml.	109
farina, quick-cooking, dry, 250 ml.	691
farina, quick-cooking, cooked 2–5 minutes, 250 ml.	111
farina, instant, dry, 250 ml.	729
farina, instant, cooked ½ minute, 250 ml.	143
oat flakes, maple-flavored, instant, dry, 250 ml.	387
oat flakes, maple-flavored, instant, cooked, 250 ml.	176
oat granules, maple-flavored, regular, dry, 250 ml.	426
oat granules, maple-flavored, regular, cooked, 250 ml.	156
oat and wheat, dry, 250 ml.	367
oat and wheat, cooked, 250 ml.	169
oatmeal or rolled oats, dry, 250 ml.	331
oatmeal or rolled oats, cooked, 250 ml.	140
rice, granulated, dry, 250 ml.	690
rice, granulated, cooked, 250 ml.	130
wheat, rolled, dry, 250 ml.	306
wheat, rolled, cooked, 250 ml.	191
wheat, whole-meal, dry, 250 ml.	448
wheat, whole-meal, cooked, 250 ml.	117
wheat and malted barley, quick-cooking, dry, 250 ml.	548
wheat and malted barley, quick-cooking, cooked, 250 ml.	169
wheat and malted barley, instant, dry, 250 ml.	465
wheat and malted barley, instant, cooked, 250 ml.	208

Cereals, ready-to-eat, dry:

bran, with malt extract, 25 g.	60
bran, with malt extract, 250 ml.	153

bran, with defatted wheat germ, 25 g. 59
bran, with defatted wheat germ, 250 ml. 190
bran flakes, 40%, 25 g. 76
bran flakes, 40%, 250 ml. 112
bran flakes with raisins, 25 g. 71
bran flakes with raisins, 250 ml. 153
corn, puffed, 25 g. 100
corn, puffed, 250 ml. 85
corn, puffed, presweetened, unflavored, 25 g. 94
corn, puffed, presweetened, unflavored, 250 ml. 121
corn, puffed, presweetened, cocoa-flavored, 25 g. 97
corn, puffed, presweetened, cocoa-flavored, 250 ml. 124
corn, puffed, presweetened, fruit-flavored, 25 g. 99
corn, puffed, presweetened, fruit-flavored, 250 ml. 126
corn flakes, 25 g. 96
corn flakes, 250 ml. 103
corn flakes, crumbs, 250 ml. 348
corn flakes, sugar-coated, 25 g. 96
corn flakes, sugar-coated, 250 ml. 163
corn flakes, with protein concentrates, 25 g. 94
corn, rice, and wheat flakes, 25 g. 97
corn, shredded, 25 g. 97
corn, shredded, 250 ml. 103
oat flakes, with soy flour and rice, 25 g. 100
oats and corn, puffed, sugar-coated, 25 g. 99
oats and corn, puffed, sugar-coated, 250 ml. 147
oats, puffed, 25 g. 100
oats, puffed, 250 ml. 105
oats, shredded, 25 g. 94
oats, shredded, 250 ml. 181
rice flakes, 25 g. 97
rice, oven-popped, 25 g. 100
rice, oven-popped, 250 ml. 124
rice, oven-popped, presweetened, 25 g. 97
rice, oven-popped, presweetened, 250 ml. 186
rice, puffed, 25 g. 100
rice, puffed, 250 ml. 64
rice, puffed, presweetened, with honey or cocoa, 25 g. 97
rice, puffed, presweetened, with honey or cocoa, 250 ml. .. 148
rice, shredded, 25 g. 98
rice, shredded, 250 ml. 104

rice, shredded, with protein concentrates, casein, 25 g.	95
rice, shredded, with protein concentrates, casein, 250 ml.	345
rice, shredded, with protein concentrates, wheat gluten, 25 g. ..	96
rice, shredded, with protein concentrates, wheat gluten, 250 ml.	82
wheat flakes, 25 g.	88
wheat flakes, 250 ml.	112
wheat germ, toasted, 25 g.	98
wheat germ, toasted, 15 ml.	23
wheat, puffed, 25 g.	91
wheat, puffed, 250 ml.	57
wheat, puffed, with sugar and/or honey, 25 g.	94
wheat, puffed, with sugar and/or honey, 250 ml.	140
wheat, shredded, 25 g.	88
wheat, shredded, 1 oblong biscuit (9.53 x 5.72 x 2.54 cm.)	89
wheat, shredded, 1 round biscuit (7.62 cm. in diam., 2.54 cm. thick)	71
wheat, shredded, spoon size, 250 ml. (about 53 biscuits)	188
wheat, shredded, crumbled, 250 ml.	131
wheat, shredded, finely crushed, 250 ml.	281
wheat, shredded, with malt and sugar, 25 g.	92
wheat, shredded, with malt and sugar, bite-size squares, 250 ml.	213
wheat, shredded, with malt and sugar, shreds, 250 ml.	155
wheat and malted barley, flakes, 25 g.	98
wheat and malted barley, flakes, 250 ml.	166
wheat and malted barley, granules, 25 g.	98
wheat and malted barley, granules, 250 ml.	456

Cervelat, dry:

150-g. roll (15.24 cm. long, 3.81 cm. in diam.)	677
4 slices (3.81 cm. in diam., .32 cm. thick)	54
25 g.	113

Cervelat, soft, see Thuringer cervelat

Chard, Swiss:

raw, whole, 500 g.	124
raw, trimmed, 500 g.	114
boiled, drained, leaves and stalks, 250 ml.	28
boiled, drained, leaves only, 250 ml.	34

Cheese food, processed:

American, 25 g.	81
American, 2.54-cm. cube	57
American, 15 ml.	45

Cheeses, natural:

bleu or blue, 25 g.	92
bleu or blue, 2.54-cm. cube	64
bleu or blue, crumbled, 250 ml. loosely packed	527
bleu or blue, crumbled, 250 ml. packed	971
brick, 25 g.	93
brick, 2.54-cm. cube	64
brick, packaged, 1 slice (11 slices per 500 g.)	167
Camembert, domestic, 25 g.	75
Camembert, domestic, 2.54-cm. cube	51
Camembert, domestic, packaged, 1 piece (13 pieces per 500 g.)	114
Cheddar, domestic, 25 g.	100
Cheddar, domestic, 2.54-cm. cube	68
Cheddar, domestic, packaged, 1 slice (11 slices per 500 g.)	179
Cheddar, domestic, diced, 250 ml.	552
Cheddar, domestic, shredded, 250 ml.	477
Cheddar, domestic, grated, 15 ml.	28
cottage, creamed, large- or small-curd, 25 g.	27
cottage, creamed, 340-g. container	360
cottage, creamed, large-curd, 250 ml. loosely packed	253
cottage, creamed, small-curd, 250 ml. loosely packed	236
cottage, uncreamed, 25 g.	22
cottage, uncreamed, 340-g. container	292
cottage, uncreamed, 250 ml. loosely packed	133
cottage, uncreamed, 250 ml. packed	182
cream, 25 g.	94
cream, 2.54-cm. cube	60
cream, 250 ml.	920
cream, 15 ml.	52
cream, whipped, 25 g.	94
cream, whipped, 250 ml.	615
cream, whipped, 15 ml.	37
Edam, 25 g.	93
Fontina, 25 g.	101
Gorgonzola, 25 g.	99
Gouda, 25 g.	95
Gruyère, 25 g.	97
Limburger, 25 g.	86
Limburger, 2.54-cm. cube	62
Monterey Jack, 25 g.	91
mozzarella, low-moisture, part skim, 25 g.	75

Muenster, 25 g. 88
Parmesan, 25 g. 98
Parmesan, grated, 25 g. 116
Parmesan, grated, 250 ml. loosely packed 495
Parmesan, grated, 250 ml. packed 693
Parmesan, grated, 15 ml. 23
Parmesan, shredded, 25 g. 106
Parmesan, shredded, 250 ml. loosely packed 358
Parmesan, shredded, 250 ml. packed 492
Parmesan, shredded, 15 ml. 21
Port du Salut, 25 g. 88
Provolone, 25 g. 87
ricotta, moist, 25 g. 40
Roquefort, 25 g. 92
Roquefort, 2.54-cm. cube 64
Roquefort, crumbled, 250 ml. loosely packed 527
Roquefort, crumbled, 250 ml. packed 971
Swiss, domestic, 25 g. 93
Swiss, domestic, 2.54-cm. cube 56
Swiss, domestic, packaged, 1 slice (16 slices per 500 g.) 130

Cheeses, processed:
American, 25 g. 93
American, 2.54-cm. cube 65
American, diced, 250 ml. loosely packed 549
American, shredded, 250 ml. loosely packed 443
American, diced or shredded, 250 ml. packed 1,000
American, grated, 15 ml. 28
Muenster, 25 g. 90
pimento, American, 25 g. 93
pimento, American, 2.54-cm. cube 65
Swiss, 25 g. 89
Swiss, 2.54-cm. cube 64

Cheese spread, processed:
American, 25 g. 72
American, 2.54-cm. cube 50
American, diced, 250 ml. loosely packed 427
American, shredded, 250 ml. loosely packed 345
American, diced or shredded, 250 ml. packed 778
American, 15 ml. 40
American, canned, pressurized, 114-g. can 389

Cheese straws:
10 pieces (12.70 cm. long) 272
25 g. 113
Cherimoyers, raw:
whole, with skin and seeds, 500 g. 272
peeled and seeded, 125 g. 118
Cherries, fresh:
sour, red, whole, with pits and stems, 500 g. 204
sour, red, whole, 250 ml. 64
sour, red, pitted, 250 ml. 95
sweet, whole, with pits and stems, 500 g. 315
sweet, whole, 250 ml. 87
sweet, pitted, 250 ml. 108
sweet, 10 cherries 47
Cherries, canned, with liquid:
sour, red, in water, pitted, 250 g. 108
sour, red, in water, pitted, 250 ml. 111
sweet, in water, with pits, 250 g. 101
sweet, in water, with pits, 250 ml. 116
sweet, in heavy syrup, with pits, 250 g. 170
sweet, in heavy syrup, with pits, 250 ml. 202
sweet, in heavy syrup, pitted, 250 g. 208
sweet, in heavy syrup, pitted, 250 ml. 220
Cherries, frozen:
sour, red, unsweetened, unthawed, 250 g. 138
sour, red, sweetened, unthawed, 250 g. 279
Cherries, candied:
25 g. 85
10 cherries 119
Cherries, maraschino, bottled:
with liquid, 25 g. 29
1 average cherry 8
Cherry pie, see Pies
Chervil:
raw, 25 g. 14
Chestnut flour:
125 g. 453
Chestnuts, fresh:
in shell, 500 g. 784
in shell, 250 ml. 200
in shell, 10 nuts 141

Chestnuts, fresh, continued

shelled, 125 g.	242
shelled, 250 ml.	329

Chestnuts, dried:

shelled, 125 g.	471

Chewing gum, sweetened:

25 g.	79
1 stick	9
candy-coated, 1 piece (1.91 x 1.27 x .64 cm.)	5

Chicken, fresh:

broilers:

broiled, with skin, giblets, 221 g. (yield from 500 g. raw)	300
broiled, meat only, 125 g.	169
capon, raw, ready-to-cook, 500 g.	1,031

fryers:

raw, ready-to-cook, 500 g.	420
fried, with skin, giblets, 275 g. (yield from 500 g. raw)	622
fried, dark meat, without skin, 125 g.	274
fried, light meat, without skin, 125 g.	245
fried, 1 back (60 g.)	139
fried, ½ whole breast (94 g.)	160
fried, 1 drumstick (56 g.)	88
fried, 1 neck (60 g.)	127
fried, ½ rib section (20 g.)	41
fried, 1 thigh (65 g.)	122
fried, 1 wing (50 g.)	82
fried, skin only, 25 g.	105

roasters:

raw, ready-to-cook, 500 g.	870
roasted, with skin, giblets, 262 g. (yield from 500 g. raw)	634
roasted, dark meat, without skin, 125 g.	224
roasted, dark meat, without skin, chopped or diced, 250 ml.	273
roasted, dark meat, without skin, ground, 250 ml.	214
roasted, light meat, without skin, 125 g.	228
roasted, light meat, without skin, chopped or diced, 250 ml.	270
roasted, light meat, without skin, ground, 250 ml.	212

stewing hens or cocks:

raw, ready-to-cook, 500 g.	1,086
stewed, with skin, giblets, 250 g. (yield from 500 g. raw)	779
stewed, dark meat, without skin, 125 g.	259
stewed, dark meat, without skin, chopped or diced, 250 ml.	307

stewed, dark meat, without skin, ground, 250 ml. 242
stewed, light meat, without skin, 125 g. 224
stewed, light meat, without skin, chopped or diced, 250 ml. . 267
stewed, light meat, without skin, ground, 250 ml. 210

Chicken, boned, canned:
156-g. can 309
125 g. 248
250 ml. 430

Chicken, potted, canned:
156-g. can 387
250 ml. 591
15 ml. 32
25 g. 62

Chicken à la king, home recipe:
250 g. 476
250 ml. 496

Chicken chow mein, see Chow mein, chicken
Chicken fricassee, home recipe:
250 g. 402
250 ml. 409

Chicken gizzards, see Gizzards
Chicken hearts, see Hearts
Chicken livers, see Liver
Chicken pot pie, home recipe:
baked, 1 whole pie (22.86 cm. in diam.) 1,640
baked, ⅓ of 22.86-cm. pie 545
baked, 250 g. 586

Chicken pot pie, frozen:
227-g. pie 497

Chicken soup, see Soups
Chick-peas (garbanzos), dry:
raw, 250 g. 800
raw, 250 ml. 763

Chicory, witloof, see Endive, French or Belgian
Chicory greens, fresh:
untrimmed, 500 g. 81
cuts, 250 ml. 12
10 inner leaves 5

Chili con carne, canned:
with beans, 250 g. 332

Chow mein, chicken, canned:
    without noodles, 250 g. 95
    without noodles, 250 ml. 101
Chutney, Major Grey's, bottled:
    15 ml. 50
Cider, see Apple juice
Cisco, see Lake herring
Citron, candied:
    25 g. 78
Clam chowder, see Soups
Clam fritters, home recipe:
    1 fritter (5.08 cm. in diam., 4.45 cm. thick) 124
Clam juice or liquor, canned or bottled:
    250 ml. 49
Clams, fresh, raw:
    hard or round, meat only, 454-g. container 363
    hard or round, meat only, 250 g. 200
    hard or round, meat only, 4 cherrystones or 5 littlenecks 56
    soft, meat only, 454-g. container 372
    soft, meat only, 250 g. 197
Clams, canned:
    with liquid, 250 g. 130
    drained, 250 g. 245
    drained, chopped or minced, 250 ml. 166
Club soda, see Soft drinks
Cocoa and chocolate-flavored mixes, dry:
    high-fat or breakfast, processed, 25 g. 74
    high-fat or breakfast, processed, 15 ml. 18
    medium-fat, processed, 25 g. 65
    medium-fat, processed, 15 ml. 16
    low-medium-fat, processed, 25 g. 54
    low-medium-fat, processed, 15 ml. 13
    low-fat, 25 g. 47
    low-fat, 15 ml. 11
    mix, with nonfat dry milk, 25 g. 90
    mix, with nonfat dry milk, 15 ml. 32
    mix, without milk, 25 g. 86
    mix, without milk, 15 ml. 31
    mix, for hot chocolate, 25 g. 98
    mix, for hot chocolate, 15 ml. 35

Coconut, fresh:

in shell, 1 coconut (11.75 cm. in diam.; 763 g.) 1,373
shelled, meat only, 125 g. 431
shelled, meat only, 1 piece (5.08 x 5.08 x 1.27 cm.) 156
shredded or grated, 250 ml. loosely packed 294
shredded or grated, 250 ml. packed 477

Coconut, dried, shredded:

unsweetened, 125 g. 826
unsweetened, 250 ml. 659
sweetened, 125 g. 683
sweetened, 250 ml. 546

Coconut, chocolate-covered, see Candy

Coconut cream (liquid from grated coconut meat):

250 ml. 850
15 ml. 50

Coconut milk (liquid from grated coconut meat and coconut water):

250 ml. 641

Coconut water (liquid from coconuts):

250 ml. 56

Coconut custard pie, see Pies

Cod, fresh:

raw, fillets, 250 g. 194
broiled, with butter, 1 steak (13.97 x 10.16 x 3.18 cm.) 352
broiled, with butter, fillets, 125 g. 211
broiled, with butter, 1 fillet (12.70 x 6.35 x 2.22 cm.) 111

Cod, canned:

drained, 240 g. (yield from 312-g. can with liquid) 204
drained, 125 g. 107
drained, flaked, 250 ml. 126

Cod, frozen:

cakes, breaded, reheated, 125 g. 339
fillets, 2 average fillets (114 g.) 84
sticks, breaded, 5 average sticks (114 g.) 276

Cod, dehydrated and dried:

dehydrated, lightly salted, 125 g. 466
dehydrated, lightly salted, shredded, 250 ml. 167
dried, salted, 125 g. 163
dried, salted, 1 piece (13.97 x 3.81 x 1.27 cm.) 104

Codfish cakes, see Cod, frozen, and Fish cakes

Coffee, instant:

regular, dry, 15 ml. 3

      regular, dry, 5 ml. 1
      freeze-dried, dry, 15 ml. 5
      freeze-dried, dry, 5 ml. 1
Cola, see Soft drinks
Coleslaw:
      homemade, with French dressing, 125 g. 162
      homemade, with French dressing, 250 ml. 164
      commercial, with French dressing, 125 g. 119
      commercial, with French dressing, 250 ml. 121
      commercial, with mayonnaise, 125 g. 180
      commercial, with mayonnaise, 250 ml. 183
      commercial, with mayonnaise-type salad dressing, 125 g. 124
      commercial, with mayonnaise-type salad dressing, 250 ml. 126
Collards, fresh:
      raw, with stems, 500 g. 199
      raw, leaves only, 500 g. 224
      leaves only, boiled in small amount water, drained, 250 ml. .. 67
      leaves only, boiled in large amount water, drained, 250 ml. .. 63
      with stems, boiled in small amount water, drained, 250 ml. .. 45
Collards, frozen:
      chopped, unthawed, 284-g. pkg. 91
      chopped, boiled, drained, 250 g. (yield from 284-g. pkg.) 75
      chopped, boiled, drained, 250 ml. 54
Consommé, see Soups
Cookie crumbs:
      gingersnap, 250 ml. 512
      graham cracker, 250 ml. loosely packed 346
      graham cracker, 250 ml. packed 427
      vanilla wafer, 250 ml. 392
Cookies:
      animal crackers, 25 g. 113
      animal crackers, 10 average 112
      assorted, 312-g. pkg. (about 36 cookies) 1,498
      assorted, 25 g. 120
      brownies with nuts, home recipe, 25 g. 121
      brownies with nuts, home recipe, 1 brownie
            (7.62 x 2.54 x 2.22 cm.) 97
      brownies with nuts, iced, frozen, 25 g. 105
      brownies with nuts, iced, frozen, 1 brownie
            (3.81 x 4.45 x 2.22 cm.) 103
      butter, thin, rich, 25 g. 115

butter, thin, rich, 10 cookies
   (5.08–5.4 cm. in diam., .64 cm. thick) 229
chocolate, 25 g. 111
chocolate chip, home recipe, 25 g. 129
chocolate chip, home recipe, 4 cookies (5.93 cm. in diam.) 206
chocolate chip, commercial, 25 g. 118
chocolate chip, commercial, 10 cookies (5.72 cm. in diam.) 495
chocolate chip, commercial, 10 cookies
   (4.45 cm. in diam., 1.27 cm. thick) 344
chocolate chip, commercial, 10 cookies
   (4.45 cm. in diam., .95 cm. thick) 250
coconut bars, 1 oz. 123
coconut bars, 10 cookies (7.62 x 3.18 x .64 cm.) 445
cream sandwiches, 25 g. 123
cream sandwiches, oval, 4 cookies (7.94 x 3.18 x .95 cm.) 297
cream sandwiches, round, 4 cookies
   (4.45 cm. in diam., .95 cm. thick) 198
fig bars, 25 g. 89
fig bars, 4 cookies (4.13 x 4.13 x .95 cm.) 200
gingersnaps, 25 g. 105
gingersnaps, 10 cookies (5.08 cm. in diam., .64 cm. thick) 294
graham crackers, plain, 25 g. 96
graham crackers, plain, 1 large (12.70 x 6.35 x .48 cm.) 55
graham crackers, plain, crumbs, see **Cookie crumbs**
graham crackers, chocolate-coated, 25 g. 119
graham crackers, chocolate-coated, 1 piece
   (6.35 x 5.08 x .64 cm.) 62
graham crackers, sugar honey, 25 g. 102
graham crackers, sugar honey, 1 large (12.70 x 6.35 x .48 cm.) 58
ladyfingers, 25 g. 90
ladyfingers, 4 cookies (8.26 x 3.49 x 2.86 cm.) 158
macaroons, 25 g. 119
macaroons, 2 cookies (6.99 cm. in diam., .64 cm. thick) 181
marshmallow, coconut- or chocolate-coated, 25 g. 102
marshmallow, coconut-coated, 4 cookies
   (5.4 cm. in diam., 2.86 cm. thick) 294
marshmallow, chocolate-coated, 4 cookies
   (4.45 cm. in diam., 1.91 cm. thick) 213
molasses, 25 g. 106

molasses, 1 cookie (9.21 cm. in diam., 1.91 cm. thick) 137
oatmeal with raisins, 25 g. 108
oatmeal with raisins, 4 cookies (6.67 cm. in diam., .64 cm. thick) 235
peanut, sandwich- or sugar-wafer-type, 25 g. 118
peanut, sandwich, 4 cookies (4.45 cm. in diam., 1.27 cm. thick) 232
peanut, sugar wafer, 10 cookies (4.45 x 3.49 x .95 cm.) 331
raisin, biscuit-type, 25 g. 94
raisin, biscuit-type, 4 cookies (5.72 x 6.35 x .64 cm.) 269
raisin, biscuit-type, 4 cookies (5.72 x 5.08 x .64 cm.) 216
shortbreads, 25 g. 124
shortbreads, 10 cookies (4.13 x 4.13 x .64 cm.) 374
sugar, soft, home recipe, 25 g. 111
sugar, soft, home recipe, 10 cookies
   (5.72 cm. in diam., .64 cm. thick) 355
sugar wafers, 25 g. 121
sugar wafers, 10 cookies (8.89 x 2.54 x 1.27 cm.) 461
sugar wafers, 10 cookies (4.45 x 3.81 x 1.91 cm.) 437
sugar wafers, 10 cookies (8.89 x 3.81 x .64 cm.) 340
sugar wafers, 10 cookies (6.35 x 1.91 x .64 cm.) 170
vanilla wafers, regular, brown-edge- or biscuit-type, 25 g. 116
vanilla wafers, regular, 10 cookies
   (4.45 cm. in diam., .64 cm. thick) 185
vanilla wafers, brown edge, 10 cookies
   (6.99 cm. in diam., .64 cm. thick) 268
vanilla wafers, biscuit, 10 cookies (5.72 x 3.81 x .64 cm.) 217

Cookies, baked from mix:
brownies, made with nuts and water, 25 g. 101
brownies, made with nuts, egg, and water, 25 g. 107
brownies, made with nuts and egg, 1 brownie
   (7.62 x 2.54 x 2.22 cm.) 86
plain, made with egg and water, 25 g. 123
plain, made with egg and water, 10 cookies
   (4.23 cm. in diam., .95 cm. thick) 276
plain, made with milk, 25 g. 123

Cookies, plain, refrigerated dough:
baked, 25 g. 124
baked, 4 cookies (6.35 cm. in diam., .64 cm. thick) 238

Corn, sweet, fresh:
raw, on the cob, with husks, 500 g. 173
raw, on the cob, without husks, 500 g. 264

Corn, sweet, fresh, continued
  on the cob, boiled, drained, 1 ear
    (12.70 cm. long., 4.45 cm. in diam.) 70
  kernels cut from cob, boiled, drained, 250 ml. 146
Corn, sweet, canned:
  cream-style, 250 g. 205
  cream-style, 250 ml. 223
  vacuum pack, kernels, with liquid, 250 g. 207
  vacuum pack, kernels, with liquid, 250 ml. 184
  wet pack, kernels, with liquid, 250 g. 165
  wet pack, kernels, with liquid, 250 ml. 179
  wet pack, kernels, drained, 250 g. 210
  wet pack, kernels, drained, 250 ml. 148
  dietary (low-sodium) pack, cream-style, 250 g. 205
  dietary (low-sodium) pack, cream-style, 250 ml. 223
  dietary (low-sodium) pack, kernels, with liquid, 250 g. 143
  dietary (low-sodium) pack, kernels, with liquid, 250 ml. 155
  dietary (low-sodium) pack, kernels, drained, 250 g. 190
  dietary (low-sodium) pack, kernels, drained, 250 ml. 161
Corn, sweet, frozen:
  on the cob, unthawed, 1 ear (12.70 cm. long) 122
  on the cob, unthawed, 1 ear trimmed (8.89 cm. long) 61
  on the cob, boiled, drained, 1 ear (12.70 cm. long) 118
  on the cob, boiled, drained, 1 ear trimmed (8.89 cm. long) 59
  kernels, unthawed, 284-g. pkg. 233
  kernels, boiled, drained, 275 g. (yield from 284-g. pkg.) 217
  kernels, boiled, drained, 250 ml. 138
Cornbread:
  baked from mix, with egg and milk, 125 g. 405
  baked from mix, with egg and milk, 1 piece
    (6.35 x 6.35 x 3.49 cm.) 178
  baked from mix, with egg and milk, 2.54-cm. cube 21
  corn pone, home recipe, with whole-ground corn meal, 125 g. . 255
  johnnycake, home recipe, with degermed corn meal, 125 g. 334
  southern, home recipe, with degermed corn meal, 125 g. 281
  southern, home recipe, with degermed corn meal, 2.54-cm. cube 18
  southern, home recipe, with whole-ground corn meal, 125 g. .. 260
  southern, home recipe, with whole-ground corn meal,
    2.54 cm. cube 17
  spoonbread, home recipe, with whole-ground corn meal, 125 g. 244
  spoonbread, home recipe, with whole-ground corn meal, 250 ml. 496

Corned beef, see Beef, corned
Corn flakes, see Cereals, ready-to-eat
Cornflour, see Flour
Corn fritters, home recipe:
  1 fritter (5.08 cm. in diam., 3.81 cm. thick) 132
Corn grits, degermed:
  dry, 250 g. 903
  dry, 250 ml. 614
  cooked, 250 g. 128
  cooked, 250 ml. 133
Corn meal, white or yellow:
  whole-ground, unbolted, dry, 250 g. 887
  whole-ground, unbolted, dry, 250 ml. 459
  bolted, dry, 250 g. 904
  bolted, dry, 250 ml. 469
  degermed, dry, 250 g. 909
  degermed, dry, 250 ml. 532
  degermed, cooked, 250 ml. 127
  self-rising, whole-ground, dry, 250 g. 867
  self-rising, whole-ground, dry, 250 ml. 493
  self-rising, degermed, dry, 250 g. 869
  self-rising, degermed, dry, 250 ml. 520
Corn muffins, see Muffins
Corn salad:
  raw, whole, 500 g. 100
  raw, trimmed, 500 g. 106
Cornstarch:
  125 g. 454
  stirred, 250 ml. 491
  stirred, 15 ml. 29
Corn syrup, see Syrups
Cowpeas (black-eyed peas):
  immature seeds, in pods, raw, 500 g. 349
  immature seeds, shelled, raw, 250 g. 317
  immature seeds, shelled, raw, 250 ml. 195
  immature seeds, boiled, drained, 250 ml. 189
  young pods, with seeds, raw, 500 g. 200
  young pods, with seeds, boiled, drained, 250 ml. 163
  mature seeds, dry, uncooked, 250 g. 857
  mature seeds, dry, uncooked, 250 ml. 618
  mature seeds, dry, cooked, 250 ml. 201

Cowpeas (black-eyed peas), canned:
with liquid, 250 g. 175
with liquid, 250 ml. 190
Cowpeas (black-eyed peas), frozen:
unthawed, 284-g. pkg. 372
boiled, drained, 260 g. (yield from 284-g. pkg.) 338
boiled, drained, 250 ml. 234
Crab, fresh:
steamed, in shell, 500 g. 222
steamed, meat only, 250 g. 232
steamed, meat only, pieces, 250 ml. loosely packed 153
steamed, meat only, flaked, 250 ml. loosely packed 123
steamed, meat only, pieces or flaked, 250 ml. packed 207
Crab, canned:
drained, 250 g. 252
claw, drained, 250 ml. loosely packed 123
white or king, drained, 250 ml. loosely packed 144
claw, white, or king, drained, 250 ml. packed 172
Crab, deviled, home recipe:
250 g. 470
250 ml. 478
Crab imperial, home recipe:
250 g. 367
250 ml. 342
Crab apples, raw:
whole, 500 g. 312
trimmed, flesh only, 250 g. 169
Cracker crumbs:
butter, 250 ml. 388
cheese, 250 ml. 431
graham, see **Cookie crumbs**
saltines, 250 ml. 321
soda, 250 ml. 325
Crackers:
animal, see **Cookies**
bacon-flavor, 25 g. 112
barbecue-flavor, 25 g. 125
butter, 25 g. 115
butter, rectangular, 10 crackers (6.35 x 3.49 x .32 cm.) 174
butter, round, 10 crackers (4.76 cm. in diam., .48 cm. thick) .. 151

cheese, 25 g. 120
cheese, assorted shapes, 10 crackers (about 4.76 cm. in diam.) 150
cheese, rectangular sticks, 10 crackers
   (4.13 cm. long, .64 cm. wide) 44
cheese, round, 10 crackers (4.76 cm. in diam., .48 cm. thick) .. 165
cheese, square, 10 crackers (2.54 cm. square, .32 cm. thick) .. 52
graham, see Cookies
matzos, 25 g. 100
oyster or soup, 25 g. 99
oyster or soup, 250 ml. 210
peanut-butter-and-cheese sandwiches, 25 g. 123
peanut-butter-and-cheese sandwiches, 1 sandwich
   (4.13 cm. in diam. or square) 35
rusks, 25 g. 105
rusks, 1 piece (8.57 cm. in diam., 1.27 cm. thick) 38
rye wafers, whole-grain, 25 g. 86
rye wafers, whole-grain, 10 wafers (8.89 x 4.76 x .64 cm.) ... 224
saltines, 25 g. 108
saltines, 4 crackers (4.76 cm. square) 48
soda, 25 g. 109
soda, 10 biscuits (6.03 x 5.40 x 1.64 cm.) 221
soda, 10 crackers (4.75 cm. square) 125
whole-wheat, 25 g. 101
zwiebacks, 25 g. 107
zwiebacks, 1 piece (8.89 x 3.81 x 1.27 cm.) 30
Cranberries:
fresh, whole, with stems, 500 g. 220
fresh, without stems, 250 ml. 55
fresh, chopped, 250 ml. 54
dehydrated, 25 g. 92
Cranberry juice cocktail, canned or bottled:
177-ml. can 124
250 ml. 174
Cranberry-orange relish:
uncooked, 125 g. 222
uncooked, 250 ml. 528
Cranberry sauce:
canned, strained, 25 g. 36
canned, strained, 250 ml. 428
homemade, unstrained, 250 ml. 523

Crayfish:
raw, in shell, 500 g. 43
raw, meat only, 125 g. 90
Cream:
half and half, 250 ml. 343
half and half, 15 ml. 20
light, table or coffee, 250 ml. 536
light, table or coffee, 15 ml. 32
whipping, light, 250 ml. unwhipped 760
whipping, light, 15 ml. unwhipped 45
whipping, light, 250 ml. whipped 378
whipping, light, 15 ml. whipped 23
whipping, heavy, 250 ml. unwhipped 887
whipping, heavy, 15 ml. unwhipped 53
whipping, heavy, 250 ml. whipped 444
whipping, heavy, 15 ml. whipped 27
Cream, imitation:
creamer, powdered, 15 ml. 30
creamer, frozen, liquid, 15 ml. 20
sour-cream dressing, 15 ml. 20
Cream, sour:
250 ml. 514
15 ml. 26
Cress, garden:
raw, untrimmed, 500 g. 113
raw, trimmed, 125 g. 40
boiled in small amount water, drained, 250 ml. 33
boiled in large amount water, drained, 250 ml. 32
Cress, water, see **Watercress**
Croaker, Atlantic:
raw, whole, 500 g. 163
raw, meat only, 125 g. 120
baked, 125 g. 167
Croaker, white:
raw, meat only, 125 g. 105
Croaker, yellow:
raw, meat only, 125 g. 111
Cucumber, fresh:
with skin, 500 g. 72
with skin, 1 large (20.96 cm. long; 310 g.) 45
with skin, 1 small (16.19 cm. long; 175 g.) 25

with skin, sliced, 6 large or 8 small slices (28 g.) 4
with skin, sliced, 250 ml. 17
pared, 500 g. 70
pared, 1 large (20.96 cm. long; 280 g.) 39
pared, 1 small (16.19 cm. long; 158 g.) 22
pared, sliced, 6½ large or 9 small slices (28 g.) 4
pared, sliced or diced, 250 ml. 21

Cucumber, pickled, see Pickles

Cupcakes, baked from home recipe:
chocolate, without icing, 1 cupcake (6.99 cm. in diam.) 121
chocolate, without icing, 1 cupcake (6.35 cm. in diam.) 92
chocolate, with chocolate icing, 1 cupcake (6.99 cm. in diam.) 162
chocolate, with chocolate icing, 1 cupcake (6.35 cm. in diam.) 125
chocolate, with uncooked white icing, 1 cupcake
    (6.99 cm. in diam.) 162
chocolate, with uncooked white icing, 1 cupcake
    (6.35 cm. in diam.) 122
plain, without icing, 1 cupcake (6.99 cm. in diam.) 120
plain, without icing, 1 cupcake (6.35 cm. in diam.) 91
plain, with chocolate icing, 1 cupcake (6.99 cm. in diam.) 173
plain, with chocolate icing, 1 cupcake (6.35 cm. in diam.) 132
plain, with boiled white icing, 1 cupcake (6.99 cm. in diam.) .. 155
plain, with boiled white icing, 1 cupcake (6.35 cm. in diam.) .. 116
plain, with uncooked white icing, 1 cupcake (6.99 cm. in diam.) 172
plain, with uncooked white icing, 1 cupcake (6.35 cm. in diam.) 128

Cupcakes, baked from mix:
with egg, milk, without icing, 1 cupcake (6.99 cm. in diam.) .. 116
with egg, milk, without icing, 1 cupcake (6.35 cm. in diam.) .. 88
with egg, milk, chocolate icing, 1 cupcake (6.99 cm. in diam.) . 172
with egg, milk, chocolate icing, 1 cupcake (6.35 cm. in diam.) . 129
yellow, with eggs, chocolate icing, 1 cupcake (6.99 cm. in diam.) 155
yellow, with eggs, chocolate icing, 1 cupcake (6.35 cm. in diam.) 118

Currants, fresh:
black, with stems, 500 g. 264
black, trimmed, 250 ml. 64
red or white, with stems, 500 g. 242
red or white, trimmed, 250 ml. 58

Cusk:
raw, meat only, 125 g. 94
steamed, meat only, 125 g. 132

Custard, see Pies and Puddings

D

Dandelion greens, fresh:
  raw, fully trimmed, 500 g. 224
  boiled, drained, 250 ml. loosely packed 37
  boiled, drained, 250 ml. packed 74
Danish pastry, plain, commercial:
  ring, 340-g. pkg. (20.32 cm. in diam.; 5.08 cm.-diam. hole) 1,435
  ring, ⅛ of 340-g. ring (7.94-cm. arc) 179
  ring, 142-g. pkg. (17.78 cm. in diam.; 10.16 cm.-diam. hole) ... 599
  ring, ¼ of 142-g. ring (13.97-cm. arc) 150
  rectangular, 1 piece (16.51 x 6.99 x 1.91 cm.) 317
  round, 1 piece (20.96 cm. in diam., 2.54 cm. thick) 274
  125-g. piece 528
Dates, Chinese, see Jujubes
Dates, domestic:
  with pits, 500 g. 1,189
  pitted, 500 g. 1,367
  chopped, 250 ml. 517
  10 average dates 219
Deviled ham, see Ham, deviled
Dewberries, see Blackberries
Dinners, frozen, see Plate dinners
Distilled liquor, see Alcoholic beverages
Dock or sorrel:
  raw, with stems, 500 g. 98
  boiled, drained, 250 ml. 42
Doughnuts, cake-type, plain:
  1 doughnut (9.21 cm. in diam., 3.18 cm. thick; 58 g.) 227
  1 doughnut (8.89 cm. in diam., 2.54 cm. thick; 42 g.) 164
  1 doughnut (8.26 cm. in diam., 2.54 cm. thick; 25 g.) 98
  1 doughnut (3.81 cm. in diam., 1.91 cm. thick; 14 g.) 55
Doughnuts, yeast, plain:
  1 doughnut (9.53 cm. in diam., 3.18 cm. thick; 42 g.) 176
Drum:
  freshwater, raw, whole, 500 g. 157
  freshwater, raw, meat only, 125 g. 152

red, raw, whole, 500 g. 164
red, raw, meat only, 125 g. 100
Duck:
  domesticated, raw, meat only, 125 g. 207
  domesticated, roasted, meat only, 125 g. 387
  wild, raw, meat only, 125 g. 173

E

food and measure	calories

Eclairs, custard-filled:
  with chocolate icing, 1 éclair (12.70 x 5.08 x 4.45 cm.) 239
  with chocolate icing, 125 g. 299
Eel:
  domestic, raw, meat only, 125 g. 290
  smoked, 125 g. 414
Eggnog, commercial, dairy-packed:
  6% butterfat, 250 ml. 318
  8% butterfat, 250 ml. 363
Eggplant, fresh:
  raw, whole, 500 g. 100
  raw, diced, 250 ml. 53
  boiled, drained, 125 g. 24
  boiled, drained, diced, 250 ml. 40
Eggs, chicken, fresh:
  raw, whole, 500 g. (8½ extra large, 10 large, or
    11 medium eggs) 813
  raw, whole, 1 extra large egg 94
  raw, whole, 1 large egg 82
  raw, whole, 1 medium egg 72
  raw, white of 1 extra large egg 19
  raw, white of 1 large egg 17
  raw, white of 1 medium egg 15
  raw, yolk of 1 extra large egg 66
  raw, yolk of 1 large egg 59
  raw, yolk of 1 medium egg 52
  boiled or poached, 1 extra large egg 94
  boiled or poached, 1 large egg 82
  boiled or poached, 1 medium egg 72

fried, 1 extra large egg	112
fried, 1 large egg	99
fried, 1 medium egg	86
scrambled or omelet, 1 extra large egg	126
scrambled or omelet, 1 large egg	111
scrambled or omelet, 1 medium egg	97

Eggs, chicken, dried:

whole, 250 ml.	339
whole, 25 g.	148
whole, 15 ml.	41
white, flakes, 25 g.	87
white, powdered, 25 g.	93
white, powdered, 15 ml.	26
yolk, 25 g.	166
yolk, 15 ml.	47

Eggs, duck, fresh:

raw, whole, 500 g. (about 7 eggs)	953
raw, whole, 1 egg	134

Eggs, goose, fresh:

raw, whole, 500 g. (about 3½ eggs)	923
raw, whole, 1 egg	266

Eggs, turkey, fresh:

raw, whole, 500 g. (about 6¼ eggs)	848
raw, whole, 1 egg	135

Elderberries, fresh:

with stems, 500 g.	338
without stems, 125 g.	90

Endive, curly, see Escarole

Endive, French or Belgian, bleached, fresh:

trimmed, 500 g.	75
1 head (12.70–17.75 cm. long)	8
10 small leaves	5
chopped (1.27-cm. pieces), 250 ml.	15

Escarole, fresh:

untrimmed, 500 g.	88
4 large outer leaves	20
7 small leaves	4
cuts or small pieces, 250 ml.	11

Eulachon (smelt), raw:

meat only, 125 g.	149

food and measure	calories

Farina, see Cereals, cooking type

Fats, cooking (see also **Lard, Oils,** etc.):
- vegetable shortening, 250 g. 2,205
- vegetable shortening, 250 ml. 1,874
- vegetable shortening, 15 ml. 111

Fennel leaves, raw:
- untrimmed, 500 g. 130
- trimmed, 125 g. 35

Figs, raw:
- whole, 500 g. 399
- 1 large (6.35 cm. in diam.; about 8 per 500 g.) 52
- 1 medium (5.72 cm. in diam.; about 10 per 500 g.) 40
- 1 small (3.81 cm. in diam.; about 12 per 500 g.) 32

Figs, candied:
- 25 g. 75

Figs, canned:
- in water, with liquid, 250 g. 120
- in water, with liquid, 250 ml. 126
- in water, 3 figs and 25 ml. liquid 38
- in heavy syrup, with liquid, 250 g. 210
- in heavy syrup, with liquid, 250 ml. 231
- in heavy syrup, 3 figs and 25 ml. liquid 71

Figs, dried:
- 125 g. 342
- 1 fig. (5.08 x 2.54 cm.) 57

Filberts (hazelnuts):
- in shell, 125 g. 364
- in shell, 10 nuts 87
- shelled, 125 g. 790
- shelled, whole, 250 ml. 907
- shelled, whole, 25 g. (about 17½ nuts) 159
- shelled, chopped, 250 ml. 773
- shelled, chopped, 15 ml. 44
- shelled, ground, 250 ml. 490

Finnan haddie:
meat only, 125 g. 129
Fish, see individual listings
Fish cakes, fried, home recipe:
made with canned fish, potato, egg, 125 g. 215
made with canned fish, potato, egg, 1 cake
(7.62 cm. in diam., 1.59 cm. thick) 103
made with canned fish, potato, egg, 1 bite-size cake
(3.18 cm. in diam.) 21
Fish cakes, fried, frozen:
reheated, 125 g. 337
reheated, 1 cake (7.62 cm. in diam., 1.59 cm. thick;
or 6.35 cm. in diam., 2.22 cm. thick) 162
reheated, 1 bite-size cake (3.18 cm. in diam., 1.59 cm. thick) .. 33
Fish flakes, canned:
198-g. can 220
250 ml. 194
Fish flour:
from whole fish, 25 g. 86
from fish fillets, 25 g. 100
from fish-fillet waste, 25 g. 76
Fish loaf, home recipe, cooked:
whole loaf (22.23 x 10.40 x 6.35 cm.) 1,507
1 slice (10.48 x 6.35 x 2.54 cm.; ⅛ of whole loaf) 186
Fish sticks, breaded, fried, frozen:
reheated, 227-oz. pkg. 400
reheated, 1 stick (1.16 x 2.54 x 1.27 cm.) 50
Flat fish, see **Flounder, Sand dab,** and **Sole**
Flounder, fillets:
raw, 125 g. 98
baked with butter, 125 g. 252
baked with butter, 1 fillet (20.96 x 6.99 x .64 cm.) 202
baked with butter, 1 fillet (15.24 x 6.35 x .64 cm.) 115
Flour (see also individual listings):
buckwheat:
whole-grain, 125 g. 420
whole-grain, sifted, 250 ml. 355
dark, 125 g. 418
dark, sifted, spooned into cup, 250 ml. 346
light, 125 g. 435
light, sifted, spooned into cup, 250 ml. 360

Flour, continued
wheat, whole (hard wheat), 125 g. 418
wheat, whole (hard wheat), stirred, spooned into cup, 250 ml. .. 424

Frankfurters, canned:
340-g. can (7 frankfurters) 751
1 frankfurter (12.38 cm. long, 2.22 cm. in diam.; 48 g.) 106

Frankfurters, chilled or refrigerated:
without binders (all meat):
not smoked, 454-g. pkg. (8 or 10 frankfurters) 1,343
not smoked, 156-g. pkg. (about 16 frankfurters) 462
not smoked, 1 frankfurter
  (12.70 cm. long, 2.22 cm. in diam.; 57 g.) 169
not smoked, 1 frankfurter
  (12.70 cm. long, 1.91 cm. in diam.; 45 g.) 133
not smoked, 1 frankfurter
  (4.45 cm. long, 1.27 cm. in diam.; 10 g.) 30
half smoked, 312-g. pkg. (about 5 frankfurters) 924
half smoked, 1 frankfurter (12.70 cm. long, 2.54 cm. in diam.) 184
smoked, 340-g. pkg. (8 or 10 frankfurters) 1,006
smoked, 142-g. pkg. (about 16 frankfurters) 420
smoked, 1 frankfurter
  (12.07 cm. long, 1.91 cm. in diam.; 57 g.) 124
smoked, 1 frankfurter
  (11.43 cm. long, 1.91 cm. in diam.; 45 g.) 101
smoked, 1 frankfurter
  (4.45 cm. long, 1.59 cm. in diam.; 10 g.) 27
with nonfat dry milk:
454-g. pkg. (8 or 10 frankfurters) 1,361
1 frankfurter (12.70 cm. long, 2.22 cm. in diam.; 57 g.) 171
1 frankfurter (12.70 cm. long, 1.91 cm. in diam.; 45 g.) 135
with cereal:
454-g. pkg. (8 or 10 frankfurters) 1,125
1 frankfurter (12.70 cm. long, 2.22 cm. in diam.; 57 g.) 141
1 frankfurter (12.70 cm. long, 1.91 cm. in diam.; 45 g.) 112

Frogs' legs, raw:
whole, with bone, 500 g. 237
meat only, 125 g. 91

Frostings, see **Icings**

Frozen dinners, see **Plate dinners**

Fruit, see individual listings

Fruit, mixed, frozen:
  sweetened, 227-g. pkg. 250
Fruitcake, see Cakes
Fruit cocktail, canned:
  in water, with liquid, 250 g. 92
  in water, with liquid, 250 ml. 96
  in heavy syrup, with liquid, 250 g. 190
  in heavy syrup, with liquid, 250 ml. 206
Fruit salad, canned:
  in water, with liquid, 250 g. 88
  in water, with liquid, 250 ml. 91
  in heavy syrup, with liquid, 250 g. 187
  in heavy syrup, with liquid, 250 ml. 202
Fruit salad, dairy-packed:
  250 g. 150
Fudge syrup, see Chocolate syrup

G

food and measure	calories

Garbanzos, see Chick-peas
Garlic, raw:
  whole, with skin, 50 g. 60
  peeled, 25 g. 34
  peeled, 5 cloves 14
Gelatin:
  unflavored, dry, 25 g. 84
  unflavored, dry, 15 ml. 00
Gelatin dessert, flavored, commercial:
  dry, 85-g. pkg. 315
  prepared with water, 250 ml. 151
  prepared, fruit (bananas and grapes) added, 250 ml. 171
Ginger, crystallized (candied):
  25 g. 85
Ginger root, fresh:
  unpeeled, 500 g. 228
  peeled, 25 g. 12

Gizzards:

chicken, raw, 500 g. 564
chicken, simmered, 370 g. (yield from 500 g. raw) 547
chicken, simmered, 125 g. 185
chicken, simmered, chopped or diced, 250 ml. 228
goose, raw, 500 g. 694
turkey, raw, 500 g. 783
turkey, simmered, 370 g. (yield from 500 g. raw) 725
turkey, simmered, 125 g. 245
turkey, simmered, chopped or diced, 250 ml. 301

Gluten flour, see Flour, wheat

Goat's milk, see Milk, goat's

Goose, domesticated:

raw, whole, ready-to-cook, 500 g. 1,289
roasted, whole, 264 g. (yield from 500 g. raw) 1,124
roasted, meat only, 125 g. 293
roasted, meat and skin, 125 g. 553

Gooseberries, fresh:

500 g. 195
250 ml. 63

Gooseberries, canned:

in water, with liquid, 250 g. 65
in heavy syrup, with liquid, 250 g. 224

Gourd, see Towel gourd

Granadillas, purple (passion fruit), raw:

whole, in shell, 500 g. 233
whole, 1 average fruit 16
shelled, 125 g. 112

Grape drink, canned:

250 ml. 143

Grapefruit, fresh:

pink or red, seeded:
  whole, with skin, 500 g. 96
  ½ large (11.11 cm. in diam.) 68
  ½ medium (10.64 cm. in diam.) 58
  ½ small (10.00 cm. in diam.) 51
  sections, 250 ml. 85
  sections, with 32 ml. juice, 250 ml. 98
pink or red, seedless:
  whole, with skin, 500 g. 102
  ½ large (10.00 cm. in diam.) 55

½ medium (9.53 cm. in diam.) 49
½ small (9.05 cm. in diam.) 41
sections, 250 ml. 85
sections, with 32 ml. juice, 250 ml. 98
white, seeded:
  whole, with skin, 500 g. 92
  ½ large (11.11 cm. in diam.) 66
  ½ medium (10.64 cm. in diam.) 56
  ½ small (10.00 cm. in diam.) 49
  sections, 250 ml. 87
  sections, with 32 ml. juice, 250 ml. 100
white, seedless:
  whole, with skin, 500 g. 96
  ½ large (10.00 cm. in diam.) 51
  ½ medium (9.53 cm. in diam.) 46
  ½ small (9.05 cm. in diam.) 38
  sections, 250 ml. 83
  sections, with 32 ml. juice, 250 ml. 95
Grapefruit, canned:
  sections, in water, with liquid, 250 g. 175
  sections, in water, with liquid, 250 ml. 189
Grapefruit juice, fresh:
  pink or red, seeded:
    250 ml. 99
    juice from 1 large grapefruit 130
    juice from 1 medium grapefruit 110
    juice from 1 small grapefruit 98
  pink or red, seedless:
    250 ml. 102
    juice from 1 large grapefruit 107
    juice from 1 medium grapefruit 96
    juice from 1 small grapefruit 80
  white, seeded:
    250 ml. 104
    juice from 1 large grapefruit 129
    juice from 1 medium grapefruit 108
    juice from 1 small grapefruit 96
  white, seedless:
    250 ml. 99
    juice from 1 large grapefruit 100

Grapefruit juice, fresh, continued

juice from 1 medium grapefruit	90
juice from 1 small grapefruit	75

Grapefruit juice, canned:

unsweetened, 177-ml. can	76
unsweetened, 250 ml.	107
sweetened, 177-ml. can	99
sweetened, 250 ml.	141

Grapefruit juice concentrate, frozen:

unsweetened, undiluted, 207-g. can	300
unsweetened, diluted with 3 parts water, 250 ml.	107
sweetened, undiluted, 212-g. can	350
sweetened, diluted with 3 parts water, 250 ml.	124

Grapefruit juice, dehydrated (crystals):

dry form, 25 g.	95
dry form, 15 ml.	30
diluted with water, 250 ml.	105

Grapefruit-orange juice, see Orange-grapefruit juice
Grapefruit-pineapple juice drink, see Pineapple-grapefruit juice drink
Grapefruit peel, candied:

25 g.	79

Grape juice, canned or bottled:

250 ml.	177

Grape juice concentrate, frozen:

sweetened, undiluted, 177-ml. can	395
sweetened, diluted with 3 parts water, 250 ml.	141

Grapes, fresh:

all varieties, seeds removed, halves, 250 ml.	124
American-type (slipskin), Concord, Delaware, Niagara, etc.:	
seeded, whole, 500 g.	217
seeded, 250 ml.	74
seeded, 10 grapes (1.91 cm. in diam.)	18
European type (adherent skin), Malaga, muscat,	
Thompson seedless, etc.:	
whole, 500 g.	297
seeded, 250 ml.	108
seedless, 250 ml.	113
seedless, 10 grapes (1.59 cm. in diam.)	34

Grapes, canned (Thompson seedless):

in water, with liquid, 250 g.	128
in water, with liquid, 250 ml.	133

in heavy syrup, with liquid, 250 g. 193
in heavy syrup, with liquid, 250 ml. 209
Griddlecakes, see Pancakes
Grits, see Corn grits
Ground cherries (cape gooseberries or pohas):
raw, with husks, 500 g. 243
raw, without husks, 500 g. 264
raw, without husks, 250 ml. 78
Grouper, raw:
whole, 500 g. 187
meat only, 125 g. 109
Guavas, common, fresh:
whole, with stems, 500 g. 300
trimmed, 125 g. 77
1 small (about 80 g.) 48
Guavas, strawberry, fresh:
whole, with stems, 500 g. 318
trimmed, 125 g. 81
Guinea hen, raw:
whole, ready-to-cook, 500 g. 653
meat and skin, 125 g. 197
Gum, see Chewing gum

H

food and measure	calories

Haddock, fresh:
raw, whole, 500 g. 189
raw, fillets, 500 g. 396
fillets, breaded, fried, 398 g. (yield from 500 g. raw) 657
fillets, breaded, fried, 125 g. 206
Haddock, frozen:
fillets, 125 g. 97
Haddock, smoked, see Finnan haddie
Half and half, see Cream
Halibut, Atlantic or Pacific, fresh:
raw, whole, 500 g. 295

raw, fillets, 500 g. 497
fillets, broiled with butter, 400 g. (yield from 500 g. raw) 686
fillets, broiled with butter, 125 g. 213

Halibut, frozen:
steak, 125 g. 158

Halibut, smoked:
125 g. 279

Ham, retail cuts (see also **Pork**):
fresh, lean with fat:
raw, with bone and skin, 500 g. 1,307
baked, with bone and skin, 288 g. (yield from 500 g. raw) ..1,078
raw, without bone and skin, 500 g. 1,537
baked, without bone and skin, 338 g. (yield from 500 g. raw) .1,267
baked, without bone and skin, 125 g. 466
baked, chopped or diced, 250 ml. 555
baked, ground, 250 ml. 436
fresh, lean only (trimmed of fat):
baked, with bone and skin, 213 g.
(yield from 500 g. raw with fat) 463
baked, without bone and skin, 251 g.
(yield from 500 g. raw with fat) 545
baked, without bone and skin, 125 g. 271
baked, chopped or diced, 250 ml. 322
baked, ground, 250 ml. 253
light-cured, lean with fat:
raw, with bone and skin, 500 g. 1,210
baked, with bone and skin, 352 g. (yield from 500 g. raw) ..1,018
raw, without bone and skin, 500 g. 1,407
baked, without bone and skin, 409 g. (yield from 500 g. raw) .1,183
baked, without bone and skin, 125 g. 361
baked, chopped or diced, 250 ml. 429
baked, ground, 250 ml. 337
light-cured, lean only (trimmed of fat):
baked, with bone and skin, 271 g.
(yield from 500 g. raw with fat) 506
baked, without bone and skin, 317 g.
(yield from 500 g. raw with fat) 593
baked, without bone and skin, 125 g. 233
baked, chopped or diced, 250 ml. 278
baked, ground, 250 ml. 218

long-cured, dry, unbaked:

    medium-fat, lean with fat, with bone and skin, 125 g. 422

    relatively lean, with fat, with bone and skin, 125 g. 332

  picnic, see **Pork**

Ham, boiled:

  packaged, 227-g. pkg. (about 8 slices) 531

  packaged, 1 slice (15.88 x 10.16 x .16 cm.; 28 g.) 66

Ham, canned:

  cured, boneless, 454-g. can 875

  cured, boneless, 125 g. 241

Ham, deviled, canned:

  64-g. can 225

  250 ml. 837

  25 g. 88

  15 ml. 46

Ham, minced:

  125 g. 285

Ham, spiced, canned:

  198-g. can 582

  1 slice (7.62 x 5.08 x 1.27 cm.; ⅓ of 198-g. can) 176

Hamburger, see Beef, ground

Ham croquettes, home recipe:

  pan-fried, 1 croquette (2.54 cm. in diam., 7.62 cm. thick) 163

Hazelnuts, see Filberts

Head cheese:

  packaged, 227-g. pkg. (about 8 slices) 608

  packaged, 1 slice (10.16 x 10.16 x .24 cm.; 28 g.) 76

Hearts, fresh:

  beef, lean only, raw, 250 g. 270

  beef, lean only, braised, 125 g. 234

  beef, lean only, braised, chopped or diced, 250 ml. 289

  calf, raw, 250 g. 309

  calf, braised, 125 g. 280

  calf, braised, chopped or diced, 250 ml. 320

  chicken, raw, 250 g. 334

  chicken, simmered, 125 g. 216

  chicken, simmered, chopped or diced, 250 ml. 266

  hog, raw, 250 g. 283

  hog, braised, 125 g. 243

  hog, braised, chopped or diced, 250 ml. 300

  lamb, raw, 250 g. 405

Hearts, continued

lamb, braised, 125 g. 325
lamb, braised, chopped or diced, 250 ml. 400
turkey, raw, 250 g. 427
turkey, simmered, 125 g. 270
turkey, simmered, chopped or diced, 250 ml. 332

Herring:

fresh, Atlantic, raw, whole, 500 g. 448
fresh, Atlantic, raw, meat only, 125 g. 220
fresh, Pacific, raw, meat only, 125 g. 122
canned, plain, with liquid, 425-g. can 884
canned, plain, with liquid, 125 g. 260
canned, in tomato sauce, 125 g. 220
canned, in tomato sauce, 15 ml. sauce, 1 herring
   (12.70 x 2.86 x 1.59 cm.) 97
pickled, Bismarck or marinated, 125 g. 278
pickled, Bismarck, 1 herring (17.78 x 3.81 x 1.27 cm.) 112
pickled, marinated pieces, 1 piece (4.45 x 2.22 x 1.27 cm.) ... 33
salted or brined, 125 g. 272
smoked, bloaters, 125 g. 244
smoked, hard, 125 g. 374
smoked, kippered, 125 g. 263
smoked, kippered, canned, drained, 125 g. 268
smoked, kippered, canned, drained, 1 fillet
   (17.78 x 5.72 x .64 cm.) 137
smoked, kippered, canned, drained, 1 fillet
   (11.11 x 4.45 x .64 cm.) 84
smoked, kippered, canned, drained, 1 fillet
   (6.03 x 3.49 x .64 cm.) 42

Herring, lake, see **Lake Herring**

Hickory nuts:

in shell, 125 g. 294
shelled, 125 g. 839

Hominy grits, see **Corn grits**

Honey:

strained or extracted, 125 g. 380
strained or extracted, 250 ml. 1,093
strained or extracted, 15 ml. 64
strained or extracted, 1 packet (14 g.) 43

Honeydew melon, fresh:

whole, with rind and seeds, 500 g. 103

1 wedge (5.08 x 17.78 cm.) 49
cubed or diced, 250 ml. 59
Horseradish:
raw, whole, 500 g. 317
raw, pared, 25 g. 22
prepared, 25 g. 10
prepared, 15 ml. 6
prepared, 5 ml. 2
Hot dogs, see Frankfurters
Hyacinth beans, raw:
young pods, untrimmed, 500 g. 154
young pods, cuts (1.27-cm. pieces), 250 ml. 34
mature seeds, dry, 125 g. 421

I

food and measure	calories

Ice cream:
hardened, 10% fat, 250 ml. 272
hardened, 12% fat, 250 ml. 292
hardened, rich, 16% fat, 250 ml. 349
soft-serve (frozen custard), 250 ml. 354
Ice-cream cone:
25 g. 94
1 average 19
rolled sugar, 1 average 37
Ice milk:
hardened, 5.1% fat, 250 ml. 211
soft-serve, 5.1% fat, 250 ml. 282
Ices, water:
lime, 250 ml. 262
Icings, cake, home recipe:
caramel, 125 ml. 649
chocolate, 125 ml. 548
coconut, 125 ml. 320
white, uncooked, 125 ml. 636
white, boiled, 125 ml. 158

Icings, cake, prepared from mix:
chocolate fudge, 125 ml. 621
creamy fudge, made with water, 125 ml. 441
creamy fudge, made with water and table fat, 125 ml. 497
Inconnu (sheefish), raw:
whole, 500 g. 459
meat only, 125 g. 183

J

food and measure	calories

Jack fruit, fresh:
whole, 500 g. 136
peeled and seeded, 125 g. 122
Jack mackerel, raw:
meat only, 125 g. 178
Jams and preserves, commercial:
all flavors, 25 g. 68
all flavors, 15 ml. 54
all flavors, 1 packet (14 g.) 38
Jellies, commercial:
all flavors, 25 g. 68
all flavors, 15 ml. 49
all flavors, 1 packet (14 g.) 38
Jerusalem artichokes, fresh:
whole, with skin, 500 g. 228
pared, 125 g. 83
Juices, see individual listings
Jujubes (Chinese dates):
fresh, whole, 500 g. 487
fresh, seeded, 125 g. 131
dried, whole, with seeds, 500 g. 1,275
dried, seeded, 125 g. 359

K

Kale, fresh:
raw, whole, with stems, 500 g. 141
raw, whole, without stems, 500 g. 169
raw, trimmed, leaves only, 125 g. 88
boiled, drained, with stems, 250 ml. 33
boiled, drained, leaves only, 250 ml. 46

Kale, frozen:
unthawed, 284-g. pkg. 91
boiled, drained, 218 g. (yield from 284-g. pkg.) 68
boiled, drained, 250 ml. 42

Kidneys, fresh:
beef, raw, 250 g. 323
beef, braised, 125 g. 315
beef, braised, pieces (1.27 x 1.27 x .64 cm.), 250 ml. 374
calf, raw, 250 g. 282
hog, raw, 250 g. 264
lamb, raw, 250 g. 262

Kingfish, fresh:
raw, whole, 500 g. 231
raw, meat only, 125 g. 131

Kippers, see Herring

Knockwurst:
packaged, 340-g. pkg. (about 5 links) 945
packaged, 1 link (10.16 cm. long, 2.86 cm. in diam.) 189

Kohlrabi, fresh:
raw, whole, without leaves, 500 g. 105
raw, pared, 125 g. 36
raw, pared, diced, 250 ml. 43
boiled, drained, 125 g. 30
boiled, drained, diced, 250 ml. 42

Kumquats, fresh:
whole, with seeds, 500 g. 301
with seeds, trimmed, 125 g. 81
1 medium 12

L

Lake herring (cisco), raw:

  whole, 500 g. 249

  meat only, 125 g. 120

Lake trout, raw:

  drawn, 500 g. 310

  meat only, 125 g. 210

Lake trout (siscowet), raw:

  under 3 kg., whole, 500 g. 444

  under 3 kg., meat only, 125 g. 300

  over 3 kg., whole, 500 g. 942

  over 3 kg., meat only, 125 g. 653

Lamb, retail cuts:

  leg, lean with fat:

    raw, with bone, 500 g. 930

    roasted, with bone, 294 g. (yield from 500 g. raw) 820

    raw, boneless, 500 g. 1,108

    roasted, boneless, 350 g. (yield from 500 g. raw) 976

    roasted, boneless, 125 g. 349

    roasted, chopped or diced, 250 ml. 414

  leg, lean only (trimmed of fat):

    roasted, with bone, 243 g. (yield from 500 g. raw with fat) .. 452

    roasted, boneless, 290 g. (yield from 500 g. raw with fat) .. 540

    roasted, boneless, 125 g. 232

    roasted, chopped or diced, 250 ml. 276

  loin chops, with bone, lean with fat:

    raw, 500 g. 1,261

    broiled, 314 g. (yield from 500 g. raw) 1,125

    broiled, 125 g. 448

    broiled, 1 chop (95 g.) 341

    broiled, 1 chop (71 g.) 255

  loin chops, with bone, lean only (trimmed of fat):

    broiled, 216 g. (yield from 500 g. raw with fat) 405

    broiled, 125 g. 234

    broiled, 1 chop (65 g.) 122

    broiled, 1 chop (49 g.) 92

rib chops, with bone, lean with fat:
```
raw, 500 g. ............................................1,352
broiled, 295 g. (yield from 500 g. raw) ..................1,200
broiled, 125 g. .........................................  508
broiled, 1 chop (89 g.) .................................  362
broiled, 1 chop (67 g.) .................................  273
```
rib chops, with bone, lean only (trimmed of fat):
```
broiled, 100 g. (yield from 500 g. raw with fat) ...........  397
broiled, 125 g. .........................................  263
broiled, 1 chop (57 g.) .................................  120
broiled, 1 chop (43 g.) .................................   91
```
shoulder, lean with fat:
```
raw, with bone, 500 g. .................................1,190
roasted, with bone, 297 g. (yield from 500 g. raw) ........1,004
raw, boneless, 500 g. ..................................1,403
roasted, boneless, 350 g. (yield from 500 g. raw) .........1,183
roasted, boneless, 125 g. ..............................  421
roasted, chopped or diced, 250 ml. .....................  501
```
shoulder, lean only (trimmed of fat):
```
roasted, with bone, 220 g. (yield from 500 g. raw with fat) ..  451
roasted, boneless, 259 g. (yield from 500 g. raw with fat) ...  530
roasted, boneless, 125 g. ..............................  256
roasted, chopped or diced, 250 ml. .....................  304
```
Lamb's-quarters:
```
raw, trimmed, 500 g. ...................................  215
boiled, drained, 125 g. .................................   40
boiled, drained, 250 ml. ................................   68
```
Lard:
```
250 g. ................................................2,250
250 ml. ...............................................2,034
15 ml. ................................................  117
```
Leeks:
```
raw, untrimmed, 500 g. .................................  135
raw, bulb and lower leaf, 125 g. ........................   65
raw, 3 average ........................................   52
```
Lemonade, frozen:
```
undiluted, 177-ml. can .................................  427
diluted with 4⅓ parts water, 250 ml. ...................  113
```
Lemon Juice, fresh:
```
250 ml. ...............................................   65
15 ml. ................................................    4
```

Lemon juice, canned or bottled, unsweetened:

177-ml. can	42
250 ml.	59
15 ml.	3

Lemon juice, frozen, unsweetened:

single-strength, 177-ml. can	40
single-strength, 15 ml.	3

Lemon peel, candied:

25 g.	79

Lemons, fresh:

whole, 500 g.	99
pulp only, 1 large (6.03 cm. in diam.)	29
pulp only, 1 medium (5.40 cm. in diam.)	20
1 slice (.48 cm. thick)	2
1 wedge, ¼ of large lemon	7
1 wedge, 1/6 of large lemon	5
1 wedge, ¼ of medium lemon	5
1 wedge, 1/6 of medium lemon	3

Lentils:

whole, dry, 250 g.	848
whole, dry, 250 ml.	685
whole, cooked, 250 ml.	225
split, without seed coat, dry, 250 g.	861
split, without seed coat, dry, 250 ml.	695

Lettuce, fresh:

Boston or bibb, untrimmed, 500 g.	52
Boston or bibb, 1 head (12.70 cm. in diam.)	23
Boston or bibb, 1 large, 2 medium, or 3 small leaves	2
Boston or bibb, chopped or shredded, 250 ml.	8
iceberg, untrimmed, 500 g.	62
iceberg, 1 head trimmed (15.24 cm. in diam.)	70
iceberg, 1 leaf (12.70 x 11.43 cm.)	3
iceberg, 1 wedge (¼ of 15.24 cm. head)	18
iceberg, 1 wedge (1/6 of 15.24 cm. head)	12
iceberg, small chunks, 250 ml.	11
iceberg, chopped or shredded, 250 ml.	7
loose leaf, untrimmed, 500 g.	57
loose leaf, 2 large leaves	9
loose leaf, chopped or shredded, 250 ml.	11
romaine or cos, untrimmed, 500 g.	57

romaine or cos, 3 leaves (20.32 cm. long) 5
romaine or cos, chopped or shredded, 250 ml. 11
Lichee nuts:
raw, in shell, 500 g. 191
raw, shelled, 125 g. 80
raw, 6 average nuts 41
dry, in shell, 500 g. 636
dry, shelled, 125 g. 348
Lima beans, see Beans, lima
Limeade, frozen:
undiluted, 177-ml. can 408
diluted with 4⅓ parts water, 250 ml. 108
Lime juice, fresh:
250 ml. 68
15 ml. 4
Lime juice, canned or bottled, unsweetened:
250 ml. 68
15 ml. 4
Limes, fresh:
whole, 500 g. 118
pulp only, 1 lime (5.08 cm. in diam.) 19
Ling cod, raw:
whole, 500 g. 143
meat only, 125 g. 105
Liquor, see Alcoholic beverages
Liver, fresh:
beef, raw, 500 g. 699
beef, fried, 125 g. 286
beef, fried, 1 slice (16.50 x 6.03 x .95 cm.) 195
calves', raw, 500 g. 699
calves', fried, 125 g. 326
calves', fried, 1 slice (16.50 x 6.03 x .95 cm.) 222
chicken, raw, 500 g. 644
chicken, simmered, 125 g. 206
chicken, simmered, 1 liver (5.08 x 5.08 x 1.59 cm.) 41
chicken, simmered, chopped, 250 ml. 254
goose, raw, 500 g. 909
hog, raw, 500 g. 653
hog, fried, 125 g. 300
hog, fried, 1 slice (16.50 x 6.03 x .95 cm.) 205
lamb, raw, 500 g. 679

Liver, continued

Liver paste, see **Pâté de foie gras**

Liverwurst:

smoked, see **Braunschweiger**

Lobster, northern:

Lobster Newburg, home recipe:

Lobster paste, canned:

Loganberries, fresh:

Loganberries, canned:

Longans:

Loquats, fresh:

Luncheon meat, see individual listings

Lychees, see **Lichee nuts**

food and measure	calories

Macadamia nuts:
in shell, 500 g. 1,069
shelled, 125 g. 862
6 average nuts 104

Macaroni:
dry, 227-g. pkg. 838
dry, 250 ml. 532
cooked, firm stage (8–10 minutes), hot, 250 ml. 204
cooked, tender stage (14–20 minutes), hot, 250 ml. 164
cooked, tender stage (14–20 minutes), cold, 250 ml. 124

Macaroni and cheese, home recipe:
baked, 250 g. 537
baked, 250 ml. 456

Macaroni and cheese, canned:
250 g. 237
250 ml. 242

Mackerel, Atlantic, fresh:
raw, whole, 500 g. 515
raw, fillets, 500 g. 953
fillets, broiled with butter, 402 g. (yield from 500 g. raw) 947
fillets, broiled with butter, 125 g. 295
fillets, broiled with butter, 1 fillet (21.59 x 6.35 x 1.27 cm.) .. 248

Mackerel, Atlantic, canned:
with liquid, 250 g. 458

Mackerel, Jack, see Jack mackerel

Mackerel, Pacific, fresh:
raw, dressed, 500 g. 571
raw, meat only, 125 g. 199

Mackerel, Pacific, canned:
drained, 425-g. can 765
drained, 125 g. 224

Mackerel, salted:
fillets, 125 g. 380
fillets, 1 piece (19.69 x 6.35 x 1.27 cm.) 342

Mackerel, smoked:
meat only, 125 g. 273

Malt:
dry, 25 g. 92

Malt extract:
dry, 25 g. 92

Mandarin oranges, see Tangerines

Mangoes, fresh:
whole, 500 g. 221
whole, 1 average (about 300 g.) 152
diced or sliced, 250 ml. 116

Maple syrup, see Syrups

Margarine, regular:
250 g. 1,800
250 ml. 1,732
1 stick (114 g.) 816
15 ml. 102
5 ml. 34
1 pat (2.54 x .85 cm.; 100 pats per 500 g.) 36

Margarine, whipped:
227-g. container 1,634
250 ml. 1,152
1 stick (75 g.) 544
15 ml. 68
5 ml. 23
1 pat (3.18 x .85 cm.; 132 pats per 500 g.) 27

Marmalade, citrus:
25 g. 64
15 ml. 51
1 packet (14 g.) 36

Marmalade plums, see Sapotes

Marshmallows, see Candy

Matai, see Water chestnuts, Chinese

Mayonnaise, see Salad dressings

Meat, see individual listings

Meat, potted, see individual listings

Meat loaf (luncheon meat):
125 g. 250

Melon, see individual listings

Melon balls (cantaloupe and honeydew), frozen:

   in syrup, unthawed, 340-g. pkg. 211

   in syrup, unthawed, 250 ml. 152

Milk, canned:

   condensed, sweetened, 250 ml. 1,041

   condensed, sweetened, 30 ml. 123

   evaporated, unsweetened, 250 ml. 366

   evaporated, unsweetened, 30 ml. 43

Milk, chocolate, canned or dairy-packed:

   made with skim milk, 250 ml. 201

   made with whole milk (3.5% fat), 250 ml. 226

Milk, cow's, fluid:

   whole, 3.5% fat, 250 ml. 169

   whole, 3.7% fat, 250 ml. 171

   buttermilk, cultured, made from skim milk, 250 ml. 93

   half and half, see **Cream**

   skim, 250 ml. 93

   skim, partially (with 2% nonfat solids added), 250 ml. 154

Milk, dry (dry form):

   whole, regular, dry, 250 ml. 682

   whole, regular, dry, 15 ml. 35

   whole, instant, low-density

     (120 g. to 873 ml. water), dry, 250 ml. 372

   whole, instant, high-density

     (62 ml. to 250 ml. water), dry, 250 ml. 559

   nonfat, regular, dry, 250 ml. 462

   nonfat, instant, 1 envelope (91 g) 327

   nonfat, instant, low-density (91 g. yields 317 ml.), dry, 250 ml. 259

   nonfat, instant, high-density (91 g. yields 207 ml.), dry, 250 ml. 395

   buttermilk, cultured, dry, 250 ml. 492

   buttermilk, cultured, dry, 15 ml. 25

Milk, goat's:

   whole, 250 ml. 173

Milk, malted:

   dry powder, 15 ml. (heaping) (28 g.) 116

   beverage, 250 ml. 259

Milk, reindeer:

   250 ml. 615

Millet:

   whole-grain, 125 g. 408

Mince pie, see **Pies**

Mints, see Candy
Miso, see Soybeans, fermented
Molasses:
first extraction (light), 250 ml. 877
first extraction (light), 15 ml. 50
second extraction (medium), 250 ml. 807
second extraction (medium), 15 ml. 46
third extraction (blackstrap), 250 ml. 741
third extraction (blackstrap), 15 ml. 43
Barbados, 250 ml. 942
Barbados, 15 ml. 54
Mortadella:
125 g. 393
1 slice (12.38 cm. in diam., .24 cm. thick) 79
Muffins, baked from home recipe:
plain, 125 g. 367
plain, 1 muffin (about 40 g.) 118
blueberry, 125 g. 351
blueberry, 1 muffin (about 40 g.) 112
bran, 125 g. 326
bran, 1 muffin (about 40 g.) 104
corn, from degermed corn meal, 125 g. 393
corn, from degermed corn meal, 1 muffin (about 40 g.) 126
corn, from whole-ground corn meal, 125 g. 360
corn, from whole-ground corn meal, 1 muffin (about 40 g.) 115
Muffins, baked from mix:
corn, made with egg and milk, 125 g. 405
corn, made with egg and milk, 1 muffin (about 40 g.) 130
Mullet, raw:
whole, 500 g. 386
meat only, 125 g. 183
Mung beans, see Beans, mung and Bean sprouts, mung
Mushrooms, fresh (commercial variety):
raw, untrimmed, 500 g. 135
raw, sliced, chopped, or diced, 250 ml. 21
Mushrooms, canned:
with liquid, 250 g. 42
with liquid, 250 ml. 43
Muskellunge, raw:
whole, 500 g. 266
meat only, 125 g. 136

Muskmelon, see Cantaloupe, Casaba melon, and Honeydew melon
Muskrat:
    roasted, 125 g. 191
Mussels, Atlantic and Pacific, fresh:
    raw, in shell, 500 g. 168
    raw, meat only, 125 g. 119
Mussels, canned:
    meat only, drained, 125 g 143
Mustard, prepared:
    brown, 250 ml. 242
    brown, 25 g. 23
    brown, 5 ml. or 1 serving packet 5
    yellow, 250 ml. 199
    yellow, 25 g. 19
    yellow, 5 ml. or 1 serving packet 4
Mustard greens, fresh:
    raw, untrimmed, 500 g. 108
    raw, trimmed, 125 g. 39
    leaves, boiled, drained, 250 g. 57
    leaves, boiled, drained, 250 ml. 34
Mustard greens, frozen:
    chopped, unthawed, 284-g. pkg. 57
    chopped, boiled, drained, 212 g. (yield from 284-g. pkg.) 42
    chopped, boiled, drained, 250 ml. 32
Mustard spinach (tendergreens), fresh:
    raw, 500 g. 110
    boiled, drained, 250 g. 41
    boiled, drained, 250 ml. 31

N

food and measure	calories

Natal plums, see Carissas
Natto, see Soybeans, fermented
Nectarines, fresh:
    whole, 500 g. 294
    whole, 1 nectarine (6.35 cm. in diam.) 88
    pitted, 125 g. 80

New Zealand spinach, fresh:
raw, 500 g. 95
boiled, drained, 250 g. 33
boiled, drained, 250 ml. 24
Noodles, chow mein, canned:
142-g. can 694
250 ml. 233
Noodles, egg:
dry, 227-g. pkg. 881
cooked, 250 ml. 212
Nuts, see individual listings

O

Oats or oatmeal, see Cereals
Ocean perch, Atlantic (redfish), fresh:
raw, whole, 500 g. 136
raw, meat only, 125 g. 110
breaded, fried, 125 g. 284
Ocean perch, Atlantic (redfish), frozen:
fillets, breaded, fried, reheated, 125 g. 420
fillets, breaded, fried, reheated, 1 fillet (17.15 x 4.45 x 1.59 cm.) 281
Ocean perch, Pacific, fresh:
raw, whole, 500 g. 128
raw, meat only, 125 g. 119
Octopus:
raw, 125 g. 91
Oils, cooking or salad:
corn, cottonseed, safflower, sesame, or soybean, 250 ml. 2,043
corn, cottonseed, safflower, sesame, or soybean, 15 ml. 120
olive or peanut, 250 ml. 2,024
olive or peanut, 15 ml. 119
Okra, fresh:
raw, untrimmed, 500 g. 154
raw, fully trimmed, 125 g. 45

raw, crosscut slices, 250 ml. 38
boiled, drained, crosscut slices, 250 ml. 49
boiled, drained, 10 pods (7.62 x 1.59 cm.) 31
boiled, drained, 125 g. 36

Okra, frozen:
cuts and pods, unthawed, 284-g. pkg. 111
cuts and pods, boiled, drained, 255 g. (yield from 284-g. pkg.) . 97
cuts, boiled, drained, 250 ml. 74

Oleomargarine, see Margarine

Olive oil, see Oils

Olives, pickled, canned or bottled, drained:
green, 50 g. 58
green, 10 giant (2.22 cm. in diam., 2.86 cm. long) 76
green, 10 large (1.91 cm. in diam., 2.40 cm. long) 45
green, 10 small (1.59 cm. in diam., 2.08 cm. long) 33
ripe, Ascolano, pitted, 50 g. 65
ripe, Ascolano, pitted, sliced, 250 ml. 184
ripe, Ascolano, 10 jumbo (2.40 cm. in diam., 3.02 cm. long) ... 105
ripe, Ascolano, 10 giant (2.08 cm. in diam., 2.86 cm. long) 89
ripe, Ascolano, 10 mammoth (2.08 cm. in diam., 2.70 cm. long) . 72
ripe, Ascolano, 10 extra large (1.91 cm. in diam., 2.54 cm. long) 61
ripe, Manzanilla, pitted, 50 g. 65
ripe, Manzanilla, pitted, sliced, 250 ml. 184
ripe, Manzanilla, 10 extra large (1.91 cm. in diam., 2.54 cm. long) 61
ripe, Manzanilla, 10 large (1.91 cm. in diam., 2.40 cm. long) ... 51
ripe, Manzanilla, 10 medium (1.76 cm. in diam., 2.22 cm. long) . 44
ripe, Manzanilla, 10 small (1.59 cm. in diam., 2.08 cm. long) ... 38
ripe, Mission, pitted, 50 g. 92
ripe, Mission, pitted, sliced, 250 ml. 263
ripe, Mission, 10 extra large (1.91 cm. in diam., 2.54 cm. long) 87
ripe, Mission, 10 large (1.91 cm. in diam., 2.40 cm. long) 73
ripe, Mission, 10 medium (1.76 cm. in diam., 2.22 cm. long) ... 63
ripe, Mission, 10 small (1.59 cm. in diam., 2.08 cm. long) 54
ripe, Sevillano, pitted, 50 g. 47
ripe, Sevillano, pitted, sliced, 250 ml. 134
ripe, Sevillano, 10 supercolossal
(2.70 cm. in diam., 3.49 cm. long) 114
ripe, Sevillano, 10 colossal (2.54 cm. in diam., 3.20 cm. long) .. 95
ripe, Sevillano, 10 jumbo (2.40 cm. in diam., 3.02 cm. long) ... 76
ripe, Sevillano, 10 giant (2.08 cm. in diam., 2.86 cm. long) 64
ripe, salt-cured, Greek-style, pitted, 50 g. 169

Olives, pickled, continued

    ripe, salt-cured, Greek-style, 10 extra large (150 per 500 g.) ..   89
    ripe, salt-cured, Greek-style, 10 medium (about 207 per 500 g.)   65

Onions, dehydrated:

    flakes, 250 ml.   237
    flakes, 25 g.   88

Onions, mature, fresh:

    raw, untrimmed, 500 g.   173
    raw, trimmed, 125 g.   47
    raw, 1 medium onion (6.35 cm. in diam.)   40
    raw, chopped, 250 ml.   69
    raw, chopped or minced, 15 ml.   4
    raw, grated or ground, 250 ml.   94
    raw, sliced, 250 ml.   47
    large, boiled, drained, halves, 250 ml.   55
    large, boiled, drained, whole, 250 ml.   65
    pearl, boiled, drained, whole, 250 ml.   57

Onions, young green, fresh:

    bulb and entire top, untrimmed, 500 g.   173
    bulb and entire top, trimmed, 500 g.   179
    bulb and entire top, chopped or sliced, 250 ml.   38
    bulb and entire top, chopped, 15 ml.   2
    bulb and white portion of top, 2 medium (10.48 cm. long)   14
    bulb and white portion of top, chopped or sliced, 250 ml.   48
    bulb and white portion of top, chopped, 15 ml.   3
    tops only (green portion), chopped, 250 ml.   29
    tops only (green portion), chopped, 15 ml.   2

Onions, Welsh:

    raw, untrimmed, 500 g.   110
    raw, trimmed, 125 g.   43

Opossum:

    roasted, meat only, 125 g.   277

Orange-apricot juice drink, canned:

    250 ml.   133

Orange-cranberry relish, see Cranberry-orange relish

Orange-grapefruit juice, canned:

    unsweetened, 177-ml. can   80
    unsweetened, 250 ml.   112
    sweetened, 177-ml. can   93
    sweetened, 250 ml.   133

Orange-grapefruit juice concentrate, frozen:
unsweetened, undiluted, 177-ml. can 330
unsweetened, diluted with 3 parts water, 250 ml. 116
Orange juice, fresh:
all commercial varieties, 250 ml. 119
California, navels (winter oranges):
250 ml. 127
juice from 1 large orange (7.78 cm. in diam.) 50
juice from 1 medium orange (7.30 cm. in diam.) 41
juice from 1 small orange (6.03 cm. in diam.) 26
California, Valencias (summer oranges):
250 ml. 124
juice from 1 large orange (7.78 cm. in diam.) 58
juice from 1 medium orange (6.67 cm. in diam.) 37
juice from 1 small orange (6.03 cm. in diam.) 30
Florida, all commercial varieties, 250 ml. 112
Florida, early and midseason (Hamlin, parson Brown, etc.):
250 ml. 104
juice from 1 large orange (7.48 cm. in diam.) 49
juice from 1 medium orange (6.84 cm. in diam.) 39
juice from 1 small orange (6.35 cm. in diam.) 31
Florida, late season (Valencias):
250 ml. 119
juice from 1 large orange (7.48 cm. in diam.) 60
juice from 1 medium orange (6.84 cm. in diam.) 48
juice from 1 small orange (6.35 cm. in diam.) 38
Florida, temple:
250 ml. 142
juice from 1 large orange (7.94 cm. in diam.) 87
juice from 1 medium orange (7.30 cm. in diam.) 65
juice from 1 small orange (6.52 cm. in diam.) 48
Orange juice, canned:
unsweetened, 177-ml. can 89
unsweetened, 250 ml. 127
sweetened, 177-ml. can 97
sweetened, 250 ml. 138
Orange juice concentrate, canned:
unsweetened, undiluted, 29 ml. 84
unsweetened, diluted with 5 parts water, 250 ml. 121

Orange juice concentrate, frozen:
  unsweetened, undiluted, 177-ml. can 362
  unsweetened, diluted with 3 parts water, 250 ml. 119
Orange juice, dehydrated:
  crystals, dry, 25 g. 95
  crystals, prepared with water, 250 ml. 121
Orange peel, candied:
  25 g. 79
Orange-pineapple juice drink, see Pineapple-orange juice drink
Oranges, fresh:
  all commercial varieties:
    whole, 500 g. 178
    whole, 1 orange (6.67 cm. in diam.) 64
    sections, without membranes, 250 ml. 93
    bite-size pieces, 250 ml. 86
    diced, 250 ml. 109
  California, navels (winter oranges):
    whole, 500 g. 173
    whole, 1 large orange (7.78 cm. in diam.) 87
    whole, 1 medium orange (7.30 cm. in diam.) 71
    whole, 1 small orange (6.03 cm. in diam.) 45
    sections, with membranes, 250 ml. 82
    sections, without membranes, 250 ml. 89
    bite-size pieces, peeled, with membranes, 250 ml. 82
    bite-size pieces, pared, without membranes, 250 ml. 87
    diced, 250 ml. 113
    sliced, peeled, 1 slice (6.35 cm. in diam., .64 cm. thick) 11
    sliced, peeled, 1 slice (5.72 cm. in diam., .64 cm. thick) 9
    wedge, ¼ of medium orange 18
    wedge, 1/6 of medium orange 12
  California, Valencias (summer oranges):
    whole, 500 g. 191
    whole, 1 large orange (7.78 cm. in diam.) 96
    whole, 1 medium orange (6.67 cm. in diam.) 62
    whole, 1 small orange (6.03 cm. in diam.) 50
    sections, without membranes, 250 ml. 98
    bite-size pieces, peeled, with membranes, 250 ml. 84
    bite-size pieces, pared, without membranes, 250 ml. 89
    diced, 250 ml. 113
    sliced, peeled, 1 slice (6.03 cm. in diam., .64 cm. thick) 10
    sliced, pared, 1 slice (5.08 cm. in diam., .64 cm. thick) 8

wedge, ¼ of medium orange 15
wedge, 1/6 of medium orange 10
Florida, all commercial varieties:
  whole, 500 g. 174
  whole, 1 large orange (7.48 cm. in diam.) 89
  whole, 1 medium orange (6.84 cm. in diam.) 71
  whole, 1 small orange (6.35 cm. in diam.) 57
  sections, without membranes, 250 ml. 92
  bite-size pieces, 250 ml. 83
  diced, 250 ml. 105
  sliced, peeled, 1 slice (6.35 cm. in diam., .64 cm. thick) 10
  sliced, peeled, 1 slice (5.08 cm. in diam., .64 cm. thick) 7
  wedge, ¼ of medium orange 18
  wedge, 1/6 of medium orange 12
Oyster plant, see **Salsify**
Oysters, raw:
  eastern, in shell, 500 g. 33
  eastern, meat only, 250 g. 165
  eastern, meat only, 250 ml.
    (13–20 medium or 20–33 small oysters) 167
  eastern, meat only, 50 g. (3½ medium or 5 small oysters) 34
  eastern, canned, drained, 355-ml. can 224
  Pacific and western, meat only, 250 g. 228
  Pacific, meat only, 250 ml.
    (4–7 medium or 7–10 small oysters) 231
  Pacific, canned, drained, 355-ml. can 309
Oysters, cooked:
  breaded, fried, 125 g. 299
  breaded, fried, 4 medium (select) oysters 108
Oyster stew, home recipe (see also **Soups, frozen**):
  1 part oysters to 1 part milk, 250 ml. 260
  1 part oysters to 2 parts milk, 250 ml. 247
  1 part oysters to 3 parts milk, 250 ml. 218

P

food and measure	calories

Pancakes, made from home recipe:
  1 pancake (15.24 cm. in diam., 1.27 cm. thick) 169
  1 pancake (10.16 cm. in diam., .95 cm. thick) 62

Pancakes, made from mix:
  plain and buttermilk:
    dry form, 250 ml. loosely packed 510
    dry form, 250 ml. packed 554
    baked, made with egg and milk, 1 pancake
      (15.24 cm. in diam., 1.27 cm. thick) 164
    baked, made with egg and milk, 1 pancake
      (10.16 cm. in diam., .95 cm. thick) 61
  buckwheat and other cereal flours:
    dry form, 250 ml. loosely packed 452
    dry form, 250 ml. packed 470
    baked, made with egg and milk, 1 pancake
      (15.24 cm. in diam., 1.27 cm. thick) 146
    baked, made with egg and milk, 1 pancake
      (10.16 cm. in diam., .95 cm. thick) 54

Pancake syrup, see Syrups

Pancreas, raw:
  beef, fat, 125 g. 394
  beef, medium fat, 125 g. 353
  beef, lean, 125 g. 176
  calf, 125 g. 201
  hog (hog sweetbreads), 125 g. 301

Papaw, North American-type, fresh:
  whole, 500 g. 318
  whole, 1 papaw (9.53 cm. long, 5.08 cm. in diam.) 83
  peeled and seeded, 125 g. 106
  peeled and seeded, mashed, 250 ml. 226

Papayas, fresh:
  whole, 500 g. 131
  whole, 1 papaya (13.02 cm. long, 8.89 cm. in diam.) 119
  peeled and seeded, 125 g. 48
  peeled and seeded, mashed, 250 ml. 95
  peeled and seeded, cubed (1.27-cm. pieces), 250 ml. 58

Parsley, fresh:
  whole, 500 g. 220
  chopped, 250 ml. 28
  chopped, 15 ml. 2
  1 sprig (about 6.35 cm. long) 4

Parsnips, fresh:
  raw, whole, 500 g. 322

whole, boiled, drained, 1 large
(22.86 cm. long, 5.72 cm. in diam.) 106
whole, boiled, drained, 1 small
(15.24 cm. long, 2.86 cm. in diam.) 23
boiled, drained, diced (5.08-cm. lengths), 250 ml. 108
boiled, drained, mashed, 250 ml. 147

Passion fruit, see Granadillas

Pastini, dry:

carrot, 250 g. 924
egg, 250 g. 955
egg, 250 ml. 690
spinach, 250 g. 920

Pastry, see individual listings

Pastry shell, see Pie crust

Pâté de foie gras, canned:

25 g. 116
15 ml. 60
5 ml. 18

Peach nectar, canned:

163-ml. can 82
250 ml. 127

Peach pie, see Pies

Peaches, fresh:

whole, 500 g. 165
peeled, 1 peach (6.99 cm. in diam.; 175 g.) 58
peeled, 1 peach (6.35 cm. in diam.; 115 g.) 38
pared, 1 peach (6.99 cm. in diam.; 175 g.) 51
pared, 1 peach (6.35 cm. in diam.; 115 g.) 33
pared, diced, 250 ml. 74
pared, sliced, 250 ml. 69

Peaches, canned:

in water, with liquid, 250 g. 77
in water, with liquid, halves or slices, 250 ml. 81
in water, 1 peach half and 30 ml. liquid 28
in juice, with liquid, 250 g. 112
in juice, 2 peach halves and 30 ml. juice 45
in heavy syrup, with liquid, 250 g. 195
in heavy syrup, with liquid, halves, slices, or chunks, 250 ml. . 212
in heavy syrup, 1 peach half and 45 ml. liquid 85

Peaches, dehydrated (nuggets):

uncooked, 250 g. 848

uncooked, 250 ml.	360
cooked, sweetened, with liquid, 250 g.	303
cooked, sweetened, with liquid, 250 ml.	372

Peaches, dried (halves):

uncooked, 250 g.	653
uncooked, 250 ml.	444
uncooked, 10 large halves	380
uncooked, 10 medium halves	341
cooked, unsweetened, with liquid, 250 g.	205
cooked, unsweetened, with liquid, 250 ml.	217
cooked, sweetened, with liquid, 250 g.	297
cooked, sweetened, with liquid, 250 ml.	340

Peaches, frozen:

sliced, sweetened, unthawed, 284-g. pkg.	250
sliced, sweetened, thawed, 250 ml.	233

Peanut butter, commercial variety:

125 g.	1,470
250 ml.	1,611
15 ml.	94

Peanut flour, defatted:

250 g.	926
250 ml.	236

Peanut oil, see **Oils**

Peanuts:

raw, in shell, 500 g.	2,055
raw, shelled, 125 g.	704
roasted, in shell, 500 g.	1,946
roasted, in shell, 10 peanuts	105
roasted, shelled, 125 g.	726
roasted, shelled, halves, 250 ml.	893
roasted, shelled, chopped, 250 ml.	888
roasted, shelled, chopped, 15 ml.	52
chocolate-coated, see **Candy**	

Peanut spread:

125 g.	754
15 ml.	84

Pear nectar, canned:

163-ml. can	89
250 ml.	138

Pears, fresh:
   whole, 500 g. 277
   Bartlett, whole, 1 pear (8.89 cm. long, 6.35 cm. in diam.; 180 g.) 100
   bosc, whole, 1 pear (8.26 cm. long, 6.35 cm. in diam.; 155 g.) . 86
   D'Anjou, whole, 1 pear (7.62 cm. long, 7.62 cm. in diam.; 220 g.) 122
   sliced or cubed, 250 ml. 107

Pears, canned:
   in water, with liquid, 250 g. 80
   in water, with liquid, 250 ml. 83
   in water, 1 pear half and 15 ml. liquid 14
   in water, 1 pear half and 30 ml. liquid 29
   in juice, with liquid, 250 g. 116
   in heavy syrup, with liquid, 250 g. 190
   in heavy syrup, with liquid, 250 ml. 206
   in heavy syrup, 1 pear half and 15 ml. liquid 36
   in heavy syrup, 1 pear half and 30 ml. liquid 71

Pears, dried (halves):
   uncooked, 250 g. 669
   uncooked, 250 ml. 511
   uncooked, 10 pear halves 469
   cooked, unsweetened, with liquid, 250 g. 315
   cooked, unsweetened, with liquid, 250 ml. 340
   cooked, sweetened, 250 g. 377
   cooked, sweetened, 250 ml. 448

Pears, candied:
   25 g. 76

Pears, prickly, see **Prickly pears**
Peas, black-eyed, see **Cowpeas**
Peas, green, immature, fresh:
   raw, in pods, 500 g. 160
   raw, shelled, 250 g. 210
   raw, shelled, 250 ml. 129
   boiled, drained, 250 g 178
   boiled, drained, 250 ml. 121

Peas, green, immature, canned:
   Alaska (early or June peas):
      with liquid, 250 g. 165
      with liquid, 250 ml. 174
      drained, 250 g. 220
      drained, 250 ml. 159
      dietary (low-sodium) pack, with liquid, 250 g. 138

    dietary (low-sodium) pack, with liquid, 250 ml. 145
    dietary (low-sodium) pack, drained, 250 g. 195
    dietary (low-sodium) pack, drained, 250 ml. 141
  sweet (sweet wrinkled or sugar peas):
    with liquid, 250 g. 143
    with liquid, 250 ml. 151
    drained, 250 g. 200
    drained, 250 ml. 144
    dietary (low-sodium) pack, with liquid, 250 g. 118
    dietary (low-sodium) pack, with liquid, 250 ml. 124
    dietary (low-sodium) pack, drained, 250 g. 180
    dietary (low-sodium) pack, drained, 250 ml. 129

Peas, green, immature, frozen:
  unthawed, 284-g. pkg. 207
  unthawed, 250 ml. 112
  boiled, drained, 253 g. (yield from 284-g. pkg.) 172
  boiled, drained, 250 ml. 116

Peas, mature seeds, dry:
  whole, uncooked, 250 g. 848
  whole, uncooked, 250 ml. 721
  split, without seed coat, uncooked, 250 g. 869
  split, without seed coat, uncooked, 250 ml. 738
  split, without seed coat, cooked, 250 g. 287
  split, without seed coat, cooked, 250 ml. 244

Peas and carrots, frozen:
  unthawed, 284-g. pkg. 156
  unthawed, 250 ml. 82
  boiled, drained, 278 g. (yield from 284-g. pkg.) 147
  boiled, drained, 250 ml. 90

Pecan pie, see Pies
Pecans:
  in shell, 500 g. 1,817
  in shell, 10 oversize nuts (60 or less per 500 g.) 299
  in shell, 10 extra large nuts (62–70 per 500 g.) 277
  in shell, 10 large nuts (70–85 per 500 g.) 236
  shelled, 500 g. 3,435
  shelled, 25 g. 172
  shelled, 250 ml. 787
  shelled, 10 mammoth nuts (275 or less per 500 g.) 124
  shelled, 10 jumbo nuts (330–385 per 500 g.) 96

shelled, 10 large nuts (495–605 per 500 g.)	62
shelled, chopped, 250 ml.	860
shelled, chopped, 15 ml.	52
shelled, ground, 250 ml.	692

Pepper, black:
| 2.5 ml. | 2 |

Pepper, hot chili, green (immature):
raw, whole, 500 g.	135
raw, seeded, 125 g.	46
pods, canned, with liquid, 125 g.	31
chili sauce, canned, 4 oz.	25
chili sauce, canned, 250 ml.	52

Pepper, hot chili, red (mature):
raw, whole, 500 g.	446
raw, pods with seeds, 125 g.	116
raw, pods, seeded, 125 g.	81
chili sauce, canned, 125 g.	26
chili sauce, canned, 250 ml.	54
dried pods, 25 g.	80
dried pods, 15 ml.	26
dried, powder, see **Chili powder**	

Peppers, sweet, green (immature):
raw, whole, 500 g.	90
raw, cored and seeded, 125 g.	28
raw, 1 pepper fancy grade	
(9.53 cm. long, 7.62 cm. in diam.; 200 g.)	36
raw, 1 pepper No. 1 grade	
(6.99 cm. long, 6.35 cm. in diam.; 90 g.)	16
raw, chopped or diced, 250 ml.	35
raw, cut in strips, 250 ml.	23
raw, sliced, 250 ml.	19
raw, 1 ring (7.62 cm. in diam., .64 cm. thick)	2
boiled, drained, 1 pepper fancy grade	
(0.59 cm. long, 7.62 cm. in diam.)	29
boiled, drained, 1 pepper No. 1 grade	
(6.99 cm. long, 6.35 cm. in diam.)	13
boiled, drained, strips, 250 ml.	25
boiled, drained, 125 g.	23

Peppers, sweet, red (mature):
| raw, whole, 500 g. | 123 |
| raw, cored and seeded, 125 g. | 39 |

    raw, 1 pepper fancy grade
        (9.53 cm. long, 7.62 cm. in diam.; 200 g.) 51

    raw, 1 pepper No. 1 grade
        (6.99 cm. long, 6.35 cm. in diam.; 90 g.) 23

    raw, chopped or diced, 250 ml. 50

    raw, cut in strips, 250 ml. 33

    raw, sliced, 250 ml. 27

    raw, 1 ring (7.62 cm. in diam., .64 cm. thick) 3

    canned, see **Pimientos**

Perch, raw:

    white, whole, 500 g. 212

    white, meat only, 125 g. 147

    yellow, whole, 500 g. 177

    yellow, meat only, 125 g. 113

Perch, ocean, see **Ocean perch**

Persimmons, fresh:

    Japanese or kaki, with seeds, 500 g. 315

    Japanese or kaki, seedless, whole, 500 g. 322

    Japanese or kaki, seedless, trimmed, 125 g. 96

    Japanese or kaki, seedless, 1 average
        (7.62 cm. long, 6.35 cm. in diam.) 129

    native, whole, 500 g. 519

    native, trimmed and seeded, 125 g. 158

    native, 1 average 31

Pheasant, raw:

    whole, ready-to-cook, 500 g. 656

    meat only, 125 g. 202

Pickerel, chain, raw:

    whole, 500 g. 213

    meat only, 125 g. 105

Pickle relish:

    sour, 125 g. 24

    sour, 15 ml. 3

    sweet, 125 g. 145

    sweet, 250 ml. 358

    sweet, 15 ml. 21

Pickles, chowchow (with cauliflower):

    sour, 125 g. 36

    sour, 250 ml. 74

Boston cream, 1 whole pie (22.86 cm. in diam.) 2,492
Boston cream, 7.94-cm. arc (⅛ of 22.86-cm. pie) 311
butterscotch, 1 whole pie (22.86 cm. in diam.) 2,430
butterscotch, 12.07-cm. arc (1/6 of 22.86-cm. pie) 406
butterscotch, 8.89-cm. arc (⅛ of 22.86-cm. pie) 304
cherry, 1 whole pie (22.86 cm. in diam.) 2,466
cherry, 12.07-cm. arc (1/6 of 22.86-cm. pie) 412
cherry, 8.89-cm. arc (⅛ of 22.86-cm. pie) 308
chocolate chiffon, 1 whole pie (22.86 cm. in diam.) 2,125
chocolate chiffon, 12.07-cm. arc (1/6 of 22.86-cm. pie) 354
chocolate chiffon, 8.89-cm. arc (⅛ of 22.86-cm. pie) 266
chocolate meringue, 1 whole pie (22.86 cm. in diam.) 2,293
chocolate meringue, 12.07-cm. arc (1/6 of 22.86-cm. pie) 383
chocolate meringue, 8.89-cm. arc (⅛ of 22.86-cm. pie) 287
coconut custard, 1 whole pie (22.86 cm. in diam.) 2,139
coconut custard, 12.07-cm. arc (1/6 of 22.86-cm. pie) 357
coconut custard, 8.89-cm. arc (⅛ of 22.86-cm. pie) 268
custard, 1 whole pie (22.86 cm. in diam.) 1,984
custard, 12.07-cm. arc (1/6 of 22.86-cm. pie) 331
custard, 8.89-cm. arc (⅛ of 22.86-cm. pie) 249
lemon chiffon, 1 whole pie (22.86 cm. in diam.) 2,028
lemon chiffon, 12.07-cm. arc (1/6 of 22.86-cm. pie) 338
lemon chiffon, 8.89-cm. arc (⅛ of 22.86-cm. pie) 254
lemon meringue, 1 whole pie (22.86 cm. in diam.) 2,142
lemon meringue, 12.07-cm. arc (1/6 of 22.86-cm. pie) 357
lemon meringue, 8.89-cm. arc (⅛ of 22.86-cm. pie) 268
mince, 1 whole pie (22.86 cm. in diam.) 2,561
mince, 12.07-cm. arc (1/6 of 22.86-cm. pie) 428
mince, 8.89-cm. arc (⅛ of 22.86-cm. pie) 320
peach, 1 whole pie (22.86 cm. in diam.) 2,410
peach, 12.07-cm. arc (1/6 of 22.86-cm. pie) 403
peach, 8.89-cm. arc (⅛ of 22.86-cm. pie) 301
pecan, 1 whole pie (22.86 cm. in diam.) 3,449
pecan, 12.07-cm. arc (1/6 of 22.86-cm. pie) 577
pecan, 8.89-cm. arc (⅛ of 22.86-cm. pie) 431
pineapple, 1 whole pie (22.86 cm. in diam.) 2,391
pineapple, 12.07-cm. arc (1/6 of 22.86-cm. pie) 400
pineapple, 8.89-cm. arc (⅛ of 22.86-cm. pie) 299
pineapple chiffon, 1 whole pie (22.86 cm. in diam.) 1,866
pineapple chiffon, 12.07-cm. arc (1/6 of 22.86-cm. pie) 311

Pike, raw:
blue, whole, 500 g. 198
blue, meat only, 125 g. 112
northern, whole, 500 g. 114
northern, meat only, 125 g. 110
walleye, whole, 500 g. 264
walleye, meat only, 125 g. 117

Pili nuts:
in shell, 500 g. 601
shelled, 125 g. 839

Pimientos, canned:
with liquid, 114-g. can or jar 31
drained, 1 average 10

Pineapple, fresh:
whole, 500 g. 135
trimmed, 125 g. 65
diced, 250 ml. 86
sliced, 1 slice (8.89 cm. in diam., 1.91 cm. thick) 44

Pineapple, candied:
114-g. container (2 slices or 118 ml. chunks) 357
227-g. container (4 slices or 236 ml. chunks) 717
25 g. 79

Pineapple, canned:
in water, with liquid, 250 g. 98
in water, tidbits, with liquid, 250 ml. 102
in juice, with liquid, 250 g. 145
in juice, 1 slice and 30 ml. juice 71
in heavy syrup, with liquid, 250 g. 185
in heavy syrup, chunks, crushed, or tidbits, with liquid, 250 ml. 200
in heavy syrup, 1 large slice or 8 chunks and 33 ml. syrup ... 78
in heavy syrup, 1 medium slice or 4 chunks and 18 ml. syrup . 43
in extra heavy syrup, with liquid, 250 g. 224
in extra heavy syrup, chunks or crushed, 250 ml. 248
in extra heavy syrup, 1 large slice or 8 chunks and 35 ml. syrup 95
in extra heavy syrup, 1 medium slice or 4 chunks
   and 18 ml. syrup 52

Pineapple, frozen:
chunks, sweetened, 250 g. 212
chunks, sweetened, 250 ml. 220

Pineapple juice, canned:

unsweetened, 177-ml. can 103

unsweetened, 250 ml. 146

Pineapple juice concentrate, frozen:

unsweetened, undiluted, 177-ml. can 387

unsweetened, diluted with 3 parts water, 250 ml. 138

Pineapple-grapefruit juice drink (50% fruit juices), canned:

177-ml. can 101

250 ml. 143

Pineapple-orange juice drink (40% fruit juices), canned:

177-ml. can 101

250 ml. 143

Pineapple pie, see **Pies**

Pine nuts:

pignolias, shelled, 125 g. 692

piñons, in shell, 500 g. 1,838

piñons, shelled, 125 g. 796

Pistachio nuts:

in shell, 500 g. 1,482

shelled, 125 g. 741

shelled, 250 ml. 788

shelled, chopped, 15 ml. 53

Pitangas (Surinam cherries), raw:

whole, 500 g. 206

whole, 2 average 5

pitted, 250 ml. 92

Pizza, baked from home recipe:

cheese topping, 1 whole pizza (34.93 cm. in diam.) 1,227

cheese topping, 1 sector, 13.55-cm. arc (⅛ of 34.93-cm. pizza) 153

sausage topping, 1 whole pizza (34.93 cm. in diam.) 1,252

sausage topping, 1 sector, 13.55-cm. arc (⅛ of 34.93-cm. pizza) 157

Pizza, chilled, commercial:

cheese, baked, 1 whole pizza (30.48 cm. in diam.) 1,179

cheese, baked, 1 sector, 12.07-cm. arc (⅛ of 30.48-cm. pizza) 147

Pizza, frozen, commercial:

cheese, baked, 1 whole pizza (25.40 cm. in diam.) 973

cheese, baked, 1 sector, 11.43-cm. arc (1/7 of 25.40-cm. pizza) 139

cheese, baked, 1 whole small pizza (13.34 cm. in diam.) 179

Plantains (baking bananas), raw:

whole, with skin, 500 g. 428

raw, fillets, 500 g. 474
cooked, creamed with flour, butter, and milk, 250 ml. 339
Pomegranates, fresh:
whole, 500 g. 176
whole, 1 average (8.57 cm. in diam., 6.99 cm. high) 97
Pompano, raw:
whole, 500 g. 464
meat only, 125 g. 207
Popcorn:
unpopped, 125 g. 452
unpopped, 250 ml. 787
popped, plain, 50 g. 193
popped, plain, large-kernel, 250 ml. 24
popped, with oil and salt added, 50 g. 228
popped, with oil and salt added, large-kernel, 250 ml. 43
popped, sugar-coated, 50 g. 192
popped, sugar-coated, 250 ml. 142
Popovers, baked from home recipe:
1 popover (10.16 cm. high; about 40 g.) 90
Porgy, raw:
whole, 500 g. 229
meat only, 125 g. 140
Pork, fresh, retail cuts (see also Ham and Pork, cured):
Boston butt (shoulder), with bone and skin, lean with fat:
raw, 500 g. 1,342
roasted, 319 g. (yield from 500 g. raw) 1,126
Boston butt (shoulder), without bone and skin, lean with fat:
raw, 500 g. 1,432
roasted, 339 g. (yield from 500 g. raw) 1,196
roasted, 3 pieces (6.35 x 6.35 x .64 cm.) 300
roasted, chopped or diced, 250 ml. loosely packed 524
roasted, ground, 250 ml. loosely packed 411
Boston butt (shoulder), with bone and skin, lean only
(trimmed of fat):
roasted, 252 g. (yield from 500 g. raw with fat) 615
Boston butt (shoulder), without bone and skin, lean only
(trimmed of fat):
roasted, 268 g. (yield from 500 g. raw with fat) 655
roasted, chopped or diced, 250 ml. loosely packed 363
roasted, ground, 250 ml. loosely packed 284
loin chops, with bone, lean with fat:

    raw, 500 g. 1,172
    broiled, 256 g. (yield from 500 g. raw) 1,002
    broiled, 1 chop (78 g.) 305
    broiled, 1 chop (58 g.) 227
 loin chops, without bone, lean with fat:
    raw, 500 g. 1,487
    broiled, 325 g. (yield from 500 g. raw) 1,268
    broiled, 125 g. 452
 loin chops, with bone, lean only (trimmed of fat):
    broiled, 185 g. (yield from 500 g. raw with fat) 499
    broiled, 1 chop (56 g.) 151
    broiled, 1 chop (42 g.) 113
 loin chops, without bone, lean only (trimmed of fat):
    broiled, 233 g. (yield from 500 g. raw with fat) 629
    broiled, 125 g. 317
 loin roast, with bone, lean with fat:
    raw, 500 g. 1,172
    baked or roasted, 268 g. (yield from 500 g. raw) 971
 loin roast, without bone, lean with fat:
    raw, 500 g. 1,487
    baked or roasted, 339 g. (yield from 500 g. raw) 1,227
    baked or roasted, 125 g. 452
    baked or roasted, 1 piece (6.35 x 6.35 x 1.91 cm.) 308
    baked or roasted, chopped or diced, 250 ml. loosely packed . 537
 loin roast, with bone, lean only (trimmed of fat):
    baked or roasted, 315 g. (yield from 500 g. raw with fat) ... 545
    baked or roasted, 1 piece (6.35 x 6.35 x 1.91 cm.) 216
    baked or roasted, chopped or diced, 250 ml. loosely packed . 377
 loin roast, without bone, lean only (trimmed of fat):
    baked or roasted, 272 g. (yield from 500 g. raw with fat) ... 690
    baked or roasted, 125 g. 317
    baked or roasted, chopped or diced, 250 ml. loosely packed . 377
 picnic (shoulder), with bone and skin, lean with fat:
    raw, 500 g. 1,191
    simmered, 262 g. (yield from 500 g. raw) 979
 picnic (shoulder), without bone and skin, lean with fat:
    raw, 500 g. 1,447
    simmered, 319 g. (yield from 500 g. raw) 1,194
    simmered, 125 g. 466

simmered, 3 pieces (6.35 x 6.35 x .64 cm.) 318
    simmered, chopped or diced, 250 ml. loosely packed 555
picnic (shoulder), with bone and skin, lean only (trimmed of fat):
    simmered, 194 g. (yield from 500 g. raw with fat) 410
picnic (shoulder), without bone and skin, lean only
    (trimmed of fat):
    simmered, 237 g. (yield from 500 g. raw with fat) 502
    simmered, 125 g. ....,,, 265
    simmered, 3 pieces (6.35 x 0.35 x .64 cm.) 180
    simmered, chopped or diced, 250 ml. loosely packed 315
spareribs, with bone, lean with fat:
    raw, 500 g. 1,074
    braised, 198 g. (yield from 500 g. raw) 871
    braised, 125 g. 549

Pork, cured, retail shoulder cuts (see also **Bacon** and **Ham**):
Boston butt, with bone and skin, lean with fat:
    unbaked, 500 g. 1,350
    baked or roasted, 343 g. (yield from 500 g. unbaked) 1,133
Boston butt, without bone and skin, lean with fat:
    unbaked, 500 g. 1,452
    baked or roasted, 370 g. (yield from 500 g. unbaked) 1,220
    baked or roasted, 125 g. 411
    baked or roasted, 3 pieces (6.35 x 6.35 x .64 cm.) 281
    baked or roasted, chopped or diced, 250 ml. loosely packed . 490
    baked or roasted, ground, 250 ml. loosely packed 385
Boston butt, with bone and skin, lean only (trimmed of fat):
    baked or roasted, 285 g. (yield from 500 g. unbaked with fat) 692
Boston butt, without bone and skin, lean only (trimmed of fat):
    baked or roasted, 307 g. (yield from 500 g. unbaked with fat) 746
    baked or roasted, 125 g. 304
    baked or roasted, 3 pieces (6.35 x 6.35 x .64 cm.) 207
    baked or roasted, chopped or diced, 250 ml. loosely packed . 360
    baked or roasted, ground, 250 ml. loosely packed ...., 283
picnic, with bone and skin, lean with fat:
    unbaked, 500 g. ....,,,........1,186
    baked or roasted, 303 g. (yield from 500 g. unbaked) 977
picnic, without bone and skin, lean with fat:
    unbaked, 500 g. 1,422
    baked or roasted, 370 g. (yield from 500 g. unbaked) 1,194
    baked or roasted, 125 g. 403
    baked or roasted, 3 pieces (6.35 x 6.35 x .64 cm.) 275

    baked or roasted, chopped or diced, 250 ml. loosely packed . 479

    baked or roasted, ground, 250 ml. loosely packed 376

  picnic, with bone and skin, lean only (trimmed of fat):

    baked or roasted, 211 g. (yield from 500 g. unbaked with fat) 446

  picnic, without bone and skin, lean only (trimmed of fat):

    baked or roasted, 259 g. (yield from 500 g. unbaked with fat) 546

    baked or roasted, 125 g. 263

    baked or roasted, 3 pieces (6.35 x 6.35 x .64 cm.) 179

    baked or roasted, chopped or diced, 250 ml. loosely packed . 313

    baked or roasted, ground, 250 ml. loosely packed 246

Pork, cured, canned, see Ham

Pork, salt, see Salt pork

Pork and beans, see Beans, baked

Pork and gravy, canned:

  250 g. 639

Pork sausage, see Sausages

Potato chips:

  smooth or corrugated surface, 50 g. 284

  smooth or corrugated surface, 10 chips (.16 x 4.45 x 6.35 cm.) . 114

Potatoes, fresh:

  raw, whole, 500 g. 307

  raw, peeled, chopped, diced, or sliced, 250 ml. 121

  baked in skin, 125 g. 89

  baked in skin, 1 long (12.07 cm. long, 5.93 cm. in diam.) 145

  boiled in skin, 125 g. 87

  boiled in skin, 1 long (12.07 cm. long, 5.93 cm. in diam.) 173

  boiled in skin, 1 round (6.35 cm. in diam.) 104

  boiled in skin, diced or sliced, 250 ml. 125

  boiled, peeled, 125 g. 81

  boiled, peeled (split-knife peeler), 1 long

    (12.07 cm. long, 5.93 cm. in diam.) 146

  boiled, peeled (split-knife peeler), 1 round (6.35 cm. in diam.) . 88

  boiled, peeled, diced or sliced, 250 ml. 107

  French-fried, 125 g. 342

  French-fried, 10 strips (8.89–10.16 cm. long) 214

  French-fried, 10 strips (5.08–8.89 cm. long) 137

  French-fried, 10 strips (2.54–5.08 cm. long) 96

  fried, 125 g. 334

  fried, 250 ml. 483

  hash brown, 125 g. 286

hash brown, 250 ml. 376
mashed, with milk, 125 g. 81
mashed, with milk, 250 ml. 145
mashed, with milk and butter, 125 g. 118
mashed, with milk and butter, 250 ml. 209
scalloped or au gratin, with cheese, 125 g. 182
scalloped or au gratin, with cheese, 250 ml. 376
scalloped or au gratin, without cheese, 125 g. 130
scalloped or au gratin, without cheese, 250 ml. 270

Potatoes, canned:
with liquid, 250 g. 110
with liquid, 250 ml. 117

Potatoes, dehydrated:
flakes, dry form, 125 g. 454
flakes, dry form, 250 ml. 174
flakes, prepared with water, milk, butter, 125 g. 117
flakes, prepared with water, milk, butter, 250 ml. 207
granules without milk, dry form, 125 g. 439
granules without milk, dry form, 250 ml. 746
granules without milk, prepared with water, milk, butter, 125 g. 120
granules without milk, prepared with water, milk, butter, 250 ml. 214
granules with milk, dry form, 125 g. 447
granules with milk, dry form, 250 ml. 759
granules with milk, prepared with water, milk, butter, 125 g. .. 98
granules with milk, prepared with water, milk, butter, 250 ml. . 176

Potatoes, frozen:
diced, shredded, or crinkle-cut for hash browning:
   unthawed, 340-g. pkg. 248
   unthawed, crinkle-cut, 250 ml. 85
   unthawed, diced or shredded, 250 ml. 108
cooked (hash brown), 250 ml. 368
French-fried, straight and crinkle cut strips (1.27 cm. in diam.):
   unthawed, 255-g. pkg. 434
   unthawed, 10 strips (8.89–10.16 cm. long) 170
   unthawed, 10 strips (5.08–8.89 cm. long) 111
   unthawed, 10 strips (2.54–5.08 cm. long) 77
   oven heated, 198 g. (yield from 255-g. pkg.) 434
   oven heated, 10 strips (8.89–10.16 cm. long unheated) 172
   oven heated, 10 strips (5.08–8.89 cm. long unheated) 110
   oven heated, 10 strips (2.54–5.08 cm. long unheated) 77

Potatoes, sweet, see **Sweet potatoes**

Potato flour:

125 g. 440

Potato salad, home recipe:

made with cooked salad dressing, seasonings:

250 g. 248

250 ml. 263

made with mayonnaise and French dressing,

hard-cooked eggs, seasonings:

250 g. 362

250 ml. 385

Potato sticks:

50 g. 272

250 ml. 201

Poultry, see individual listings

Preserves, see **Jams and preserves**

Pretzels, commercial varieties:

all varieties, 50 g. 195

logs, 10 pretzels (7.62 cm. long, 1.27 cm. in diam.) 195

rods, 1 pretzel (19.05–19.69 cm. long, 1.27 cm. in diam.) 55

sticks, 10 pretzels (7.94 cm. long, .32 cm. in diam.) 23

sticks, 10 pretzels (5.72 cm. long, .32 cm. in diam.) 12

twisted, Dutch, 1 pretzel (6.99 x 6.67 x 1.59 cm.) 62

twisted, rings (1-ring), 10 pretzels

(3.81 cm. in diam., 2.54 cm.-diam. hole) 78

twisted, rings (3-ring), 10 pretzels (4.76 x 4.45 x .64 cm.) 117

twisted, thins, 10 pretzels (8.26 x 5.72 x .64 cm.) 234

Prickly pears:

raw, whole, 500 g. 92

peeled and seeded, 125 g. 53

Prune juice, canned or bottled:

118-ml. bottle 99

250 ml. 209

Prune whip, home recipe:

baked, served hot, 250 ml. 148

baked, served cold, 250 ml. 215

Prunes, dehydrated (nugget type):

uncooked, 250 g. 858

uncooked, 250 ml. 365

cooked, sweetened, with liquid, 250 g. 449

cooked, sweetened, with liquid, 250 ml. 534

Prunes, dried, "softenized":
  uncooked, whole, with pits:
    extra large size (up to 47 per 500 g.), 250 g. 560
    extra large size (up to 47 per 500 g.), 10 prunes 274
    large size (up to 58 per 500 g.), 250 g. 551
    large size (up to 58 per 500 g.), 10 prunes 215
    medium size (up to 74 per 500 g.), 250 g. 548
    medium size (up to 74 per 500 g.), 10 prunes 164
  uncooked, whole, pitted, 8 oz. 637
  uncooked, whole, pitted, 250 ml. 487
  uncooked, whole, pitted, 10 prunes 260
  uncooked, chopped or ground, 250 ml. loosely packed 432
  uncooked, chopped or ground, 250 ml. packed 703
  cooked, with pits, unsweetened, with liquid, cold, 250 g. 253
  cooked, with pits, unsweetened, with liquid, cold, 250 ml. 268
  cooked, with pits, sweetened, with liquid, cold, 250 g. 365
  cooked, with pits, sweetened, with liquid, cold, 250 ml. 434

Pudding, rennin, see **Rennin dessert**

Pudding, vegetable gum base, mix:
  custard, cooked with milk, 250 ml. 403

Puddings, starch base, home recipe:
  chocolate, prepared, 250 ml. 408
  vanilla (blancmange), prepared, 250 ml. 300

Puddings, starch base, mix:
  chocolate, dry form, 114-g. pkg. 408
  chocolate, cooked with milk, 250 ml. 341
  chocolate, instant, dry form, 128-g. pkg. 457
  chocolate, instant no-cook, prepared with milk, 250 ml. 345

Pumpkin, fresh:
  raw, whole, 500 g. 91
  raw, pulp only, 125 g. 88

Pumpkin, canned:
  250 g. 83
  250 ml. 86

Pumpkin pie, see **Pies**

Pumpkinseed kernels, dry:
  hulled, 125 g. 690
  hulled, 250 ml. 820
  whole, weighed in hull, 125 g. 510

Purslane leaves, fresh:
raw, whole, with stems, 500 g. 105
boiled, drained, 250 ml. 29

Q

food and measure	calories

Quail, raw:
whole, ready-to-cook, 500 g. 755
meat and skin only, 125 g. 216
giblets, 50 g. 88
Quinces, fresh:
whole, 500 g. 174
peeled and seeded, 125 g. 72

R

food and measure	calories

Rabbit, domesticated:
raw, whole, ready-to-cook, 500 g. 639
raw, meat only, 125 g. 202
stewed, whole, 270 g. (yield from 500 g. raw, ready-to-cook) .. 582
stewed, meat only, 125 g. 270
stewed, chopped or diced, 250 ml. 320
stewed, ground, 250 ml. 252
Rabbit, wild, raw:
whole, ready-to-cook, 500 g. 539
meat only, 125 g. 168
Raccoon, roasted:
meat only, 125 g. 319
Radishes, raw:
with tops, 500 g. 54
without tops, prepackaged, 170-g. pkg. 26

whole, 10 large radishes (over 2.54–3.18 cm. in diam.)	14
whole, 10 medium radishes (1.91–2.54 cm. in diam.)	8
sliced, 250 ml.	21

Radishes, Oriental, raw:

with tops, 500 g.	63
without tops, 500 g.	74
pared, 125 g.	24

Raisin pie, see Pies

Raisins, natural (unbleached), seedless:

uncooked, 250 g.	722
uncooked, 43-g. pkg.	124
uncooked, 14-g. pkg.	40
uncooked, whole, 250 ml. loosely packed	444
uncooked, whole, 250 ml. packed	506
uncooked, whole, 15 ml.	26
uncooked, chopped, 250 ml. loosely packed	413
uncooked, chopped, 250 ml. packed	582
uncooked, ground, 250 ml. loosely packed	613
uncooked, ground, 250 ml. packed	827
cooked, sweetened, with liquid, 250 g.	532
cooked, sweetened, with liquid, 250 ml.	666

Raspberries, fresh:

black, 500 g.	364
black, 250 ml.	104
red, 500 g.	285
red, 250 ml.	74

Raspberries, canned:

black, in water, with liquid, 250 g.	128
red, in water, with liquid, 250 g.	88
red, in water, with liquid, 250 ml.	90

Raspberries, frozen:

red, sweetened, unthawed, 284-g. pkg.	278
red, sweetened, unthawed, 250 ml	260

Red and gray snapper, raw:

whole, 500 g.	241
meat only, 125 g.	117

Redfish, see Drum, red and Ocean perch, Atlantic

Red horse, silver, raw:

drawn, 500 g.	224
meat only, 125 g.	122

Reindeer, raw:

lean meat only, 125 g. 158

Relish, see Pickle relish

Rennin dessert, mix:

chocolate, dry form, 57-g. pkg. 221
chocolate, prepared with milk, 250 ml. 276
vanilla, caramel, or fruit flavor, dry form, 42-g. pkg. 165
vanilla, caramel, or fruit flavor, prepared with milk, 250 ml. .. 252

Rhubarb, fresh:

raw, with leaves, 500 g. 36
raw, well trimmed, 500 g. 68
raw, diced, 250 ml. 21
cooked, sweetened, 250 ml. 404

Rhubarb, frozen:

sweetened, unthawed, 284-g. pkg. 213
sweetened, cooked with added sugar, 250 ml. 409

Rhubarb pie, see Pies

Rice, brown:

raw, long-grain, 250 ml. 706
raw, short-grain, 250 ml. 763
cooked, long-grain, 250 ml. hot rice 246
cooked, long-grain, 250 ml. cold rice 183

Rice, Spanish, see Spanish rice

Rice, white:

raw, long-grain, 250 ml. 712
raw, medium-grain, 250 ml. 750
raw, short-grain, 250 ml. 770
cooked, long-grain, 250 ml. hot rice 236
cooked, long-grain, 250 ml. cold rice 167
parboiled, dry form, 250 ml. 724
parboiled, cooked, 250 ml. hot rice 197
parboiled, cooked, 250 ml. cold rice 163
precooked (instant), dry form, 250 ml. 376
precooked (instant), ready-to-serve (fluffed), 250 ml. hot rice .. 191
precooked (instant), ready-to-serve (fluffed), 250 ml. cold rice . 151

Rice, wild, see Wild rice

Rice bran:

125 g. 344

Rice cereal, see Cereals

Rice polish:
125 g. 331
stirred, spooned into cup, 250 ml. 295
Rice pudding, home recipe:
with raisins, 250 ml. 410
Rockfish (fillets):
raw, meat only, 500 g. 484
oven steamed, with onions, 405 g. (yield from 500 g. raw) 436
oven steamed, with onions, 125 g. 133
oven steamed, with onions, 1 fillet (17.78 x 8.57 x 1.59 cm.) .. 123
Roe:
raw, carp, cod, haddock, herring, pike, and shad, 125 g. 163
raw, salmon, sturgeon, and turbot, 125 g. 260
baked or broiled with butter, cod and shad, 125 g. 158
canned, with liquid, cod, haddock, and herring, 125 g. 149
Rolls, frozen dough:
unraised, 25 g. 67
baked, 25 g. 78
Parker House, baked, 1 roll (6.03 x 5.08 x 3.49 cm.) 75
Rolls, mix:
dry form, 25 g. 98
baked, made with water, 25 g. 75
cloverleaf, baked, made with water, 1 roll
(6.35 cm. in diam., 5.08 cm. high) 105
Rolls and buns, baked from home recipe:
cloverleaf, 34-g. roll (6.35 cm. in diam., 5.08 cm. high) 119
Rolls and buns, commercial:
ready-to-serve:
cloverleaf, 28-g. roll (6.35 cm. in diam., 5.08 cm. high) 83
dinner, 28-g. roll (5.08 cm. square, 5.08 cm. high) 83
frankfurter or hot-dog, 34-g. roll (15.24 x 5.08 x 3.81 cm.) .. 119
hamburger, 34-g. roll (8.89 cm. in diam., 3.81 cm. high) ... 119
hard, round or kaiser, 50 g. roll
(9.53 cm. in diam., 5.08 cm. high) 156
hard, rectangular, 25-g. roll (9.53 x 6.35 x 4.45 cm.) 78
hoagie or submarine, see **Breads, French or Vienna**
plain (pan rolls), 28-g. roll (5.08 cm. square, 5.08 cm. high) . 83
raisin, 28-g. roll 78
sweet, 28-g. roll 89
whole-wheat, 28-g. roll 73

S

food and measure	calories

Salad dressings, commercial (see also **Salad dressings, dietary**):

blue cheese, 250 ml. 1,309
blue cheese, 15 ml. 76
French, 250 ml. 1,087
French, 15 ml. 66
Italian, 250 ml. 1,375
Italian, 15 ml. 83
mayonnaise, 250 ml. 1,675
mayonnaise, 15 ml. 101
Roquefort cheese, 250 ml. 1,309
Roquefort cheese, 15 ml. 76
Russian, 250 ml. 1,283
Russian, 15 ml. 74
salad dressing (mayonnaise-type), 250 ml. 1,083
salad dressing (mayonnaise-type), 15 ml. 65
Thousand Island, 250 ml. 1,330
Thousand Island, 15 ml. 80

Salad dressings, dietary (low-calorie), commercial:

blue cheese (about 5 calories per 5 ml.), 250 ml. 206
blue cheese (about 5 calories per 5 ml.), 15 ml. 12
blue cheese (about 1 calorie per 5 ml.), 250 ml. 50
blue cheese (about 1 calorie per 5 ml.), 15 ml. 3
French (about 5 calories per 5 ml.), 250 ml. 265
French (about 5 calories per 5 ml.), 15 ml. 15
Italian (about 2 calories per 5 ml.), 250 ml. 127
Italian (about 2 calories per 5 ml.), 15 ml. 8
mayonnaise-type (about 8 calories per 5 ml.), 250 ml. 360
mayonnaise-type (about 8 calories per 5 ml.), 15 ml. 22
Roquefort cheese (about 5 calories per 5 ml.), 250 ml. 206
Roquefort cheese (about 5 calories per 5 ml.), 15 ml. 12
Roquefort cheese (about 1 calorie per 5 ml.), 250 ml. 50
Roquefort cheese (about 1 calorie per 5 ml.), 15 ml. 3
Thousand Island (about 10 calories per 5 ml.), 250 ml. 467
Thousand Island (about 10 calories per 5 ml.), 15 ml. 27

Salad oil, see **Oils**

Salami:

dry, roll, 234-g. roll 1,053
dry, roll, 1 slice (4.45 cm. in diam., .32 cm. thick) 23
dry, sliced, 114-g. pkg. 560
dry, sliced, 1 slice (7.94 cm. in diam., .16 cm. thick) 45
cooked, 227-g. pkg. 706

    cooked, 1 slice (11.43 cm. in diam.; about 28 g.) 88
    cooked, 1 slice (10.16 cm. in diam.; about 20 g.) 68

Salmon, fresh:
    Atlantic, raw, whole, 500 g. 704
    Atlantic, raw, meat only, 125 g. 271
    chinook (king), raw, steak, 500 g. 975
    chinook (king), raw, meat only, 125 g. 277
    pink (humpback), raw, steak, 500 g. 523
    pink (humpback), raw, meat only, 125 g. 149
    broiled or baked with butter, meat only, 125 g. 149
    broiled or baked with butter, 1 steak (17.15 x 6.35 cm.) 232

Salmon, canned, with liquid:
    Atlantic, 220-g. can 447
    Atlantic, 125 g. 253
    chinook (king), 220-g. can 462
    chinook (king), 125 g. 262
    chum, 220-g. can 306
    chum, 125 g. 174
    coho (silver), 220-g. can 337
    coho (silver), 125 g. 191
    pink (humpback), 220-g. can 310
    pink (humpback), 125 g. 176
    sockeye (red), 220-g. can 376
    sockeye (red), 125 g. 213

Salmon, smoked:
    125 g. 220

Salmon rice loaf, home recipe:
    1 whole loaf (19.05 x 19.05 x 3.81 cm.) 1,275
    1 piece (9.53 x 6.35 x 3.18 cm.; 1/6 of whole loaf) 212

Salsify, fresh:
    freshly harvested, raw, without tops, 500 g. 56
    stored, raw, without tops, 500 g. 356
    freshly harvested, boiled, drained, cubed, 250 ml. 17
    stored, boiled, drained, cubed, 250 ml. 100

Salt, table:
    500 g. 0
    250 ml. 0

Salt pork, raw:
    with skin, 500 g. 3,751
    without skin, 25 g. 196

Salt sticks, see **Bread sticks**
Sand dab, raw:
    whole, 500 g. 130
    meat only, 125 g. 98
Sandwich spread, with chopped pickle:
    regular, 250 ml. 985
    regular, 15 ml. 57
    dietary (about 5 calories per 5 ml.), 15 ml. ...., 17
Sapodillas:
    whole, 500 g. 355
    peeled and seeded, 125 g. 111
Sapotes (marmalade plums):
    whole, 500 g. 474
    peeled and seeded, 125 g. 157
Sardines, Atlantic:
    canned in oil, 125 g. 388
    canned in oil, with liquid, 106-g. can 330
    canned in oil, drained, 92 g. (yield from 106-g. can with oil) .. 187
    canned in oil, 1 fish
        (8.89 cm. long, 3.81 cm. wide; 5 fish per can) 41
    canned in oil, 1 fish
        (7.62 cm. long, 1.27 cm. wide; 8 fish per can) 24
    canned in oil, 1 fish
        (6.78 cm. long, 1.27 cm. wide; 16–20 fish per can) 10
Sardines, Pacific:
    raw, meat only, 125 g. 199
    canned in brine or mustard, 125 g. 245
    canned in tomato sauce, 125 g. 248
Sauces, see individual listings
Sauerkraut, canned:
    with liquid, 250 g. 45
    with liquid, 250 ml. 43
Sauerkraut juice, canned:
    144 ml. can 45
    250 ml. 25
Sauger, raw:
    whole, 500 g. 146
    meat only, 125 g. 105
Sausages (see also individual listings):
    blood (pudding), 125 g. 492
    blood (pudding), 1 slice (5.72 cm. in diam., .32 cm. thick) 83

brown-and-serve, before browning:
    227-g. pkg. (8–9 patties or 10–11 links) 892
    1 link (9.84 cm. long, 1.59 cm. in diam.) 83
    1 patty (6.03 x 4.76 x 1.27 cm.) 111
brown-and-serve, browned:
    179 g. (yield from 227-g. pkg. before browning) 760
    1 link (9.84 cm. long, 1.59 cm. in diam. before browning) ... 72
    1 patty (6.03 x 4.76 x 1.27 cm. before browning) 97
    125 g. 527
country-style, 125 g. 430
Polish, 125 g. 380
Polish, 227-g. sausage (25.40 cm. long, 3.18 cm. in diam.) 690
Polish, 77-g. sausage (13.65 cm. long, 2.54 cm. in diam.) 231
pork, raw, 227-g. pkg. (4 patties or 8 links) 1,130
pork, raw, 68-g. piece (7.62 cm. long, 3.18 cm. in diam.) 339
pork, raw, 57-g. patty (9.84 cm. in diam., .64 cm. thick) 284
pork, raw, 28-g. link (10.16 cm. long, 2.22 cm. in diam.) 141
pork, cooked, 108 g. (yield from 227-g. pkg. raw) 509
pork, cooked, 1 piece (yield from 68-g. piece raw) 152
pork, cooked, 1 patty (yield from 57-g. patty raw) 129
pork, cooked, 1 link (yield from 28-g. link raw) 62
pork, cooked, 125 g. 597
pork, canned, with liquid, 227-g. can (about 14 links) 942
pork, canned, drained, 162 g. (yield from 227-g. can with liquid) 617
pork, canned, drained, 1 link (7.62 cm. long, 1.27 cm. in diam.) . 46
pork and beef, chopped, 125 g. 421
pork, smoked, see **Sausages, country-style**
scrapple, 454-g. loaf (11.43 x 6.99 x 5.40 cm.) 975
scrapple, 1 slice (6.99 x 5.40 x .64 cm.; 1/18 of 454-g. loaf) .. 54
scrapple, 125 g. 268
souse, 170-g. pkg. (about 6 slices) 308
souse, 1 slice (28 g.) 51
souse, 125 g. 226
summer sausage, see **Thuringer cervelat**
Vienna, canned, 114-g. can (about 7 sausages) 271
Vienna, canned, 1 sausage (5.08 cm. long, 2.22 cm. in diam.) .. 38
Scallions, see **Onions, young green**
Scallops, bay and sea, fresh:
raw, meat only, 125 g. 101
steamed, meat only, 125 g. 140

    drained, 250 ml. (23 large, 42 medium, or 80 small shrimp) .. 157
    drained, 10 large shrimp (about 8.25 cm. long) 67
    drained, 10 medium shrimp (about 6.35 cm. long) 37
    drained, 10 small shrimp (about 5.10 cm. long) 17

Shrimp, frozen:
    breaded, fried, 125 g. 174

Shrimp paste, canned:
    25 g. 45
    5 ml. 13

Siscowet, see **Lake trout**

Skate (Raja fish), raw:
    meat only, 125 g. 122

Smelt, Atlantic, jack or bay, raw:
    whole, 500 g. 268
    meat only, 125 g. 122

Smelt, eulachon, see **Eulachon**

Smelt, canned:
    with liquid, 250 g. 499

Snails, raw:
    meat only, 125 g. 113
    giant African, meat only, 125 g. 91

Snapper, see **Red and gray snapper**

Soft drinks, carbonated:
    club soda, 355-ml. can or bottle 0
    club soda, 250 ml. 0
    cola-type, 355-ml. can or bottle 144
    cola-type, 250 ml. 102
    cream soda, 355-ml. can or bottle 160
    cream soda, 250 ml. 111
    fruit flavor (citrus, cherry, grape, etc.), 355-ml. can or bottle .. 171
    fruit flavor (citrus, cherry, grape, etc.), 250 ml. 120
    ginger ale, pale dry or golden, 355-ml. can or bottle 113
    ginger ale, pale dry or golden, 250 ml. 81
    quinine water (tonic), 355-ml. can or bottle 113
    quinine water (tonic), 250 ml. 81
    root beer, 355-ml. can or bottle 152
    root beer, 250 ml. 106
    Tom Collins mixer, 355-ml. can or bottle 171
    Tom Collins mixer, 250 ml. 120

Sole, raw:

whole, 500 g. 130

meat only (fillets), 125 g. 99

Sorghum grain:

125 g. 416

Sorghum syrup, see **Syrups**

Sorrel, see **Dock**

Soups, canned:

asparagus, cream of:

    condensed, 298-g. can 161

    diluted with equal part water, 250 ml. 69

    diluted with equal part whole milk, 250 ml. 156

bean with pork:

    condensed, 326-g. can 437

    diluted with equal part water, 250 ml. 178

beef broth, bouillon, or consommé:

    condensed, 298-g. can 77

    diluted with equal part water, 250 ml. 33

beef noodle:

    condensed, 298-g. can 170

    diluted with equal part water, 250 ml. 71

borscht, ready-to-serve, 250 ml. 77

celery, cream of:

    condensed, 298-g. can 215

    diluted with equal part water, 250 ml. 91

    diluted with equal part whole milk, 250 ml. 179

chicken consommé:

    condensed, 298-g. can 54

    diluted with equal part water, 250 ml. 23

chicken, cream of:

    condensed, 298-g. can 235

    diluted with equal part water, 250 ml. 100

    diluted with equal part whole milk, 250 ml. 190

chicken gumbo:

    condensed, 298-g. can 137

    diluted with equal part water, 250 ml. 58

chicken noodle:

    condensed, 298-g. can 158

    diluted with equal part water, 250 ml. 66

chicken with rice:
  condensed, 298-g. can 116
  diluted with equal part water, 250 ml. 51
chicken vegetable:
  condensed, 298–305-g. can 187
  diluted with equal part water, 250 ml. 81
clam chowder, Manhattan-type:
  condensed, 305-g. can 201
  diluted with equal part water, 250 ml. 86
minestrone:
  condensed, 305-g. can 265
  diluted with equal part water, 250 ml. 111
mushroom, cream of:
  condensed, 298-g. can 331
  diluted with equal part water, 250 ml. 142
  diluted with equal part whole milk, 250 ml. 229
onion:
  condensed, 298-g. can 161
  diluted with equal part water, 250 ml. 69
pea, green:
  condensed, 312–319-g. can 335
  diluted with equal part water, 250 ml. 138
  diluted with equal part whole milk, 250 ml. 226
pea, split:
  condensed, 319-g. can 376
  diluted with equal part water, 250 ml. 154
tomato:
  condensed, 305-g. can 220
  diluted with equal part water, 250 ml. 93
  diluted with equal part whole milk, 250 ml. 183
turkey noodle:
  condensed, 298-g. can 194
  diluted with equal part water, 250 ml. 84
vegetable beef:
  condensed, 305-g. can 198
  diluted with equal part water, 250 ml. 83
vegetable with beef broth:
  condensed, 305-g. can 195
  diluted with equal part water, 250 ml. 83

vegetarian vegetable:
  condensed, 305-g. can 195
  diluted with equal part water, 250 ml. 83

Soups, dehydrated:
  beef noodle:
    mix, dry form, 57-g. pkg. 221
    prepared (57 g. mix with 3 cups water), 250 ml. 71
  chicken noodle:
    mix, dry form, 57-g. pkg 218
    prepared (57 g. mix with 4 cups water), 250 ml. 56
  chicken rice:
    mix, dry form, 43-g. pkg. 152
    prepared (43 g. mix with 3 cups water), 250 ml. 51
  onion:
    mix, dry form, 43-g. pkg. 150
    prepared (43 g. mix with 4 cups water), 250 ml. 38
  pea, green:
    mix, dry form, 114-g. pkg. 409
    prepared (114 g. mix with 3 cups water), 250 ml. 130
  tomato vegetable with noodles:
    mix, dry form, 71-g. pkg. 247
    prepared (71 g. mix with 4 cups water), 250 ml. 69

Soups, frozen:
  clam chowder, New England:
    condensed, 250 g. 267
    diluted with equal part water, 250 ml. 135
    diluted with equal part whole milk, 250 ml. 214
  oyster stew:
    condensed, 250 g. 255
    diluted with equal part water, 250 ml. 127
    diluted with equal part whole milk, 250 ml. 209
  pea, green, with ham:
    condensed, 250 g. 283
    diluted with equal part water, 250 ml. 142
  potato, cream of:
    condensed, 250 g. 217
    diluted with equal part water, 250 ml. 109
    diluted with equal part whole milk, 250 ml. 190
  shrimp, cream of:
    condensed, 250 g. 332

Soy sauce:
    250 ml. 209
    15 ml. 12

Spaghetti, plain:
    dry form, 227-g. pkg. 838
    cooked, firm stage (8–10 minutes), 250 ml. 204
    cooked, tender stage (14–20 minutes), 250 ml. 164

Spaghetti, with meatballs and tomato sauce:
    home recipe, 250 g. 334
    home recipe, 250 ml. 352
    canned, 250 g. 259
    canned, 250 ml. 273

Spaghetti, in tomato sauce, with cheese:
    home recipe, 250 g. 260
    home recipe, 250 ml. 276
    canned, 250 g. 190
    canned, 250 ml. 201

Spanish mackerel, raw:
    whole, 500 g. 539
    meat only, 125 g. 222

Spanish rice, home recipe:
    250 g. 217
    250 ml. 226

Spinach, fresh:
    raw, whole, 500 g. 94
    raw, trimmed, packaged, 500 g. 130
    raw, trimmed, leaves, 250 ml. 10
    raw, trimmed, chopped, 250 ml. 15
    boiled, drained, leaves, 250 ml. 43

Spinach, canned:
    with liquid, 250 g. 47
    with liquid, 250 ml. 47
    drained, 250 g. 61
    drained, 250 ml. 52
    dietary (low-sodium) pack, with liquid, 250 g. 53
    dietary (low-sodium) pack, with liquid, 250 ml. 52
    dietary (low-sodium) pack, drained, 250 g. 65
    dietary (low-sodium) pack, drained, 250 ml. 56

Spinach, frozen:
    chopped, unthawed, 284-g. pkg. 68
    chopped, boiled, drained, 220 g. (yield from 284-g. pkg.) 51

Spinach, frozen, continued

chopped, boiled, drained, 250 ml. 50
leaf, unthawed, 284-g. pkg. 71
leaf, boiled, drained, 220 g. (yield from 284-g. pkg.) 53
leaf, boiled, drained, 250 ml. 49

Spinach, New Zealand, see New Zealand spinach

Spiny lobster, see Crayfish

Spleen, raw:

beef or calf, 125 g. 130
hog, 125 g. 134
lamb, 125 g. 144

Spot, fresh:

raw, fillets, 125 g. 273
baked, fillets, 125 g. 369

Squab (pigeon), raw:

whole, dressed, 500 g. 626
meat only, 125 g. 178
light meat only, 125 g. 157

Squash, summer, fresh:

white and pale green, scallop varieties:

raw, whole, 500 g. 102
raw, trimmed, 250 g. 53
raw, cubed, diced, or sliced, 250 ml. 29
boiled, drained, 250 g. 41
boiled, drained, sliced, 250 ml. 31
boiled, drained, cubed or diced, 250 ml. 36
boiled, drained, mashed, 250 ml. 40

yellow, crookneck or straightneck:

raw, whole, 500 g. 98
raw, trimmed, 250 g. 51
raw, cubed, diced, or sliced, 250 ml. 28
boiled, drained, 250 g. 37
boiled, drained, sliced, 250 ml. 29
boiled, drained, cubed or diced, 250 ml. 34
boiled, drained, mashed, 250 ml. 38

zucchini or cocozelle (Italian marrow–type), green:

raw, whole, 500 g. 80
raw, trimmed, 250 g. 43
raw, cubed, diced, or sliced, 250 ml. 23
boiled, drained, 250 g. 30
boiled, drained, sliced, 250 ml. 23

Strawberries, canned:
in water, with liquid, 250 g. 55
in water, with liquid, 250 ml. 56
Strawberries, frozen:
sweetened, whole, 454-g. pkg. 417
sweetened, whole, 250 ml. 249
sweetened, sliced, 284-g. pkg. 310
sweetened, sliced, 250 ml. 295
Strawberry pie, see **Pies**
Sturgeon, fresh:
raw, meat only, 125 g. 118
steamed, meat only, 125 g. 199
Sturgeon, smoked:
125 g. 186
Succotash (corn and lima beans), frozen:
unthawed, 284-g. pkg. 275
unthawed, 250 ml. 159
boiled, drained, 250 g. 232
boiled, drained, 250 ml. 167
Sucker, carp, raw:
whole, 500 g. 216
meat only, 125 g. 139
Sucker, white and mullet, raw:
whole, 500 g. 223
meat only (fillets), 125 g. 130
Suet (beef kidney fat), raw:
25 g. 213
Sugar, beet or cane:
brown, 500 g. 1,861
brown, 250 ml. loosely packed 573
brown, 250 ml. firm packed 870
brown, 15 ml. firm packed 52
granulated, 500 g. 1,921
granulated, 250 ml. 816
granulated, 15 ml. 46
granulated, 5 ml. 15
granulated, 1 cube (1.27 cm.) 10
granulated, 1 lump (2.86 x 1.91 x .80 cm.) 19
granulated, 1 packet 23
powdered (confectioners'), 500 g. 1,921
powdered (confectioners'), unsifted, 250 ml. 490

254

Sweet potatoes, fresh, continued

    boiled in skin, 250 g. 239
    boiled in skin, 1 potato (12.70 cm. long, 5.08 cm. in diam.) ... 172
    boiled in skin, sliced, 250 ml. 192
    boiled in skin, mashed, 250 ml. 308

Sweet potatoes, candied:

    125 g. 210
    1 piece (6.35 cm. long, 5.08 cm. in diam.) 176

Sweet potatoes, canned:

    liquid pack, with liquid, 250 g. 285
    vacuum pack, 250 g. 270
    vacuum pack, 1 piece (6.99 cm. long, 2.54 cm. in diam.) 43
    vacuum pack, pieces, 250 ml. 229
    vacuum pack, mashed, 250 ml. 292
    dietary pack, with liquid, 250 g. 114

Sweet potatoes, dehydrated:

    flakes, dry form, 125 g. 475
    flakes, dry form, 250 ml. 482
    flakes, prepared with water, 250 g. 238
    flakes, prepared with water, 250 ml. 257

Sweetsop, see Sugar apples

Swiss chard, see Chard, Swiss

Swordfish, fresh:

    raw, meat only, 500 g. 589
    broiled with butter, 315 g. (yield from 500 g. raw) 549
    broiled with butter, 125 g. 205
    broiled with butter, 1 piece (11.43 x 5.40 x 2.22 cm.) 237

Swordfish, canned:

    with liquid, 250 g. 128

Syrups (see also individual listings):

    cane, 250 ml. 878
    cane, 15 ml. 53
    maple, 250 ml. 842
    maple, 15 ml. 50
    sorghum, 250 ml. 899
    sorghum, 15 ml. 53
    table blend (chiefly corn, light and dark), 250 ml. 1,008
    table blend (chiefly corn, light and dark), 15 ml. 59
    table blend (cane and maple), 250 ml. 842
    table blend (cane and maple), 15 ml. 50

food and measure	calories

Tamarinds, fresh:

   whole, 500 g. 572

   shelled and seeded, 125 g. 298

Tangelo juice, fresh:

   250 ml. 107

   juice from 1 large tangelo (6.99 cm. in diam.) 47

   juice from 1 medium tangelo (6.52 cm. in diam.) 39

   juice from 1 small tangelo (5.72 cm. in diam.) 28

Tangerine juice, fresh:

   250 ml. 112

Tangerine juice, canned:

   unsweetened, 177-ml. can 80

   unsweetened, 250 ml. 112

   sweetened, 177-ml. can 94

   sweetened, 250 ml. 133

Tangerine juice concentrate, frozen:

   unsweetened, undiluted, 177-ml. can 342

   unsweetened, diluted with 3 parts water, 250 ml. 121

Tangerines, fresh (Dancy variety):

   whole, 500 g. 169

   whole, 1 large tangerine (6.35 cm. in diam.) 46

   whole, 1 medium tangerine (6.03 cm. in diam.) 39

   whole, 1 small tangerine (5.72 cm. in diam.) 33

   sections, without membranes, 250 ml. 95

Tapioca, dry form:

   227-g. pkg. 799

   250 ml. 567

   15 ml. 30

Tapioca pudding, home recipe:

   apple, 250 ml. 311

   cream, 250 ml. 234

Taro:

   corms and tubers, whole, 500 g. 410

   corms and tubers, without skin, 125 g. 122

   leaves and stems, 500 g. 199

Tartar sauce:

250 ml. 1,294

15 ml. 74

dietary pack, 15 ml. 31

Tautog (blackfish), raw:

whole, 500 g. 164

meat only, 125 g. 111

Tea, instant:

dry form, 25 g. 73

dry form, 5 ml. 1

Tendergreens, see Mustard spinach

Terrapin (diamondback), raw:

in shell, 500 g. 117

meat only, 125 g. 139

Thuringer cervelat (summer sausage):

227-g. pkg. 697

1 slice (11.11 cm. in diam., .32 cm. thick; 28 g.) 87

1 slice (10.48 cm. in diam., .32 cm. thick; 25 g.) 68

1 slice (7.30 cm. in diam., .16 cm. thick; 7 g.) 23

Tilefish:

raw, whole, 500 g. 201

raw, meat only, 125 g. 99

baked, meat only, 125 g. 172

Tofu, see Soybean curd

Tomato catsup, see Catsup

Tomato chili sauce, see Chili sauce

Tomato juice, canned or bottled:

163-ml. can 32

250 ml. 49

dietary (low-sodium) pack, 340-g. can 69

dietary (low-sodium) pack, 250 ml. 49

Tomato juice, dehydrated:

crystals, dry form, 25 g. 76

crystals, prepared with water, 250 ml. 52

Tomato juice cocktail, canned or bottled:

250 ml. 54

Tomato paste, canned:

250 g. 205

170-g. can 139

250 ml. 228

Tomato purée, canned:
250 g. 98
250 ml. 104
dietary (low-sodium) pack, 250 g. 98
Tomato soup, see **Soups**
Tomatoes, green, fresh:
whole, 500 g. 109
Tomatoes, ripe, fresh:
raw, whole, 500 g. 110
raw, whole, 1 tomato (about 6.60 cm. in diam.) 27
raw, whole, 1 tomato (about 6.10 cm. in diam.) 20
raw, whole, peeled, 1 tomato (6.10 cm. in diam.) 19
raw, sliced, 250 ml. 42
boiled, 250 ml. 67
Tomatoes, ripe, canned:
with liquid, 250 g. 53
with liquid, 250 ml. 54
dietary (low-sodium) pack, with liquid, 250 g. 51
dietary (low-sodium) pack, with liquid, 250 ml. 51
Tomcod, Atlantic, raw:
whole, 500 g. 150
meat only, 125 g. 97
Tom Collins mix, see **Soft drinks**
Tongue, fresh:
beef, very fat, raw, trimmed, 250 g. 677
beef, fat, raw, trimmed, 250 g. 576
beef, medium-fat, raw, trimmed, 250 g. 517
beef, medium-fat, braised, 125 g. 305
beef, medium-fat, braised, 1 slice (7.62 x 5.08 x .32 cm.) 49
calf, raw, trimmed, 250 g. 325
calf, braised, 125 g. 199
calf, braised, 1 slice (7.62 x 5.08 x .32 cm.) 32
hog, raw, trimmed, 250 g. 537
hog, braised, 125 g. 316
hog, braised, 1 slice (7.62 x 5.08 x .32 cm.) 51
lamb, raw, trimmed, 250 g. 497
lamb, braised, 125 g. 317
lamb, braised, 1 slice (7.62 x 5.08 x .32 cm.) 51
sheep, raw, trimmed, 250 g. 662
sheep, braised, 125 g. 403
sheep, braised, 1 slice (7.62 x 5.08 x .32 cm.) 65

Tongue, canned or cured:
canned or pickled, 125 g. 333
potted or deviled, 125 g. 362
Towel gourd:
whole, 500 g. 76
pared, 125 g. 22
Tripe, beef:
commercial, 125 g. 124
pickled, 125 g. 77
Trout, brook, raw:
whole, 500 g. 246
meat only, 125 g. 127
Trout, lake, see Lake trout
Trout, rainbow, fresh:
raw, meat with skin, 125 g. 243
Trout, rainbow, canned:
125 g. 261
Tuna, raw:
bluefin, meat only, 125 g. 182
yellowfin, meat only, 125 g. 166
Tuna, canned:
in oil, all styles, with liquid, 250 g. 718
in oil, solid pack, with liquid, 198-g. can 570
in oil, chunk-style, with liquid, 184-g. can 530
in oil, flake- or grated-style, with liquid, 170–177-g. can 501
in oil, solid pack or chunk-style, drained, 250 g. 492
in oil, solid pack or chunk-style, drained, 250 ml. 334
in oil, solid pack, drained, 170 g. (yield from 198-g. can) 333
in oil, chunk-style, drained, 156 g. (yield from 184-g. can) 309
in water, all styles, with liquid, 250 g. 317
in water, solid pack, with liquid, 198-g. can 251
in water, solid pack, with liquid, 99-g. can 126
in water, chunk-style, with liquid, 184-g. can 234
in water, chunk-style, with liquid, 92-g. can 117
Tuna salad, home recipe:
with celery, mayonnaise, pickle, onion, and eggs, 250 g. 425
with celery, mayonnaise, pickle, onion, and eggs, 250 ml. 370
Turbot, Greenland, raw:
whole, 500 g. 378
meat only, 125 g. 183

Turkey, fresh (all classes):

raw, whole, ready-to-cook, 500 g.	794
roasted, whole, with giblets and skin, 268 g. (yield from 500 g. raw)	708
roasted, dark meat without skin:	
125 g.	253
4 pieces (6.35 x 4.13 x .64 cm.)	173
chopped or diced, 250 ml.	301
ground, 250 ml.	236
roasted, light meat without skin:	
125 g.	220
4 pieces (6.35 x 4.13 x .64 cm.)	150
chopped or diced, 250 ml.	261
ground, 250 ml.	206
roasted, skin only, 25 g.	226

Turkey, boned, canned:

156-g. can	315
125 g.	252
250 ml.	439

Turkey, potted, canned:

156-g. can	387
250 ml.	591
15 ml.	32
25 g.	62

Turkey giblets (some gizzard fat):

raw, 250 g.	374
simmered, 125 g.	290
simmered, chopped or diced, 250 ml.	358

Turkey pot pie, home recipe:

baked, 1 whole pie (22.86 cm. in diam.)	1,654
baked, ⅓ of 22.86-cm. pie	550
baked, 250 g.	592

Turkey pot pie, frozen:

227-g. pie	447

Turkey soup, see Soups

Turnip greens, fresh:

raw, whole, 500 g.	118
raw, trimmed, 500 g.	140
boiled in small amount water, short time, drained, 250 g.	51
boiled in small amount water, short time, drained, 250 ml.	31

    boiled in large amount water, long time, drained, 250 g. 47
    boiled in large amount water, long time, drained, 250 ml. 30
Turnip greens, canned:
    with liquid, 250 g. 45
    with liquid, 250 ml. 45
Turnip greens, frozen:
    chopped, unthawed, 284-g. pkg. 65
    chopped, boiled, drained, 220 g. (yield from 284-g. pkg.) 51
    chopped, boiled, drained, 250 ml. 40
Turnips, fresh:
    raw, without tops, untrimmed, 500 g. 129
    raw, cubed or sliced, 250 ml. 41
    boiled, drained, 250 g. 57
    boiled, drained, cubed, 250 ml. 38
    boiled, drained, mashed, 250 ml. 56
Turtle, green, raw:
    in shell, 500 g. 107
    meat only, 125 g. 111
Turtle, green, canned:
    125 g. 132

V

food and measure	calories

Veal, fresh, retail cuts:
  chuck cuts and boneless for stew, lean with fat:
    raw, with bone, 500 g. 691
    stewed, with bone, 262 g. (yield from 500 g. raw) 620
    raw, without bone, 500 g. 864
    stewed, without bone, 330 g. (yield from 500 g. raw) 773
    stewed, without bone, 125 g. 294
    stewed, without bone, 1 piece (6.35 x 6.35 x 1.91 cm.) 200
    stewed, chopped or diced, 250 ml. 349
  loin cuts, lean with fat:
    raw, with bone, 500 g. 749
    braised or broiled, with bone, 296 g. (yield from 500 g. raw) 692

raw, without bone, 500 g. 903
braised or broiled, without bone, 355 g.
(yield from 500 g. raw) 834
braised or broiled, without bone, 125 g. 270
braised or broiled, without bone, 1 piece
(6.35 x 6.35 x 1.91 cm.) 199
braised or broiled, without bone, chopped or diced, 250 ml. . 348
plate (breast of veal), lean with fat:
raw, with bone, 500 g. 911
braised or stewed, with bone, 259 g. (yield from 500 g. raw) . 790
raw, without bone, 500 g. 1,153
braised or stewed, without bone, 330 g. (yield from 500 g. raw) 997
braised or stewed, without bone, 125 g. 378
rib roast, lean with fat:
raw, with bone, 500 g. 795
roasted, with bone, 265 g. (yield from 500 g. raw) 713
raw, without bone, 500 g. 1,033
roasted, without bone, 343 g. (yield from 500 g. raw) 926
roasted, without bone, 125 g. 336
roasted, without bone, 2 pieces (10.48 x 5.72 x .64 cm.) 229
roasted, chopped or diced, 250 ml. 400
roasted, ground, 250 ml. 314
round with rump (roasts and leg cutlets), lean with fat:
raw, with bone, 500 g. 630
braised or broiled, with bone, 271 g. (yield from 500 g. raw) . 587
raw, without bone, 500 g. 818
braised or broiled, without bone, 352 g.
(yield from 500 g. raw) 762
braised or broiled, without bone, 125 g. 270
braised or broiled, without bone, 1 piece
(10.48 x 5.72 x 1.27 cm.) 184
braised or broiled, chopped or diced, 250 ml. 320
Vegetable fat, see Fats, cooking
Vegetable juice cocktail, canned:
177-ml. can 31
250 ml. 43
Vegetable oil, see Oils
Vegetable-oyster, see Salsify
Vegetables, see individual listings
Vegetables, mixed, frozen:
unthawed, 284-g. pkg. 185

Vegetables, mixed, continued
    boiled, drained, 275 g. (yield from 284-g. pkg.) 176
    boiled, drained, 250 ml. 123
Vegetable soup, see Soups
Venison, raw:
    lean meat only, 125 g. 157
Vienna sausage, see Sausages
Vinegar, cider:
    250 ml. 36
    15 ml. 2
Vinegar, distilled:
    250 ml. 31
    15 ml. 2
Vine spinach (Basella), raw:
    125 g. 24
Vodka, see Alcoholic beverages

W

food and measure	calories

Waffles, baked from home recipe:
    1 round waffle (17.78 cm. in diam., 1.59 cm. thick) 209
    1 square waffle (22.86 x 22.86 x 1.59 cm.) 558
    1 square piece (11.43 x 11.43 x 1.59 cm.) 140
Waffles, baked from mix:
    made with egg and milk, 1 round waffle
        (17.78 cm. in diam., 1.59 cm. thick) 206
    made with egg and milk, 1 square waffle
        (22.86 x 22.86 x 1.59 cm.) 550
    made with egg and milk, 1 square piece
        (11.43 x 11.43 x 1.59 cm.) 138
Waffles, frozen:
    prebaked, unheated, 1 waffle (11.75 x 9.53 x 1.59 cm.) 86
    prebaked, unheated, 1 waffle (8.89 x 6.99 x 1.59 cm.) 56
Waffle syrup, see Syrups
Walnuts, black:
    in shell, 500 g. 690

Y

food and measure	calories

Yam beans, tuber, raw:
   whole, with skin, 500 g. 248
   pared, 125 g. 08
Yams, canned, see **Sweet potatoes**
Yams, tuber, raw:
   whole, with skin, 500 g. 433
   pared, 125 g. 127
Yeast, baker's:
   compressed, 28 g. 24
   compressed, 1 cake 19
   dry (active), 28 g. 80
   dry (active), 1 pkg. (7 g.) or 5 ml. 20
Yeast, brewer's:
   dry, 28 g. 80
   dry, 15 ml. 23
Yellowtail, raw:
   meat only, 125 g. 173
Yogurt, plain:
   partially skim milk, 227-g. container 113
   partially skim milk, 250 ml. 130
   whole milk, 227-g. container 140
   whole milk, 250 ml. 161
Youngberries, see **Blackberries**

Z

food and measure	calories

Zucchini, see **Squash, summer**
Zwiebacks, see **Crackers**

WHAT YOU SHOULD WEIGH

	HEIGHT (without shoes)	SMALL FRAME	MEDIUM FRAME	LARGE FRAME
WOMEN	5 ft. 0 in.	92- 98	96-107	104-109
	5 ft. 1 in.	94-101	98-110	106-112
	5 ft. 2 in.	96-104	101-113	109-118
	5 ft. 3 in.	99-107	104-116	112-121
	5 ft. 4 in.	102-110	107-119	115-125
	5 ft. 5 in.	105-113	110-122	118-130
	5 ft. 6 in.	108-116	113-126	121-135
	5 ft. 7 in.	111-119	116-130	125-140
	5 ft. 8 in.	114-123	120-135	129-145
	5 ft. 9 in.	118-127	124-139	133-150
	5 ft. 10 in.	122-131	128-143	137-155
	5 ft. 11 in.	126-135	132-147	141-160
	6 ft. 0 in.	130-140	136-151	145-165
MEN	5 ft. 4 in.	115-123	121-133	129-132
	5 ft. 5 in.	118-126	124-136	132-137
	5 ft. 6 in.	121-129	127-139	135-142
	5 ft. 7 in.	124-133	130-143	138-148
	5 ft. 8 in.	128-137	134-147	142-152
	5 ft. 9 in.	132-141	138-152	147-155
	5 ft. 10 in.	136-145	142-156	151-160
	5 ft. 11 in.	140-150	146-160	155-165
	6 ft. 0 in.	144-154	150-165	159-170
	6 ft. 1 in.	148-158	154-170	164-175
	6 ft. 2 in.	152-162	158-175	168-180
	6 ft. 3 in.	156-167	162-180	173-185
	6 ft. 4 in.	160-171	167-185	178-190

DAILY MAINTENANCE CALORIES
(When you're at your desirable weight)*

	DESIRABLE WEIGHT	18-35 YEARS	35-55 YEARS	55-75 YEARS
WOMEN	99	1,700	1,500	1,300
	110	1,850	1,650	1,400
	121	2,000	1,750	1,550
	128	2,100	1,900	1,600
	132	2,150	1,950	1,650
	143	2,300	2,050	1,800
	154	2,400	2,150	1,850
	165	2,550	2,300	1,950
MEN	110	2,200	1,950	1,650
	121	2,400	2,150	1,850
	132	2,550	2,300	1,950
	143	2,700	2,400	2,050
	154	2,900	2,600	2,200
	165	3,100	2,800	2,400
	176	3,250	2,950	2,500
	187	3,300	3,100	2,600

* Based on moderate activity. If your life is very active, add 50 calories; if your life is sedentary, subtract 75 calories.

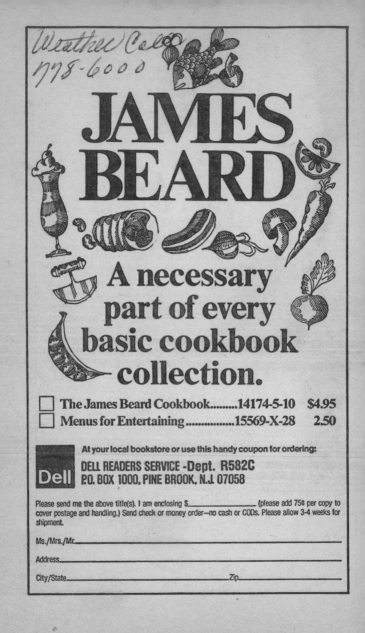